Centring the Periphery
Chaos, Order, and the Ethnohistory of Dominica

During its prehistory Dominica served as an occasional stepping-stone for small-scale, independent foraging and horticultural peoples migrating up the Antillean arc to the larger islands in the north. Its discovery by Europeans brought it into a social and economic constellation that was constructed and orchestrated largely from the metropolitan centre. Using ideas from chaos theory and world systems theory, Patrick Baker provides the unfolding story of the struggle of the Dominican people to create and order a world that is controlled from outside.

Using "centring" to mean "ordering the world," Baker links this concept to ideas in chaos theory, which views order and disorder as mutually generative phenomena rather than static antinomies. Thus strategies to control disorder and create and maintain order may suddenly precipitate change. Baker's application of these ideas to an island nation that has received little detailed attention in the past makes this a highly original work, as does his holistic, post-modern perspective.

As well as proving a sensitive historical analysis, Baker confronts the dilemma of meaning in peripheral siguations and the experience of dependency in the world system. *Centring the Periphery* provides important insights for understanding the majority of the world's peoples and makes a significant contribution to the study of society in developing nations.

PATRICK L. BAKER is associate professor of Sociology and Anthropology, Mount Allison University.

The Portuguese World Map from the Treaty of Tordesillas.
Source: Dario G. Martini, *Cristoforo Colombo: Tra Ragione E Fantasia*
(Genoa: Edizioni Culturali Internazionali 1986), 285.

Centring the Periphery

Chaos, Order, and the Ethnohistory of Dominica

PATRICK L. BAKER

McGill-Queen's University Press
Montreal & Kingston • London • Buffalo

© McGill-Queen's University Press 1994
ISBN 0-7735-1134-2

Legal deposit first quarter 1994
Bibliothèque nationale du Québec

Printed in the United States on acid-free paper

This book has been published with the help of a grant
from the Social Science Federation of Canada, using
funds provided by the Social Sciences and Humanities
Research Council of Canada.

Published simultaneously in the West Indies by
The Press – University of the West Indies.

Canadian Cataloguing in Publication Data

Baker, Patrick L., 1938–
    Centring the periphery: chaos, order, and the
    ethnohistory of Dominica
    Includes bibliographical references and index.
    ISBN 0-7735-1134-2
    1. Dominica – History. 2. Dominica – Social
    conditions. 3. Chaotic behavior in systems.
    I. Title.
    F2051.B35 1994   972.9841   C93-090507-5

The poem "Ghost in a Plantation House," by Phyllis
Shand Allfrey, is reproduced with permission of Curtis
Brown Ltd, London, on behalf of the Estate of Phyllis
Shand Allfrey. Copyright the Estate of Phyllis Shand
Allfrey.

For Cynthia,
Dominic and Stephanie,
and the people of Dominica.

Contents

Tables and Maps

MAPS

Preface

At dawn on Sunday, 3 November 1493, Christopher Columbus sighted Dominica. This book marks the quincentary of that event. It documents and interprets the impact and long-term effects of Europe's discovery of this small island, a microcosm of the massive world transformation that Columbus inaugurated.

Columbus's second voyage of discovery marked the beginning of Empire. In contrast to his first voyage into "the Sea of Darkness" (Major 1870, viii), with three small ships, no soldiers, statesmen, or ministers, and few armaments, the second voyage "was a veritable armada of supplies, men, and equipment that had had no equal in history" (Carrison 1967, 76). There were seventeen ships, a large body of well-equipped soldiers, several hundred *hidalgos*, five *religiosos*, many male colonists, and a clear mission to dominate and subdue the New World.

The impact of these events is still being felt. Columbus's legacy was to enable Europe to expand beyond its borders in an unprecedented fashion, to conquer almost every society it encountered, and to accumulate unimaginable wealth. The era of discovery set in motion colonial expansion, the exploitation of native peoples, and a "civilizing" process that incorporated the dominant characteristics of modernism – rationalism, science, materialism, secularism, capitalism, nationalism, and militarism. "Slavery, forced labour and the destruction of non-European cultures and civilizations were subsequently described as the inevitable consequences of [this] 'civilizing mission' " (Carew 1988, 37). The impact on the biota of the earth

MAP 1 The Four Voyages of Christopher Columbus

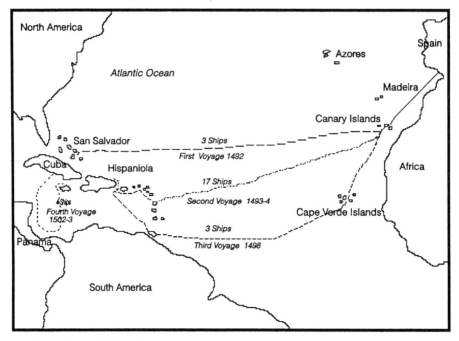

Source: Compiled from Carrison 1967, 47.

was catastrophic, entailing the alteration of environments, the extinction of species, and the decimation of vast numbers of indigenous people.[1]

The discipline of anthropology arose as an intellectual exercise to comprehend people who had been incorporated into this process by Western hegemony. So, almost five hundred years after Columbus landed in Dominica, I went there as a green anthropologist, to make sense of a local world formed from his inheritance. This work seeks to describe and account for what went on in Dominica before and after that visit.

I had been encouraged to visit Dominica. Friends and colleagues had told me that Dominica is special, that I would find it an interesting place, because it is different from the other islands. One author had commented, "It is not an obvious island: not at all. But it has the power to attract eccentrics. It has 'character' ... On my return to England, I had found myself thinking more often of Dominica than of any other island that I had visited" (Waugh 1949, 107–8). As well, I found the paucity of written material on the island intriguing. Here, in the middle of the Antillean arc, was a relatively large island, with an area of 289.8 square miles – the third-largest British Commonwealth Territory in the Caribbean – that was "different" and neglected. A disproportionate amount of what had been written about the place concerned the remnant Carib population on their reserve (see Comitas 1968).

I had also been warned that landing at the Melville Hall airfield, on the windward, *"au vent"* side of Dominica would be a hair-raising experience.[2] ("The plane has to drop off the mountains and land quickly enough before hitting the rough sea."[3] Then there would be a taxi journey at breakneck speeds on narrow, winding roads through the lush, precipitous mountains to quaint Roseau, the capital and only major town, on the leeward side of the island. "An unforgettable experience!" Alec Waugh (1949, 172) wrote. "The scenery is wonderful but I sing no praise of this road, with its bumps and potholes, its turns and twists ... each blocked by a banana truck, my horn sounding all the way, will I ever forget." In fact, Dominican roads regularly find their way into print, if not in travellers' accounts, then in consultants' reports or government requests. The high level of precipitation and rugged topography make road building a nightmare, as construction regularly gets flooded out and washed away. A government boast, when I was last in Dominica, was that all three major aid donors – Britain, Canada, and the United States – were involved in building roads on the island simultaneously.

Travellers variously glorified or vilified the island. Palgrave (1887, 119) described it glowingly: "In the wild grandeur of its towering mountains ... in the majesty of its almost impenetrable forests, in the gorgeousness of its vegetation, the abruptness of its precipices, the calm of its lakes, the violence of its torrents, the sublimity of its waterfalls, it stands without rival ... throughout the whole island catalogue of the Atlantic and Pacific combined." Waugh (1949, 134) said that it was "one of the most beautiful islands in the world." But not all were entranced by it. Waugh (1949, 134) also said that it was "one of the unluckiest [of the islands]." Early (1937, 98) wrote, "If you have a mind and don't want to use it – or you can't use it – the pleasantest place in the world is Dominica." Trollope, arriving some ninety years earlier, had lamented, "It is impossible to conceive a more distressing sight ... Everything seems to speak of desolation, apathy, and ruin" (Trollope 1860, 161).

Those who had lived there painted a puzzled picture. Jean Rhys, who was born there, wrote, "It is strange, growing up in a very beautiful place and seeing that it is beautiful ... Behind the bright

colours the softness, the hills like clouds and the clouds like fantas-
tic hills. There was something austere, sad, lost, all these things"
(Rhys 1979, 66). And "Everything is too much ... too much blue, too
much purple, too much green. The flowers too red, the mountains
too high, the hills too near. It was a beautiful place – wild, untouched, above all untouched, with an alien, disturbing, secret love-
liness. And it kept its secret" (Rhys 1966, 70, 87). Stephen Hawys, a
painter who settled in Dominica, said, "I capitulated to the island ...
Dominica is not often visited by people who happen along, and decided to stay. Very few people in the other West Indian islands have
a good word to say for it; it has a bad reputation, not entirely
unjustified, but it is an island which has been more sinned against
than sinning" (Hawys 1968, 5). And Sir Reginald St Johnston, one of
the island's earlier administrators, wrote, "But Dominica is like that.
It is a strange island of likes and dislikes and perhaps to some extent of 'nerves,' for the brooding, overhanging mountains, exhilarat-
ing enough when one is living up on the heights, exert at times a
curiously depressing effect on those living in the closed valleys" (St
Johnston 1936, 93–4). My curiosity piqued by these descriptions, I
decided to do my doctoral research there in 1972–73.

Dominica lies approximately thirty miles equidistant from
France's two island-departments, Martinique and Guadeloupe, at a
median latitude of 51°20′N and longitude of 61°22′W. As part of a
submerged volcanic mountain range, it rises from a depth of some
forty-two hundred feet to an axial range of mountains between four
and five thousand feet high and is considered the most rugged
island in the Caribbean.[4] Its geographical position puts it in the path
of the moisture-laden northeast trade winds, which cause abundant
orographic rain: 250 inches fall annually on its western slopes, over
400 inches fall in the interior, and the "dry" eastern leeward side, in
the rain shadow of the mountains, receives a minimum of 70 inches
annually (see Annual Statistical Digest No. 4; Clarke 1962, 5–6;
Harrison 1935, 66; Hodge 1954, 2–3, 10). It also lies just west of the
chief point of origin of the hurricane belt, whose winds can ruin
agriculture and devastate housing. The abundant rainfall created tremendous soil erosion (Hodge 1943, 355). Landslides and avalanches
are common, and streams can become raging torrents in a matter of
minutes, carrying away roads and bridges in their wake.

The general impression of Dominica's flora is of lush vegetation.
"The countryside is almost solid forest or else an intricate mixture
of small clearings and various types of volunteer vegetation"
(Clarke 1962, 12). However, the soil is not very fertile, and its use is
determined almost wholly by site factors. Fauna are limited in both

MAP 2   The Caribbean

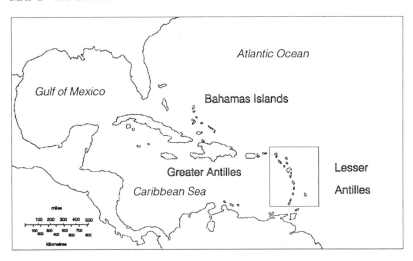

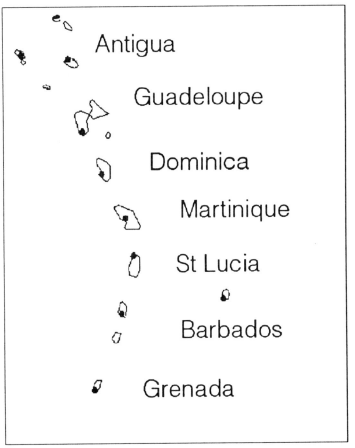

MAP 3   Dominica

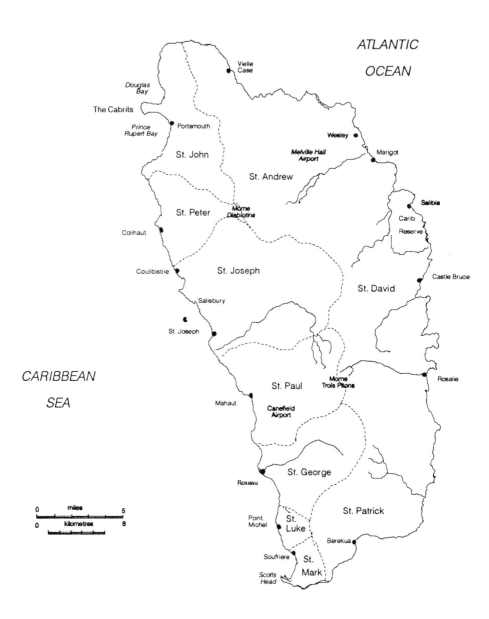

Source: Compiled from Myers (1987a), 191.

number and variety in comparison to continental regions. There are some fourteen species of reptile (Barbour 1937) and three dozen species of bat. Mammals native to Dominica are scarce; both the agouti, a rabbit-sized rodent, and the manicou, an opossum (*Marmosa mitis*), are imported species. There are 135 species of bird, the most famous of which are the diablotin (*Pterodroara kasibaba*) the siffleur montagne (*Circolocerthia ruficauda*), the sisserou (*Amazona impircates*), and the Jacquot (*Amazona arausicica*).[5]

Geographical features have inhibited Dominica's development. There are no mineral resources or sandy beaches; although tourism has increased in the last twenty-five years, the economy remains agro-horticultural. The island's topography militates against large-scale mechanized production. There were only six estates of more than one thousand acres in 1972, and these tended to be under-productive because of labour shortages. Twelve years later, in 1984, there were only two estates in production (Prins, personal communication 1984). Dominica relies on a peasant-based agricultural economy. Dominicans, in keeping with a horticultural terminology, refer to their small-scale agricultural activity as their "gardens."

Internal communications have been a perennial problem in the development of Dominica. The mountains and heavy rainfall make construction of roads very difficult and their maintenance very costly. Before 1958, there were two road networks, one in the north and the other in the south, and they were connected by a launch service operating between Roseau, in the south, and Portsmouth, in the north. Recently, most of the thirty-four peri-island villages have become accessible by road, although as late as 1962 the bananas produced in quantity near Castle Bruce, a village midway up the east coast, had to be shipped north by dugout canoe to the paved road at Marigot, and the coconut oil produced at Rosalie had to be shipped by canoe south to the paved road at Grand Bay. Historically, this has meant that large areas of the island remained, and communities developed, in isolation.

This book describes the ethnohistory of this beautiful, captivating island. It begins with an introduction to the theoretical ideas that I have used in my analysis. The next chapter deals with the pre-history of the region, makes inferences about how Dominica fitted into a general picture, and looks at first contact with Europeans from the Amerindian perspective. The third chapter deals with the island's discovery by Columbus and the contact situation from the European perspective. It is followed by two chapters describing the early settlement and British annexation of Dominica. The latter changed the demographic and structural patterns in Dominica, by attempting to introduce sugar and making Roseau and Portsmouth free ports. As a result, there was a dramatic increase in slaves passing through the island. Chapter 5 discusses slavery and emancipation on the island. Emancipation led to the emergence of a broad horticultural subsistence strategy by ex-slaves in peri-island villages; chapter 6 provides a description of these processes. Emancipation also led to changes at the élite level of society. The coloured mulatto élite succeeded in gaining more political control; their efforts are documented and analyzed in chapter 7. After a period of economic and political stagnation, early in the twentieth century, things began to change in Dominica. The next two chapters describe these changes: chapter 8 traces the emergence of the banana industry and the transforming effect this had on the peri-island villages, and chapter 9 documents the political developments from universal franchise to political independence and the relation to these processes to the extant social structure. The book concludes with a review of developments since the 1970s, using data acquired on a return visit to the island in 1984, and assesses Dominica's history in the light of the theoretical model outlined in the first chapter.

The challenge to the anthropologist, in her or his quest to comprehend other societies and other cultures, is to understand them from within. To do this, one attempts to use emic concepts and categories. One feature of Caribbean culture that lays itself open to misunderstanding is the conceptualization of colour and race.

M.G. Smith (1975, 289) observed, "Miscegenation is an old and widespread feature of Caribbean societies which has generated two important categories, the mestizos and the coloured, while affecting all racial stocks differently." Jordan notes that the particular history of miscegenation in a given society accounts for different terminology to refer to the outcome of such unions. *Mulatto* is a term used in the Caribbean, but not in the United States. The Caribbean societies developed a social hierarchy that was structured according to degrees of intermixture of African and European blood, and, accompanying this, a terminology that differentiated people on the basis of colour. In contrast, in the United States, "the mulattos were lumped with Negroes" (Jordan 1962, 184).

M.G. Smith (1965, 60) observes further that in the Caribbean, "the concept of color is critical and pervasive" – and it is also multivalent, distinguishing between phenotypical, genealogical, associational, cultural or behavioural, and structural colour in Caribbean societies. It is a modifier, rather than a determinant, of status. The following categories were used by Dominicans in Dominica during my fieldwork: *"black black"* or *negre* (dark, black), *jaune* (brown), *clair* (fair), *shabine* (very fair), *vieux blanc* (old, passing white), *blanc* (white), *mulatre* (mulatto), and coloured. Although *black black* and *vieux blanc* were used pejoratively, the other terms were often used simply to help identify people. Thus, when the terms such as *mulattoe* or *coloured* are used in this book, it is simply to help identify the players and capture important social dimensions of the situation under discussion.

I am enormously indebted to the people of Dominica, who, besides giving of their time and effort to help in my research, made my stay among them a truly memorable, enjoyable time. To name specific individuals is always unjust to those who go unnamed, but I feel I am particularly indebted to the late Misses Ritchie, Parry and Claudia Bellot, Pat and Lennox Honychurch, Hermancia Baron and Randolphe Payne, and the late Rev. Proesmans for their friendship and assistance.

There are, as well, many persons to whom I am indebted intellectually for helping me onto and along the academic road. In particular, I must mention the late Professor M.G. Smith, who inspired me to pursue a career in anthropology, Professor W.M. Williams, who introduced me to Dominica, and Mount Allison University, which has provided me with an intellectual base from which to work for the last eighteen years.

I am most grateful to the British Social Science Research Council, the Canadian International Development Research Centre, through the Canadian Association of Latin American and Caribbean Studies, and the Mount Allison University Marjorie Young Bell Fund for the financial assistance that made the research for and writing of this book possible. As well, to the Social Science Federation of Canada awarded a subvention towards the manuscript's publication. I would also like to thank Käthe Roth for her useful suggestions and great job in copy-editing the work; Joan McGilvray, at McGill-Queen's University Press, for her most efficient and friendly role as co-ordinating editor; and the Press, through Sarah Haggard, for selling an edition of the work to the University of the West Indies Press, thus making for its easier distribution within the Caribbean.

Every effort has been made to trace copyright ownership where needed. I would like to thank the following in this regard: Lennox Honychurch, for reproduction of his illustration of Amerindian tools; Phyllis Allfrey's estate for permission to reprint her poem "Ghost in a Plantation House"; the Ministry of Finance, Government of Dominica, for permission to reprint the quotation from the World

Bank Report No. 4740-DOM; ECIG, in Genoa, for reproduction of the map on the frontispiece; the Jamaican Historical Society, for a table from Joseph Boromé's article "The French and Dominica"; and the University of Wisconsin Press, for a table from Phillip D. Curtin's book *The Atlantic Slave Trade*. Finally, I would like particularly to thank Barb Porter, at the University of Toronto Press, for help in searching copyright permissions.

Finally, I owe a tremendous debt to my wife, Cynthia, and my family for tolerating the preoccupations and absences entailed in producing such a work. More than this, not only is Cynthia my soul companion and better half, but she contributed very significantly to the book with her editing skills and critical suggestions.

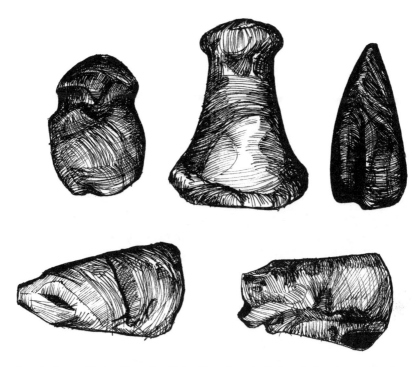

Amerindian artifacts. *Above*: Pre-Columbian stone tools found at various parts of Dominica; *below*: Arawak clay adorno used as a handle for a food bowl. It was found with other shards at a village site at Woodford Hill Bay.

An abandoned estate house.

Fortification ruins.

A paved street in Old Roseau.

The interior of Dominica.

Hurricane damage to Nassief's store.

Cannibals: detail of 1621 engraving.

Loading bananas onto a lighter at Fond Colé.

The Geest boat off Roseau.

Carnival 1972, passing Green's chemist.

Strangest of all strange things is the presence of strangers
In the rooms and the haunts and the glades of the dearly known
Small wonder the slave girl moans and the French priest talks
And Victorian Doctors stroll in the moonlight for walks.

Shallow in graves of loam in diminished acres –
Diminished by predator buyers assisted by drink –
Lie the skeletal forms of pets from an earlier period:
An occupation more gracious; a grace under God.

At last the young Laird awakens to his endowment.
"What's mine is mine!" he says. And to hell with you all.
Leave the place empty and leave it to the spirits
Until the day when my youngling son inherits.

But land is land and predators are busy.
From an enchanted enclave of long days past
Nobody wants to move. Both ghosts and lawyers are waiting
Deep in the shadows: the struggle not yet abating.

(Phyllis Shand Allfrey n.d. 20)

1 Theoretical Questions

The perceptive visitor to Caribbean societies is often struck by the everyday presence of their histories. An apparently seamless continuity binds the past to the present.

Cross and Heuman 1988, 1

The whole tradition of physics is that you isolate the mechanisms and then all the rest flows ... That's completely falling apart. Here you know the right equations but they're just not helpful. You add up all the microscopic pieces and you find that you cannot extend them to the long term. They're not what's important in the problem. It completely changes what it means to *know* something.

Feigenbaum, quoted in Gleick 1987, 175

The purpose of this book is to describe the social history of Dominica, an island that, to date, has received little anthropological or sociological attention. The book draws on my fieldwork experience in Dominica in 1972–73, a brief return visit in 1984, and on primary and secondary historical sources. It is an attempt to understand the fieldwork data as the outcome of enduring historical processes. Trouillot (1984b, 181) comments, "Once revealed, the harsh realities of neocolonialism take such grand dimensions that little else seems to matter. Is there a relevance to Ethnography?" He answers that fieldwork can provide the information that the impact of Dominica's integration into a world economy is felt differently by different subgroups in different communities. The present work attempts to show that the effect of this integration, which was evident in Dominica at the time of the fieldwork, has deep roots and is part of a more pervasive human social phenomenon. Such an exercise entails the marriage of different kinds of research and data. Information on Amerindian prehistory is derived from archaeologists' analyses of the region; that on the historical period before fieldwork is obtained from primary documents and historical commentary. Finally, the fieldwork data are based on participant observation, interviews, and local documents such as bureaucratic memoranda, business records, and the like. This means that both the nature and amount of detail in the chapters varies, but it is argued that this combination provides an understanding of the broad picture.

On my first visit to Dominica, I was particularly struck by how much effort had been expended in and on the island over the years to so little effect. Roads had been cut into mountains, only to be washed away. Bridges had been built across rivers, only to be carried off downstream. Crops had been planted up in the heights, only to be flattened by winds and ruined by hurricanes. There was also a strenuous quest for respect, reputation, and status, which, once attained, were so easily undermined. Order was discernible in Dominica, but it was transient. This book is an attempt to make sense of these observations by presenting a new slant on interpreting the social world.

APPROACHES IN CARIBBEAN SOCIAL ANALYSIS

Several theoretical perspectives have been used to interpret Caribbean societies. In the fifties, social anthropologists such as Lloyd Braithwaite (1953, 1954), for Trinidad, and Raymond Smith (1956, 1962), for Guyana, portrayed Caribbean societies as stratified systems integrated through value consensus. The origins and functions of the institutions of kinship and family received considerable attention, and the importance of ethnic and colour distinctions in the region was noted, usually with some reference to the history of plantation slavery. But, while these approaches emphasized value consensus as a major interpretive concept, the reality of coercion was difficult to ignore. To reconcile the roles of power and consensus in Caribbean society, M.G. Smith (1960, 1965) borrowed the "plural society" concept from Furnivall and represented Caribbean social systems as plural segments integrated into a society by an overarching political framework. These approaches, while capturing important dimensions of Caribbean social reality, were essentially static. They attempted to explain the contemporary situation, a product of colonial forces, in terms of the society's institutional structure.

In marked contrast, Eric Williams' (1964) seminal history of the Caribbean described the region as the historical theatre for politico-economic battles between metropolitan players in Europe. He argued that the keys to understanding changes in the Caribbean situation of the past were sugar and slaves – the preferred means for Europe to guarantee metropolitan economic success. Their interplay created a particular type of society in the Caribbean. It followed that, as the economies of sugar and slaves changed, so did Caribbean society.[1]

This Marxian-type analysis foreshadowed the dependency-theory perspective that has been developed more recently to explain the political domination and economic dependence of Caribbean societies.[2] Dependency theory had its origins in the failure of economic-development policies of the fifties and sixties, which tried to reduce the inequities between developing and developed societies by expanding the industrial sector of Third World countries.[3] To account for this failure, dependency theorists maintained that a counterproductive tendency existed. Underdeveloped societies had to participate in international trade to develop and obtain economic independence for themselves, but the very act of doing this fostered their dependence on the more economically powerful trading partners in the international arena. From this perspective, Caribbean societies are seen as economically, and therefore institutionally, dependent on a metropole or, more broadly, on the developed Western world. Brewster and Thomas (1967) attempt to document the dependency of Caribbean societies, stressing the external structural dependence of Caribbean economic systems and pointing to the plantation and the multinational corporations as the major source of development problems in the region (see Girvan 1973, 10; Levitt and Best 1975, 37–8).[4]

These ideas have been developed by Wallerstein (1974) and his associates into a world-system theory. They argue that there is a world system in which societies, like those in the Caribbean, participate. This system has boundaries, structures, rules, and coherence, and involves a competitive struggle between the member groups, each seeking its own advantage. Like an organism, its characteristics change over time. Centres (core-states) develop through impoverishing the periphery (peripheral areas), and a capitalist economic structure links the developed and underdeveloped worlds.[5] Competition over and extraction of resources create political processes called "imperium" and economic processes called "peripheralization" through which capitalists expand their operations and control and, thereby, "accumulate."[6]

In this light, Caribbean societies are viewed as partial societies, whose internal structures are fully understandable only within a world-wide stratification system conceived in terms of exploitative capitalism. Trouillot (1984a, 1984b, 1988) used this approach in an analysis of peasantries in general, and of Dominica in particular, arguing that Dominica is underdeveloped "not because of its feeble ties with capital but because of its forced integration within the world economy" (1988, 286).

Apart from Williams, a synchronic perspective has dominated Caribbean social analyses. Even dependency theorists analyse the *contemporary* plight of Third World countries within world capitalism, despite their shift in focus from consensual integration to relationships of domination and exploitation. I would argue, however, that social relationships are temporal processes. To understand them, one needs a conceptual framework that analyses social networks over time. Insights from chaos theory, which focuses on far-from-equilibrium systems, suggest that order and change, cosmos and chaos, are not independent opposites but are embedded in one another. These ideas will be drawn on in reworking the dependency theorists' concepts of centre and periphery to produce a diachronic analysis of Dominican society.

ORDER AND CHANGE: EARLY
THEORETICAL APPROACHES

Social theorists have been struggling with the phenomena of social order and social change since the nineteenth century. Early sociologists created the discipline to seek solutions for the disruptive effects of the French and industrial revolutions. The pivotal question of classical sociological theory was the Hobbesian one of how society is possible, given the natural individualism and selfishness of human beings. To legitimize the discipline, science was invoked as the preferred intellectual perspective, and the Newtonian linear, reductionist logic that followed was applied to an understanding of society as a "thing."[7] The problem of order came to be rephrased in terms of the problem of integration, and the intellectual perspective that generated it was dubbed functionalism. The functionalist approach ignored the relationship between society and its environment and that between society and its history. According to this view, the problem of order resided entirely *within* society.

Talcott Parsons, perhaps the most influential sociologist of the second half of this century, thus created a magnificent a priori theory of the human social world with little connection to its wider environment or to its past. He emphasized culture as the key concept for understanding human behaviour and the evolution of societies, but he viewed culture as a domain in itself and human action as taking place within a wider, biophysical environment, as if it could be separated from its cultural context. He saw a society's ability to control its environment as the measure of its level of evolution (Parsons 1977, 11). Although specific evolutionary breakthroughs are identified as having important effects, it is unclear why the breakthroughs occur in the first place. Social change in the Parsonian framework remains somehow aberrant, to be explained in terms of a breakdown in an internal mechanism of social control, an inadequate or faulty socialization, or perhaps a freak intervention from outside – thus remaining residual.[8]

However, social change is not a rare phenomenon, as many critics of Parsons have pointed out. It is, on the contrary, a pervasive feature of social life. By focusing on the self-determining, ordering aspect of human societies and neglecting their embedded, dependent dimensions, functionalists portrayed them as equilibrium systems in which change was foreign rather than as far-from-equilibrium systems with an inherent propensity to change. This failure of the "sociology of order" led some theorists to advocate a "sociology of control," which replaced an understanding of order with an understanding of change (see Dawe 1970). These theorists faced an opposite problem because, although the world in general, and societies in particular, certainly changes, there is an orderliness to change and to the resistance to change.[9]

Early anthropology, in contrast to early sociology, used change to understand the human social world. The central question generating its development as a discipline in the latter half of the nineteenth century was not how to account for human social order so as to restore it, but how to account for human diversity in order to control it. The key perspectives of the time were heavily influenced by the ideas of Charles Darwin and the concept of evolution. Variety could thus be accounted for in terms of stages of development. In the quest to explain societal variation, anthropological answers were frequently couched in terms of human and societal origins, and so anthropologists have traditionally been concerned with "the question of the relation between being and becoming, between permanence and change" (Prigogine and Stengers 1984, 291).

The variety among human societies has often been conceptualized by anthropologists in terms of societal and complexity, in which wholes at one level form parts at another, and the process itself develops over time. The emergence of increasingly complex forms of social organization was explained largely in terms of the role-effectiveness of culture. As know-how increased, societies adapted their social organization to maximize the effectiveness of their improving technology, thus increasing their capacity to appropriate resources from the environment. Variation from society to society was therefore associated with the nature of the environment and the society's relationship to it. A key element in explaining this relation was the society's use of energy: the greater the amount of energy it exploited, the more complex its social structure. Complexity itself became seen as a form of order that enhanced survival potential.

This linking of structural complexity to the harnessing of energy has a long pedigree. Herbert Spencer noted, in 1880, that if some societies get greater material output than others, then energy would appear to be responsible for the material differences between them. In this century, Leslie White (1949, 1959) rekindled interest in an energeticist approach by reducing evolution to cultural complexity, which was itself a simple function of energy harnessed per capita. More recently, Richard Adams (1975, 1988) has attempted to develop a comprehensive theory that links the evolution of social power to an increase in the harnessing of energy.

A major problem with the energeticist approach is that it has, generally, disregarded the "dark side" of energy exchange – the part of the energy equation, expressed in the second law of thermodynamics, that states that as energy is transformed there is always some energy lost and some entropy created. This formula suggests that the more energy-dependent a society is, the more entropy it creates and thus the more environmental disorder it experiences.

Another influential theoretical perspective that has been centrally interested in social change is Marx's dialectical materialism. Marx developed his theory of society to reveal the forces that had created capitalism in order to understand it and to demonstrate that humans did not have to live in a capitalist society (see Bloch 1983). His goal was to generate social change.[10] The value of Marx's approach is that it seeks the origins of social change within an existing social order. Societies, he argued, generate the seeds of their own destruction – notably through the creation of classes, class interest, and class conflict. Thus, Marx's scheme accounts for a series of order-disorder-order societal phenomena. But it is, paradoxically, too sociological. Like Parsons's theory, it views human societies as entities in themselves. There is no discussion of the relationship of human social action to its social and ecological environment, nor is there room for the effects of entropy.

Dependency theory, which, as noted, has been used extensively to analyse Caribbean societies, has its intellectual roots in Marx's perspectives, but its focus is on his materialism rather than on his dialectic. As with the sociology of order, the contemporary world order is the unit of analysis; interest is focused on the systemic effect of economic relationships. Those of interest to dependency theorists emerged in the sixteenth century as a particular type of economic (capitalist) activity and spread throughout the world. This

economic order is perceived as largely self-contained, with a dy- ~~no~~ nature?
namic of development that is primarily internal and has grown to
encompass the globe. It, too, fails to place the world system in a
broader material environment, as it presents change as the incre- ?
mental development of the world system generated by capitalism.)
However, societies are embedded not only in a world system, but in
their environments. Insofar as it documents the spread of capitalism
around the world, world-systems theory is perhaps more a theory of
the nature of this order than it is of the nature of social change.

REVISITING THE PROBLEM OF ORDER AND CHANGE

Today, the traditional conception of reality, expressed in terms of
Newtonian principles, is, while still dominant in our common-sense
view of things, theoretically increasingly problematic. Space is
curved, time quickens and slows, it is theoretically impossible to
capture the building blocks of matter, and investigators inevitably
affect what they are investigating. The field of cybernetics has
increased our awareness of the difference between open and closed
systems. The former, in contrast to the latter, interact with their
environments, and are therefore never stationary or in equilibrium.
In contrast to traditional science, which sought predictability in the
concept of order as the product of cause and effect through the
operation of linear equations, chaos theory attempts to understand
change, turbulence, and disorder as the products of nonlinearity,
whose most obvious characteristic is unpredictability. In this view,
unlike Newtonian mechanics, in which a small force produces a
small effect, minor turbulence can produce major, nonpredictable
effects.[11] Moreover, turbulence is not a freak event, but is intrinsic to
any situation in which there is an exchange of energy. This is the ?
scientific paradigm underlying the theoretical framework of the
present work. The perspective is nonlinear, dynamic, and holistic.)
These ideas, it will be argued, can help us solve the old problems of
order and change and the existence of social diversity, and can provide an insightful way of accounting for Dominica's history.

Far-from-Equilibrium Systems

Living things, and thus human social life and human societies, are
open systems. They are in continuous interaction with their internal
and external environments. In the language of the chaos theorist Ilya
Prigogine, this interaction with the environment makes them far-

from-equilibrium systems with a constant propensity to change. They are inherently unstable.

Order, in an open system, exists because of patterned – that is, repetitive – internal and external interactions that produce predictable relationships and outcomes. This order is always transitory and never perfect, and predictable interactions may spontaneously generate turbulence. A pattern of relationships may be repeated and repeated and then, without warning, a bifurcation occurs. The system may divide into two identical orders that repeat the original pattern, or a new, quantitatively different, order may emerge. Which direction the system will take is inherently unpredictable.

Order is not transitory simply because it is open to turbulence. In living systems, at least, it is achieved in spite of turbulence. As chaos theorists have discovered, turbulence in a system may create a new order. Erwin Schrödinger, the quantum pioneer, said almost fifty years ago that life has the "astonishing gift of concentrating a 'stream of order' on itself and thus escaping the decay into atomic chaos – of 'drinking orderliness' from a suitable environment" (Schrödinger 1944, 82). In doing this, life presents something of an enigma. It goes against the grain – against the tendency, ensconced in the second law of thermodynamics, for all things to unravel, become disordered, break down, run down, become chaotic. Life appears to have a special ability to "suck order out of chaos," to use turbulence to promote order.

The notion that social order unravels into chaos and that chaos rebuilds itself into order can lead us to identify two opposing characteristics of systems. On the one hand, they form *dissipative structures*, which show a tendency toward falling apart. "Dissipative structures are systems capable of maintaining their identity *only* by remaining continually open to the flux and flow of their environment" (Briggs and Peat 1989, 139, my italics). But societies may also be thought of as *autopoietic structures*, which are self-renewing and autonomous. Both dissipative and autopoietic features are inextricably embedded in and merged with the environment because, as open systems, they are continuously exchanging energy with it (see Briggs and Peat 1989, 154).

Attractors

The generation of a new order from repetitive, even habitual, actions, as suggested above, is paradoxically unpredictable but patterned.[12] This tendency for regularity to exist within irregularity was portrayed visually in the fractal geometry of Benoit Mandelbrot.[13] He became fascinated with "self-similarity" – the repetition of detail at descending scale. Take, for example, a range of mountains: "Seen from forty miles away the mountains' outline is quite recognizable, yet simultaneously it's irregular. The closer we drive, the more detail it presents and even when we begin to climb the mountain we notice the same pattern of irregularity and detail in the individual rocks. The complex systems of nature seem to preserve the look of their detail at finer and finer scales ... Could it be that similar mathematical laws or principles of growth and form are operating at such different scales?" (Briggs and Peat 1989, 91).

Mandelbrot came to realize that fractals were generated by simple iterations, and he proceeded to perform them on a computer using an algebraic expression (Z^2+C, where Z is a variable complex number and C is a fixed complex number). The particular set of complex numbers that he explored has since been named the "Mandelbrot set" and dubbed "the most complex object in mathematics" (Briggs and Peat 1989, 96). What is fascinating about it is that the original pattern that initiates the set of changing figures merges repeatedly at different levels as the iterations progress. Embedded in the turbulence of the changing large picture is a recurring order, with the same pattern appearing again and again. Briggs and Peat (1989, 104) ask, "If such a rich, complex, even creative world can be generated by iterating simple mathematical equations (which are in essence symbolic statements of human logic), could iteration be a key to the creative potential in nature, which has far more interesting things to iterate?"

Chaos theorists refer to phenomena that generate a pattern within disorder as "attractors." This leads to the question of whether such an attractor could account for both order and change in the social world. What follows is an attempt to show how chaos and unpredictability can be associated with the notion of the attractor and used to further our understanding of Dominica and account for both order and change in its history.

CENTRE–PERIPHERY AS AN ATTRACTOR

As we move down in societal scale and back in evolutionary time, a pattern emerges repeatedly. Underlying the flux of order and chaos in social life is the pattern of centring and peripheralizing, the dynamic that creates turbulence and re-creates order in the social world. Individuals, families, communities, villages, companies, and societies attempt to centre their world – specifically, to control the flow of energy and information through it. The very activity of centring peripheralizes elements of their environments. The interrelationship of centring and peripheralizing cuts across the chaos and cosmos of societal evolution; it is the attractor around which social relations are formed.

The concepts of centring and peripheralizing that form the elements of the attractor were developed by world-systems theorists to explain the impact of capitalist societies on the non-industrialized nations. They are used here, however, in a broader sense. First, centre and periphery go beyond capitalism and its post-seventeenth-century world impact. Second, they entail energetic and information components involved in a dynamic of exchanges. Third, they include connotations of the cultural dimensions of a "social construction of reality."

If man in society is a world-constructor this is made possible by his constitutionally given world-openness, which already implies the conflict between order and chaos. Human existence is, *ab initio*, an ongoing externalization. As man externalizes himself, he constructs the world *into* which he externalizes himself. In the process of externalization, he projects his meanings into reality. Symbolic universes, which proclaim that *all* reality is humanly meaningful and call upon the *entire cosmos* to signify the validity of human existence, constitute the farthest reaches of the projection. (Berger and Luckmann 1967, 104)

Centring and peripheralizing, then, have connections with a return to energetics and the processes of energy access and exploitation, on the one hand, and to information theory and the sociology of knowledge, on the other. This juxtaposition of materialist and mentalist interpretations of reality might appear incongruent. A holistic perspective, however, implies a continuous exchange within and between the elements of different spheres of social reality.[14] It would predict, therefore, a creative interaction between ideas and energy. Thus, for instance, using a computer to type words may appear to consume very little energy, but the process in fact relies on an indispensable, vast network of support operations rooted in an industrial society that burns up gigawatts of energy and produces billions of tons of "waste." Energy does not determine what is typed and energy exchange does not determine culture, but, just as energy is a condition of possibility for typing words on a computer, it is a condition of possibility for the emergence of culture.

The Dynamic of Centring and Peripheralizing

Centring, then, as the concept is used here, involves individual or collective efforts to accede to and control energy and information in the environment. It is the process by which we create and maintain our individual world, our village world, our ethnic world, and our national world. It involves strategies of categorizing, controlling, dominating, manipulating, absorbing, transforming, and the like, through which we create networks of support for our biological, social, psychological, and spiritual needs. The forces at work in centring may be called centripetal processes, which are predictable sets of relationships established to pull resources into the centre. By effectively funnelling energy and information toward itself, centring is an attractor: it creates order out of chaos in a system. Order is never absolute, however, because one centre never completely dominates a system. While, individually and collectively, we use all sorts of centripetal strategies to bring the world into our ambit of control, the world never capitulates. There are always other, opposing centring forces drawing information and energy and relationships away from us; that is, our centring activities compete with the centring and peripheralizing activities of others. Order co-exists with a greater or lesser amount of disorder.

The cosmos of order developed by a centre inevitably affects its environment, increasing the degree of chaos on the periphery. Chaos is manifested by a lack of predictability in system relations. Successful centring, then, produces a periphery in which the flow of energy and information is away to somewhere else, creating imbalances in the access to resources and relationships.[15] Because the centring activity involves the transformation of energy, there must be an entropic component in this process that contributes to disorder. Although both the centre and the periphery may themselves be thought of systemically, they differ in that the former is a system that is dominated by taking in energy, information, and resources from the environment, whereas the latter is a system that is dominated by giving up energy, information, and resources to the centre. But this is not all. Just as the repetitive processes of exploiting the periphery build up energy in the centre, they also build up entropy on the periphery. Not only is this entropy part of the "resources" that constitute the periphery, but, because the centre and the periphery are intrinsically interrelated, eventually the entropy returns to haunt the centre itself and has the potential to destroy it.

We have noted that the ability of life to "suck order out of chaos" depends on its ability to harness and convert energy. The larger and more complex the life form, the more energy it requires to survive. However, lurking at the heart of any energy transformation is entropy: some energy is lost and cannot be recaptured and used. Entropy has been defined as a measure of the amount of energy no longer capable of conversion into work. An increase in entropy, then, means a decrease in "available" energy (Rifkin 1980, 35). If energy is the potential for work and the underpinning of social order, then entropy reduces the potential and limits the possibilities of ordering. By using the resources of a periphery, successful centring therefore has an entropic effect on it and reduces its potential to create order. Entropy, then, is a dissipative element in a system.

The periphery is intrinsically related to the centre. This relationship is not a spatial one, although distance may play a role in it. The greater the distance, for instance, between the periphery and the centre, the longer information will take to travel back and forth, and the more energy will be involved in communication. However, a periphery exists because there is a centre that limits its ability to use energy and order its environment. As a periphery, it is destined to experience a greater degree of chaos than the centre. Peripheralizing forces emanate from the centre and may be thought of as centrifugal processes, distancing the periphery from control over energy, resources, and decisions. The result is that those on the periphery are unable freely to create their world.

While centring and peripheralizing are evident in the analysis of the colonial and post-colonial world system, a period occupying the major scope of this work, the argument presented here is that these are just special cases of a much more pervasive feature of human life. Neolithic hunters and gatherers centred their activities around bands, while horticulturalists centre their activities around lineages and around villages. Agricultural societies developed cities, which further centred human activities.[16] In these cases, there is a dynamic relationship between the centre and the periphery such that one forms the other, and the construction and the maintenance of these relationships is dependent on a flow of energy (material goods, services, personnel) and information. Following the entropy principle, the very process of energy acquisition and transformation tends to deplete the environment's store of energy and increase the amount of unusable energy.

Centring and peripheralizing, then, is a patterned activity that acts as an attractor, causes both order and disorder, and, similarly to the repetitive pattern in the Mandelbrot set, keeps re-emerging at various levels of social organization and through various changes over time. Metaphorically, centring is similar to Einstein's view of gravity: just as gravity warps the space around it, centring makes it more difficult for people on the periphery to order their world.

As a centre increases its peripheralizing effects, the resulting rise in disorder impinges on its centripetal forces and it requires further centring strategies to handle them. At some stage, the effort to maintain control at the centre becomes too great, too costly to manage. At this point, several consequences may follow. The centre may split and form smaller centres with smaller peripheries to control; or it may develop new strategies of control that enable it to maintain control, at greater energy costs and, in the long term, with greater entropic effects; or it may become the periphery or satellite of some neighbouring larger centre.

CENTRING AND PERIPHERALIZING IN DOMINICA

The metaphor of centre and periphery as an attractor creating and re-creating order and chaos will be used herein to portray the evolution of Dominican society. Dominica's history has not been a smooth linear progression in which one thing led to another, a large cause had a large effect, and a small cause had a small effect, because Dominica has not been an isolated entity. It is and has been a "world" embedded within a world. The nature of this embeddedness is such that, since the sixteenth century, it has been a periphery: metropolitan centres have created an order in Dominica that suits their interests, and predictable sets of relationships have been established in order to funnel out and control resources. Such an order is narrow and fragile and produces a high level of turbulence and entropy. Local attempts to centre the world, therefore, have been very difficult, for resources and information have continually been funnelled away to somewhere else. Moreover, local attempts to create order on the periphery by stemming metropolitan centring have always been eroded, contributing further to the turbulence and alienation of the periphery.

Over the centuries, different groups in Dominica have resisted, sometimes strenuously, the peripheralization imposed by the metropolitan centre. Their history has been a series of lurches in this direction or that, as chaotic events have had disproportionate effects on their surroundings, as turbulence has made its way through time, and as various strategies adopted to create order have made themselves felt. As time goes on – and we may note that entropy gives time its forward direction – individuals and groups have striven for order and predictability, and have laboured to centre their societies. But this very activity has often been the disproportionate force that has sent matters in a different direction, creating greater turbulence and chaos, as centripetal and centrifugal forces from the metropole continuously play havoc with their efforts.[17]

So, we have arrived at the general thrust of the book – to present the history of Dominica in a way that emphasizes processes of energy- and information-flow management, the creation of order, the making of sense in a context that is itself a periphery, the creation of a "world" in an environment that is disorganized because of its relationship to some distant centre. How do people try to centre their world in this context? What does it mean to attempt to centre the periphery, to order a peripheral situation? This book is an attempt to answer these questions. To paraphrase Max Weber, this study seeks to understand how things have come to be as they are – to understands how the structure of the present results from the actions of the past by adopting a metaphor for the forces that are embedded in key antinomies of life – chaos and cosmos, energy and entropy, order and change, and centre and periphery. While the time frame of the later chapters is telescoped, their content is the outcome of the patterns described in the more extended time frames of the earlier chapters.[18] We start with Dominica before Columbus arrived and before the cataclysmic sixteenth-century social changes that peripheralized so much of the world.

too abstract a theoretical framework to be able to judge its usefulness.

2 Indigenous Peoples and Their Contact Experience

In history, time supplies the continuum but not the principle of change.

Goveia 1956, 176–7

The history of Dominica does not begin, as some would have us believe, when Columbus sighted the island ... on Sunday, November 3, 1493. There were neither large settlements on Dominica nor numerous inhabitants, but there is evidence that the island has been frequented by Amer-Indians for at least 1500 years.

Layng 1973, 36

The written history of Dominica began with Columbus's discovery of the island on his second voyage to the New World in 1493. But the oral history of the Amerindian peoples who used the island they called Waitikabuli began some fifteen hundred years earlier, and their material culture is still speaking to us. Recent and continuing archaeological work is uncovering this pre-history, though the paucity and the nature of the material on Dominica make for contradictory interpretations and inconclusive findings. A review of this material provides an appropriate springboard from which to consider the ensuing ethnohistory of the island and to employ the ideas presented in the last chapter. The Amerindians were the first people to inhabit Dominica, and this chapter will be presented as far as possible from their point of view. Because their use of the island was sporadic, it is necessary to place the description in a wider, regional context.

The major populations of Amerindians in the region were to be found on the northern coast of mainland South America. They organized themselves into villages and tribal groups and sought their food by foraging and horticulture. These subsistence strategies posed certain difficulties for survival as their numbers grew. One solution to this population pressure was fission and migration: members of a community separated and sought new foraging and planting territories. In this context, "conditions were much more favorable for hunting and gathering peoples in the Caribbean area than in the tropical forests of the mainland. This was especially true along the coastlines of both the mainland and the islands, where the ocean provided ample subsistence" (Gorenstein 1981, 12). Whether because of population increase, pressure from hostile neighbours, or the lure of better resources, the islands of the Caribbean hosted a series of Amerindian migrations from the South American mainland.

The pre-Columbian Caribbean can best be understood as a series of migrations up the Antillean chain, in which the people replicated mainland social structures and subsistence strategies. As each Amerindian group made its way up the islands, it used the centring strategies of the mainland, forming replicas of the parent community. Each migrating community was a self-reliant society unto itself. While some trade with the mainland occurred, it did not involve subsistence goods.[1] This migratory strategy resulted in severance from, rather than interaction with, the parent community. As a renowned scholar of Dominica's Amerindians observes, "All in all, each island and even each settlement in the island was independent of others for their everyday needs" (Taylor 1972, 5).

This centring activity of absorbing the subsistence resources of the immediate environment generated little entropy in the environment. Native peoples had a good understanding of the carrying capacity of their environments and became part of the food chain, which is an efficient way for life forms to minimize their entropic effects. They had some impact on the flora and fauna of the islands, but the greatest peripheralizing effect each community generated was to define other similar communities as outsiders. Social change was produced only in competitive encounters with other, hostile Amerindian peoples. Generally, change meant either further migration away from the threatening group, or conquest. "Ethnic" identity differences could precipitate aggression, as occurred frequently, for instance, when Caribs encountered Arawaks. The centring activity of the victor was the incorporation of captives into the victorious band and the dissolution of the conquered group.[2]

THE PRE-COLUMBIAN PICTURE

The prehistory of the Caribbean region, then, is one of instability, population movement, and eclipse. Various waves of Amerindian peoples migrated into the region from the South American coast, displaced and replaced one another, and left behind, to varying degrees, traces of their movements. The major population settlements occurred in the larger northern islands of Hispaniola, Cuba, and Jamaica, while some of the smaller islands of the Lesser Antilles appear to have lacked permanent Amerindian populations altogether.

The broader context of Caribbean prehistory suggests evidence of human habitation in the circum-Caribbean region as early as 15,000 BC (Nicholson 1975, 98; Rouse 1964, 505) and paleo-Indian habitation of the Caribbean as early as 5000 BC (Rouse and Cruxent 1969, 46), but when these inhabitants arrived is unclear.[3] It is usually assumed that the major migration of Amerindian people into the Antilles originated from South America during the meso-Indian period around 4000 BC (Kirby 1975, 19), and that it continued into neo-Indian times, ending with the most recent Carib migration, which was well underway in 1200 AD (Bullen and Bullen 1972, 153).[4] Thus, when the Spanish arrived in the West Indies they found paleo-, meso-, and neo-Indian peoples living there: the Ciboney, the Taíno and Arawak, and the Carib, respectively.

The Ciboney, who, by the time of Columbus, had been relegated mainly to western Cuba, were the "simplest" of the Amerindian peoples, centring their world around nomadic hunting and gathering. They "did not know farming and fed themselves instead by fishing and gathering shellfish and wild vegetable foods" (Rouse and Cruxent 1969, 45). These people left evidence of their presence in stone and flint tools, stone containers, shell tools, and petroglyphs and pictographs, but left no trace of pottery, ritualistic religion, or complex organization. They may have been relatively numerous and may have "inhabited the Lesser Antilles for many hundreds of years before arriving in the Greater Antilles where their occupation sites have been known for some time" (Olsen 1971, 102). Their origin is uncertain, but they antedated the other Amerindian peoples and are said by Columbus to have been enslaved by the Arawak (Knight 1978, 8). They must have been on the move some seven thousand years ago. The earliest evidence of their presence was found in Trinidad, but there are a site on Martinique, several in Antigua, and many more in the Greater Antilles (see Kirby 1975, 15). Typically, such foraging peoples live in a small-band organization with a strong emphasis on kinship ties determining membership, and mutual cooperation and familial obligation determining behaviour.

The original lithic Amerindians were displaced and possibly replaced by Taíno and Arawak meso- and neo-Indians, who entered the Antilles some centuries before the time of Christ (Bullen and Bullen 1975, 1). Lévi-Strauss (1974, 252) describes the Taíno and Arawak as "a rather mysterious group, older and more refined than the other two (the Tupi and the Carib)." These people were more developed and efficient in their centring activities. They could control their energy source to a greater extent than did their forager predecessors, for they knew how to farm and make pottery and were skilled sailors (Rouse and Cruxent 1969, 42). As horticulturists, their daily life was centred around village activity. They were hierarchically organized into chiefdoms and believed in spirits, *zemis*, whose effigies in wood, stone, and bones bear witness to ritual activity and were associated with personal-status differences in the village. The ability of horticulturalists to exploit a potentially greater energy resource by producing rather than finding their food is frequently associated with the capacity to support larger popula-tions and more complex social structures, but this centring strategy is also associated with a greater peripheralization and negative impact on the environment: such slash-and-burn agriculturists must clear new ground every few years to avoid the increasing soil infertility that their gardening activity creates.

At the time of the Spanish discovery, the Taíno and Arawak were by far the most numerous people in the region, with "communities dotted from the Bahamas in the north to the Venezuela coastline" in the south (Knight 1978, 10). The Taíno people were located primar-ily in Puerto Rico and Hispaniola (Kirby 1975, 14). The size of their communities varied enormously, from a family or two to settle-ments of four thousand or so residents. The abundant archaeological evidence of their presence includes ceremonial ball courts, pottery and gourds of impressive stylization and sophistication, woodwork, and a little ironwork.[5]

The Taíno and Arawak migrated to the Caribbean in a series of waves, each documented through the distinctive pottery it left be-hind. The first wave started around the time of Christ and lasted till 300 AD. This group left a "pathognomonic" pattern of incised cross-hatched and red-and-white painted pottery – the Insular Saladoid pottery. Their settlements ranged from Trinidad, in the south, to Puerto Rico, in the north. A second migration left white-on-red-decorated pottery with a characteristic set of designs, executed by a special technique – the Modified Saladoid pottery. These people entered the Caribbean region in a series of waves between 300 and 600 AD, and left evidence of their settlement from Trinidad to Puerto Rico and eastern Hispaniola. A third wave of Taíno and Arawak mi-grants, perhaps the most important, entered the region about 700 AD. They were very mobile and seemed to prefer the conditions in the larger islands to those in the smaller ones, which they used only as way stations on their migrations. These Cayo potters introduced a brown-to-grey ware and have been found to range from Grenada to Hispaniola, Jamaica, and even Cuba. Apparently, they liked it so much in the Greater Antilles that they continued to multiply and evolve culturally until the Hispanic invasion destroyed their high Tainan culture. Finally, they were followed by the Calivignoid potters, who introduced polychrome red-and-ochre pottery with black lines. These people arrived in St Vincent about 1000 AD, and evidence of their presence is found from Grenada to, possibly, Guadeloupe.

The last Amerindian people to enter the Caribbean gave their name to the region – the Carib.[6] (They also gave us the term "cannibal" and "canoe" [Taylor 1972, 1].) They probably originated in Guyana and moved up the Lesser Antilles, employing a centring strategy in which their social order was usually maintained through warfare and the subjugation of neighbouring Taíno and Arawak. As Owen (1974, 21) observes, "Warfare and the communal ceremonies associated with it, provided the cement that bound the different segments of Carib society together." They exerted a greater entropic, disordering effect on their environment than did more peaceful groups by killing enemy males and taking women and children captive. This need to capture women may have been created by a belief in and practice of female infanticide. If so, they resemble the Yanomamo of the Venezuelan interior (made famous by Chagnon's studies), a highly belligerent people who frequently raided their neighbours, killing their men and carrying off their women.

According to the archaeological evidence, the Island Caribs, whose Suazoid pottery is judged to be inferior to that of their Arawak predecessors, arrived in St Vincent about 1200 AD and ranged from Tobago to the Virgin Islands. They were, by all accounts, a fierce people. They had subjugated or expelled all the Arawakan communities in the eastern Caribbean, except those in Trinidad, which were somewhat east of their preferred route, by 1500 AD.[7] Their expansion was halted only by the arrival of the Europeans, who found Carib settlements along the entire Antillean arc (Kirby 1975, 19).[8]

The Caribs' social organization is believed to have been less complex than that of the Arawak, perhaps a function of their emphasis on belligerence as a centring strategy. There was no elaborate ceremonial ball court, nor were there *zemis*. A simple fireplace was the focus of a village life that seems to have been on a smaller scale than that of the Taíno and Arawak. The local family head was usually the village leader, who co-ordinated fishing and cultivation and organized the serious male business of warfare. The Caribs' choice of settlement site may have been dictated as much by military strategy as by ecological suitability. By all accounts, they were hated by the Taíno and Arawak, who described them to Columbus as a belligerent, cannibalistic people, a stereotype that was readily adopted by the Spanish and has been perpetuated to this day.[9]

Based, then, on what these Amerindian people left behind in pre-Columbian times, particularly their pottery-making, the broad picture seems clear. There were series of waves of northward migrating Amerindians from the South American mainland, each proceeding until it ran out of momentum (Kirby 1975, 19). At first, a migrating group merely replicated a parent community, but as it came into contact with previous migrants, various contact strategies modified the structure and culture of some groups. There were at least three or four series of migrations during meso-Indian times, and a few sequestered remnants of earlier paleolithic Indians survived in Cuba until Hispanic times.

The reality was probably a good deal more complex than this. The use of pottery to differentiate Carib from Arawak and to document Carib progress through the Lesser Antilles is problematic. Pottery is generally believed to be women's work. The Arawak told the Spanish explorers that the Carib regularly captured and enslaved Arawak women. If this is true, much of the "Carib" pottery would have been made by captured Arawak women, and would therefore by Arawak. Rouse (1961, 39), discussing the origins of the Carib in the region, comments on this, "I personally am rather doubtful that pottery is the best way to get the answer to this problem [of when the Caribs entered the Antilles] ... We have to look to some other aspect of the culture." Haag (1961, 9) notes, "I have the conviction, but it is only a feeling, that the so-called Carib, archaeologically speaking, is greatly overestimated in the West Indies; that is, I think that the vast majority of the archaeological remains found are those of Arawaks rather than of Caribs." Others (Allaire 1980) have argued that the Carib were not a distinct people at all, but some Arawaks who had been acculturated by the Galibies on the South American mainland.[10]

The pre-contact period of Amerindian prehistory, then, comprised a series of waves of Amerindian peoples from mainland South America, each of which had varied effects on its precursors, but each group survived to some extent into the historical period. Each had a relatively low-energy subsistence technology, with the Carib having the greatest peripheralizing, entropic effect on their environment. In order to survive, their strategies had to be altered dramatically when they came into contact with the Spanish.

EUROPEAN CONTACT: THE SPANISH

The Spanish were significantly different from anything the Amerindians had previously encountered. These new people's centring strategies were far more powerful. They were acquisitive and transient. While native people experienced each other in somewhat unequal terms in their own contact situations, it was nothing in comparison with what they all experienced at the hands of the Europeans. Apart from their different appearance, language, and behaviour, Europeans had superior weaponry, armour, and ships, and they had all sorts of unimagined material goods. They also had an ideology of domination, and they forced Amerindians to "labour." They also brought new diseases. In all, local Amerindian peoples experienced a sudden inability to effectively centre and control their world.

The Taíno and Arawak were the first to come into contact with the Spanish, and they attempted to centre their changing world by conceding to Spanish demands. But they saw Spanish demands change as Columbus's plans to create trading posts in his newly discovered territories gave way to poorly executed schemes to extract gold with Amerindian labour. When ineptness and romanticism led to his replacement by Bobadilla, Amerindians experienced a new period in Spanish foreign policy – one of concerted colonization and settlement (see Knight 1978, 24). They saw Spanish governors arrive in the Caribbean with a clear intention to dominate indigenous people. They found themselves increasingly subjugated, terrorized, tortured, and exposed to lethal diseases, and their chiefs were executed. In the words of one Spaniard of the period who was sensitive to the Amerindians' plight,

Yet into this sheep fold, into this land of meek outcasts there came some Spaniards who immediately behaved like ravening wild beasts, wolves, tigers, or lions that have been starved for many days. And Spaniards have behaved in no other way during the past forty years, down to the present time, for they are still acting like ravening beasts, killing, terrorizing, afflicting, torturing, and destroying the native peoples, doing all this with the strangest and most varied new methods of cruelty, never seen or heard of before, and to such a degree that this Island of Hispaniola, once so populous (having a population that I estimated to be more than three millions), has now a population of barely two hundred persons. (de Las Casas 1981, 25)

In response to these developments, the Taíno and Arawak altered their centring strategy from accommodation to resistance to Spanish incursions. They developed new relationships with each other as they attempted to reorder their environment through co-operation and mutual support against a common enemy. Figuerdo (1979) suggests that a great Taíno uprising in 1511 was aided, and possibly even instigated, by the Caribs of St Croix, who had an interest in reversing Spanish conquest before it reached their islands. (The Taíno and Arawak and the Carib had previously been mortal enemies.)

Initially, the Taíno apparently used the Carib as shock troops. But, as Carib numbers dwindled through disease and warfare, and with no match for Spanish power, they reverted to the role of raiding and defending their own islands. Rather than submit to the Spanish, they retreated with the Carib to the smaller islands (Figueredo 1979, 395), resorting to their third strategy – retreat and refuge. It was in this context that Dominica grew in importance, for it became a major Amerindian refuge in the region, leading to a significant increase of native population on the island, and to a more mixed population of Carib and Taíno and Arawak.)

The encounter with Europeans changed Amerindian communities from being self-determined replications of parent communities, or an adaptation to local Amerindian conquests, to being part of something powerful over the horizon. They were no longer at the centre of the world, but somehow on the edge. The Spaniards they encountered represented other, more powerful people from afar who had considerable resources and were prepared to use them in their own interests. As the Amerindians came to experience and recognize themselves as a periphery, they faced the fundamental problem that has dominated Dominican society since: how to centre the world when one is a periphery. One way to do this is to remove oneself as far as possible from any contact with the centre, thereby taking oneself out of the peripheral environment.

As for the Spanish, although they discovered Dominica in 1493, they had their eyes set on grander things and chose not to settle it. Nonetheless, they visited the island from time to time to take on wood and water. Sometimes this occurred with no incident, as when the fleet of Pedro Arias stayed for four days in June of 1514 and "did not see any inhabitants" (Bayley 1832, 648).[11] At other times, however, they encountered significant resistance. On one occasion, for example, a Spanish fleet was wrecked in a storm off the island in 1567 – "not a Spanish soul survived, for the Caribs killed every last one making it to shore" (Boromé 1966, 33). The Archives of the Indies in Seville contain 130 folios concerning raids by Dominican Carib on Puerto Rico from 1558 to 1580 (Boromé 1966, 31, n.11). Evidently, the Carib sometimes took Spaniards for slaves; at other times, they took African slaves. In 1554, six Spaniards escaped after spending a year enslaved by the Dominican Carib (Myers 1978, 327). These reports of slavery mirrored a change that was occurring in the centring strategy of the Spanish. Columbus had come to the conclusion that the riches of the Caribbean lay not in gold, but in its potential Indian labour. Unfortunately, there are no native accounts of the time to draw on, and we are forced to use European accounts that are at the least ethnocentric and often outright racist.

DOMINICA, AN AMERINDIAN REFUGE

Dominica was a base of operations for much of the Carib aggression in the region. With its rugged terrain and geographic proximity to the islands to the north, it was a good spot from which the Carib could launch attacks, first on the Taíno and Arawak, and then on the Spanish during their period of resistance to these invaders. Finally, it provided a refuge for all of the Amerindians retreating from the Spanish (Figueredo 1979) as other efforts to centre their environment failed. The very "ecological limitations" that had accounted for "the sparse aboriginal settlement of Dominica" in prehistorical times and had made it a way station or temporary place of settlement for each wave of Amerindian migrants making its way up the chain of islands from the south now made it ideal as a retreat (Evans 1967, 98–101).[12] Dominica thus became "the island, more than any other, that the Carib could at one time call their own" (Luke 1950, 125).

The Carib, unlike the Taíno and Arawak, had little direct contact with the Spanish. Apart from the occasional prisoner, encounters between Carib and Europeans resulted in the death of one or the other. Yet, some 150 years after the island was discovered by Columbus, there is evidence of some Spanish words in the Carib language: "The Caribs that Father Breton met around 1650, although not under the domination of Europeans, had nevertheless not escaped their influence. The Dictionary contains many words that unquestionably came from the Spanish language. This is most notably the case of all the words applying to entities that were new to the Caribs, such as *camicha* for shirt, *bouteicha* for bottle, *bonet* for hat, *carto* for paper and *crabou* for iron" (Petitjean-Roget 1961, 44). The Carib probably learned these Spanish terms from the Taíno and Arawak who fled the larger islands and joined up with them in "opposition" to the Spanish, thus forming a composite Carib-Taíno/Arawak society. This alteration in their centring strategies to fit new circumstances transformed the Carib from an offensive vanguard into a defensive, heterogeneous remnant.

This change is evident from several European commentaries about Amerindians made at different times. When Columbus first sighted Dominica, in 1493, he encountered a formidable coastline with no obvious haven in which to weigh anchor, so he went off to explore nearby Marie Galante and left a caravel to circumnavigate the island, searching for a harbour. "A good harbour was found, and people and houses sighted" (Cohen 1969, 132). This sighting of Carib people was around Cape Capuchin, in what is now Prince Rupert's Bay – an open spot that could be considered "vulnerable" – one where they might easily be surprised. At that time, however, surprise was of little concern to the conquering Carib. In marked contrast, when a French missionary to Dominica writes, a hundred years or so later, "The choice of [Amerindian] dwelling places is greatly influenced by their fear of seeing their enemies land unexpectedly. They inhabit the eastern part of the island 'because it is more difficult of access and not so often under the lee' " (Breton 1929, 61).[13] This was the opposite side of the island, in a location that was completely inaccessible from the sea and almost inaccessible by land. In the intervening period, the Carib had altered their centring strategy from belligerence to retreat. They had experienced enormous entropic and disordering effects as they were caught up on the periphery to the Spanish centre. Their own centring strategies failed to match the new demands, and, finally, they attempted to maintain their world by removing themselves, as much as possible, from the wake of Spanish centring.

POST-HISPANIC CONTACT

As Spanish influence in the Caribbean waned, other European powers, particularly Britain, France, Denmark, and Holland, started manoeuvring for control of the region. The West Indian islands were becoming pawns in a high-stakes game being played out in Europe. The world that the Amerindians had retreated from became more complicated for them as they became aware that there were other European nationalities besides the Spanish, and that these Europeans were in competition with one another.

In the sixteenth century, the Carib seemed ready to trade with the crews of British ships that stopped at Dominica, but they were ambivalent in the face of these European strangers. In the spring of 1568, several English ships stopped at Dominica and "trafficked with the natives" (Southey 1827, 1: 327). John White records, with the inimitable spelling of his time, "Many of the Salvages came aboard our ships in the canowes, and traffique with us, we also the same day landed and entered their towne from whence we returned the same day aboard without any resistance of the Salvages or any offence den to them" (quoted in Burrage 1906, 308). Christopher Newport spent a day bartering with them in 1592 (Andrews 1959, 189). Preston stopped for six days to refresh his men in 1595, and "the Indians came unto us in canoes ... and brought in them plantains, pinos, and potatoes, and trucked with us for hatchets, knives and small beadstones" (quoted in Andrews 1959, 383). George Percy recounts that Amerindians "came to our ships with their canoas, bringing us many kinds of sundry fruits as Pines, Potatoes, Plantons, Tobacco, and other fruits, and a Roane Cloth abundance, which they had gotten out of certaine Spanish ships that were cast away upon that Iland. We gave them Knives, Hatchets, for exchange which they esteem much; we also gave them Beads, Copper Jewels which they hang through their nostrils, ears and lips" (quoted in Barbour 1969, 129–30).

Matters were not always so amicable. In 1653, "an expedition of savages from Dominica surprised the English at Antigua, plundered and burnt most of the houses, and massacred the inhabitants" (Southey 1827, 1: 332). Thirty years later, the Carib had become so hostile to the British that Sir William Stapleton rationalized a preemptive strike against them: "Necessity compels me to go-a-hunting Indians, which is worse than hunting miquelets in Catalonia or bandits in Italy, but I judge it better to prevent their design by aggression than to live in perpetual fear, which comes in the night at any hour like a thief or a robber" (Great Britain, Calendar of State Papers 1683, quoted in Myers 1978, 331). The Carib did not always lose these encounters, and sometimes they took European prisoners. Friar Blas spent sixteen months as a captive in Dominica (Southey 1827, 1: 238–9); Louisa Navarette, who had been held prisoner on Dominica for years as a slave to one of the chiefs, escaped from the Carib when they raided Puerto Rico (Boromé 1966, 35).

While the Carib might properly hate the Spanish, who had been content to refurbish their ships or raid for slaves in Dominica, and were inconsistent in their relations with the British, who stopped at the island to trade for trinkets, they seemed to be less hostile to the French, who made efforts to settle the island in the sixteenth century as part of their strategy to lay claim to some Caribbean territories on the grounds of *de facto* possession. It appears that Carib–French relations were sometimes even cordial. But there were still clear hostilities between these people; for instance, fifteen hundred or so Carib from Dominica and St Vincent united to attack the French at Martinique in 1635 (Bayley 1832, 649). Some sixty-five years later, virtually all the Carib on the French islands of Martinique and Guadeloupe had been exterminated (Myers 1978, 331). However, the fact that, in Dominica, the French resided as small-scale producers alongside the Carib before the British settled lay the groundwork for better relations with the former than with the latter.[14]

It is to the French missionaries, indeed, that the Carib today owe the most detailed written historical information on their ancestors. French accounts of the Carib come to us from Breton, du Tertre, Labat, La Borde, de Rochefort, la Paix, and Rennard – commentators who wrote over a hundred years after the first Spanish–Amerindian contact in the Caribbean. Things had changed considerably over that period. The number of Carib on the island had declined and, as already noted, they had retreated to the east coast and were much less involved in belligerent contact with Europeans. At the time, the French were interested in the number of settlers they could claim on the island; if some of these were "converted" natives, so much the better. Thus native allegiance to the French flag was seen as an asset, and, despite the hostilities, missionary effort to convert the Carib was considered a politically useful strategy.

In this context, French accounts of the Dominica Carib were considerably more sympathetic than the earlier Spanish descriptions, although there was still ambivalence and inconsistency. Some French observers tried to rectify the ferocious imagery created by the Spanish and defend the Carib against accusations of canni-balism. For instance, Labat denied their cannibalism completely:

It is a mistake to believe that the savages of our islands are cannibals, or that they go to war for the express purpose of capturing prisoners in order to devour them. I have proofs to the contrary clearer than the day ... It is true that when they kill a man, they often *boucan* his limbs and fill cala-bashes with his fat to take home with them. They do this, however, to keep as trophies and proofs of their victory and courage ... I repeat that though the Caribs do *boucan* the limbs of enemies they have slain, it is only done to preserve the memory of the fight and rouse them to future vengeance, and not with any idea of eating them. (Labat 1931, 101, 102, 103)[15]

Breton more cautiously observes, "Let us first underline a fact concerning food. The Spaniards considered the Caribs as the perfect cannibals, the perfect man-eaters. The truth is that for them human flesh is not a food as others; but having triumphed over a courage-ous enemy, they intend to appropriate his virtues by a ritual cere-mony to which they invite the whole tribe and which they top off by assuming the name of the Arawak they have killed and eaten" (Breton 1665, quoted in Petitjean-Roget 1961, 56).[16]

In contrast, other commentators preserved and even embellished the cannibal image. Du Tertre, for example, who borrowed from Breton, writes "The Caribs have tasted men from every nation that has visited them. I have heard them say several times that among all the Christians, the French were the best and the most delicate, in contrast to the Spaniards who were so tough that the Caribs had difficulty eating them" (du Tertre 1958, 38). And de Rochefort goes further still, stating that the Carib of his day found "French people delicious and by far the best of the Europeans, and next came the English. The Dutch were dull and rather tasteless, while the Spaniards were so stringy and full of gristle as to be practicably uneatable" (quoted in Ross 1970, 52).[17]

Regardless of their opinions on Carib anthropophagy, French commentators added their own biases and exaggerations. Labat (1931), for example, describes the Carib as "the most careless and lazy creatures that have ever came from the hands of God" (73) and observes of the women, "They are no more dumb than the rest of their sex" 105). The French were prone to report what they heard rather than what they saw (see Myers 1984); sometimes, when they tried to do both, the results were contradictory. Thus, Labat (1931, 98) observes, "I have never seen them quarreling or disputing, and admire their restraint in this matter, but strange to say they often kill and murder each other without any quarrel or discussion."

The situation of the Carib themselves had changed considerably by this time, and it continued to change. They had altered their "ethnic" composition considerably. As noted already, Amerindians in Dominica were in fact a mixture of the Carib and the Taíno and Arawak, a mixture not simply the result of Carib capture of Taíno and Arawak women and children, but of the immigration of Taíno and Arawak men. In addition to this, captured Europeans and African slaves were incorporated into Carib society in the sixteenth and seventeenth centuries. Labat says, for instance, that the Amerindians showed him an Englishman's arm, which belonged to one of six men they had killed in Barbuda, where they had taken a white woman and two children captive. Sixteenth- and seventeenth-century commentaries are full of tales of Carib raiders capturing African slaves and transporting them back to their islands to be used as servants.[18] There was no love lost between the Carib and the Africans: "The Caribs imagine they are far superior to the Blacks, while the latter, who are not a whit behind the former in conceit, despise the Indians and call them savages" (Labat 1931, 83–4). In fact, "there is, interestingly enough, documentation for a slave rebellion by Blacks in Dominica against their Island Carib masters" (Gullick 1978, 286).

Thus the Carib saw the number and racial composition of their population change along with their culture.[19] They occasionally resorted to traditional centring strategies – sufficiently, at least, for Labat (1970, 110–11) to observe, "One is very careful to preserve peace with the Caribs, not because we are afraid of them, they are too weak in numbers to do any serious harm to our colonies, but so that settlers in outlying districts can live without fearing the sudden raids that these Indians make on their enemies." Although their language had taken on European words, which reflected their exposure to new objects, they struggled to maintain their own culture against that of the Europeans. As Labat (1931, 79) notes, the French missionaries laboured for some thirty years in neighbouring Martinique to convert Amerindians with absolutely no success. In the end, however, the Amerindians could do little about the existence of Europeans in their world and needed to adopt some sort of *modus vivendi* to deal with them.

As the Carib in Dominica became aware of the competition between the English and the French over the island, they developed a centring strategy of playing one off against the other.[20] At one time they were split in their allegiance – the *capesterre* (windward) carib siding with the French and the *basseterre* (leeward) Carib siding with the British. Sometimes, they attacked, slaughtered, *boucanned*, and ate both the English and the French; at other times, they were on peaceful terms with both nationalities and traded for preferred goods and metal tools. Throughout this post-Hispanic period, their attempt to centre and order their world was problematic. Some of the things they wanted necessitated trade with Europeans – over which their degree of control was unpredictable. Others involved their traditional life style, and their choice of domestic location reflected this. Increasingly, they found themselves retreating from European dominance by fleeing to the inaccessible windward side of the island. Nevertheless, they continued to make contact with European settlers, and later with the descendants of African slaves, and finally with the mix of races that came to be "Dominican." By 1952, they had lost their culture to the extent that an authority on the Dominica Carib could write, "The Carib remnant in Dominica, West Indies, one hundred – or less than a quarter of whom may be reasonably regarded as 'full-blooded' Indian, lost their language at the beginning of this century, and with it, in all probability, a considerable amount of traditional folklore" (Taylor 1972, 44). As well "As might be expected, the opening of a school, church and so forth in the last thirty or forty years have brought about the loss of nearly all that remained to the Caribs of traditional characteristics, customs, and language" (Taylor 1935, 265).

THE PREHISTORICAL AMERINDIAN migrations from the mainland were centring strategies, probably adopted to handle threatened population – ecology survival ratios. As later waves came into contact with previous migrants, they had to accommodate their behaviours accordingly. Archaeological evidence suggests that some did this by moving on, others by forming alliances, and still others by attacking and subjugating competing groups. Thus, the very repetition of the initial activity generated social change in the region, from a mere replication of communities on the mainland to hybrid cultures and communities.

The Amerindians' initial attempt to centre their world was a collective response to the requirements of staying alive in sometimes rugged island environments. They were free to choose their centring activities, and their "periphery" became problematic only when game or fish grew scarce, vegetation became scant, or other Amerindian bands emerged. Each Amerindian community was self-regulating but in dynamic interplay with the environment, from which it derived its food and the wherewithal to make tools and the like. Because the populations were small and the information and energy needs low, the ordering, centring activities of these peoples generated weak entropy and peripheralization in their environments.

A French commentator described these prehistoric times in the Caribbean as "the action and reaction ... of man, nature and chance," in which the original migrants to the Caribbean were buffeted principally by nature as they moved from island to island in their quest for survival (du Tertre, quoted in Goveia 1956, 20). Whatever the reason for the waves of migrants from the South American mainland, it was not part of a continuing centring strategy of the mainland to absorb resources, information, or persons from the peripheral area. Rather, the centring strategy consisted of a parent community freeing itself of the burden of some people, who set off to centre a replica of the community somewhere else – in this case, on one or more of the islands in the Caribbean chain.

The migrating groups represented, in microcosm, the low-entropy communities from which they had come, repeating the self-sustaining and independent technological and organizational patterns of the home community in a new environment. Members of the new migrant communities found little difficulty in ordering their world;

they perpetuated the practices that had been "successful" in the home community, perhaps with some slight modifications learned from other Amerindian communities with which they came into contact. Their small-scale operations employed simple technology, had a low impact on their environment, and were independent of the parent community on the mainland. The parent community became marginal, exercising no control over the new community, and the island communities were a periphery to the mainland only in the sense that they provided new territory into which fission-groups could move.

From an Amerindian perspective, the Spanish arrival in the region appeared to be a fortuitous, chance event, but it altered irreversibly the centring pattern that had characterized the island populations. There was a significant difference between the earlier "invasions" by Amerindian peoples of the Caribbean islands and that by the Spanish and other Europeans. Whereas the Amerindian migrants came in order to make the islands their "home," the Spanish and later Europeans were looking for territories to exploit in terms of metropolitan contexts and interests.

The contact situation completely transformed the order created by the Amerindians. In relating to the Europeans, the Amerindians found themselves inexorably caught up in that larger world and became part of a periphery for a centre over the horizon. The most significant feature of the newcomers' settlements was that, unlike those established by Amerindian migrants, they did not merely replicate the communities from which they had come. They were, rather, specialized, dynamic extensions of those communities and remained very much tied to them. In a sense, they were truncated communities existing for the narrowly conceived purposes of a distant metropole. Their role was to exploit to the fullest the newly discovered territory and, in so doing, to peripheralize it.

As a periphery to a considerably higher-entropy society than their own, the Amerindian communities experienced the disorganization that such a centre generates in its environment. In the words of one observer, "Severe depopulation of tribal peoples is a characteristic of the frontier process and has been reported by observers from all parts of the world over" (Bodley 1975, 38). By the mid-eighteenth century, the Carib population had plummeted, through wars, mass suicides, emigration, and especially illness, from some five thousand, in 1647, to a mere four hundred, by 1730 (see McNeill 1976, 215).[21] There was also the beginnings of other forms of entropy affecting the natural environment – widespread deforestation, resource over-exploitation, species extinction, pollution, and soil erosion.

To combat this new entropy and disorder, the Amerindians adopted various strategies to maintain some control of their environment and to centre their own world anew. At first, groups of Taíno and Arawak responded co-operatively, whereas Carib bands reacted with the same isolated aggressive raids they had used in the past. When this failed, various groups adopted a collective, united Amerindian resistance, a strategy unknown to them before. When this also failed, they retreated, and tried to centre their society as far as possible from contact with the Europeans by blurring ethnic distinctions that had previously been important, and by maintaining a degree of autonomy through the practice of traditional customs. They moved themselves as far away as possible, to the edge of the periphery and out of the centre's orbit. In Dominica, these efforts to counter European centring were the first of a series of relatively ineffective efforts by indigenous Dominicans to centre the periphery, to create order in an entropic environment.

The scale of this centre–periphery situation during the Spanish era was small; the absolute numbers of people involved were considerably lower than the population of the region today. Moreover, the relation of the Spanish to nature was not nearly as protected by culture and technology as would be the case even a hundred years later. Although the effect of initial contact on Amerindian communities was disastrous, the radius of the entropic impact multiplied by leaps and bounds in the centuries that followed. Nevertheless, the Amerindians were able to create a centre for themselves in Dominica, albeit on a periphery, and to survive into this century. In order to appreciate this phenomenon adequately, we need to see this process from the "invaders'" point of view.

3 European Discovery and Settlement

In the Small hours of Sunday morning, November 3, 1493, the
watchman at the Admiral's mast head saw what he had been told by
his inspired pilot he would indeed see – land!   Bradford 1973, 181

A crew of cutlass-thrusting pirates on a small ship, a sudden massacre
of helpless natives, and a memorial burnt onto a fragment of wood or
scraped on a standing stone, was how Jonathan Swift wrote of the idea
of colonial expansion. But, what was indeed as satirical exaggeration
in the eighteenth century, seems less so now that the history of European expansion and Imperial ambition has been more fully researched
and related.   Knight 1978, 6

The centring strategies of native peoples in the Caribbean had been
forced to change from one in which they had considerable autonomy while depending a good deal on the biota and geography of
their immediate environment, to one in which their autonomy was
severely threatened by the more technically sophisticated and
unpredictable strangers who viewed native people and their lands
in a very different light. In keeping with their "modern" origins in
Europe, these people came to dominate and subjugate nature. Their
impact on the Caribbean is summed up by Hodge and Taylor (1957,
513): "Where local terrain in the West Indies permitted white
settlement and exploitation much of the native flora and fauna,
including man himself, disappeared."

THE EUROPEAN CONTEXT

The European societies that increasingly peripheralized territories
like Dominica were for the most part agrarian and far larger and
more complex than the Amerindian societies described in the last
chapter. Their ability to produce greater food surpluses, particularly
in areas north of the Alps, "where the introduction of triennial
rotation by means of the heavy horse-drawn plow resulted in an absolute increase of the surplus product" (Wolf 1982a, 105), translated
into an ability to support a complex social structure of non-food
producers, most of whom were to be found in larger and larger
urban centres. In addition to this, Europe's rulers increasingly

centred political power by extracting enough tribute to pay for war, which they used to attain their expansionist political objectives. There were three ways in which this expansion could be accomplished: "One was to expand externally, against enemy powers, and seize surpluses from external enemies. Another was to discover resources, either home-grown or acquired as booty, to sell to merchants in exchange for needed goods or credit. A third way was to enlarge the royal domain, the area from which the king could draw direct support without the interference of intermediaries. The developing polities of Europe followed all three strategies, in a different mix at different times, and with different results" (Wolf 1982a, 105).

By the fifteenth century, nation-states in Europe had emerged out of feuding baronies, and new national identities and ideologies were at play. Complex patterns of trade linked cities and communities throughout Europe, and trade networks extended to the Middle and Far East. Marco Polo's thirteenth-century travels and the Christian crusades to recapture the Holy Land had stimulated European attempts to find new routes to India and the Orient. The mastery of a Chinese invention, gunpowder, and the technology for building long-distance sailing ships sparked the voyages of discovery, the growth of European influence, the extension of the slave trade, and the tendency of the world's resources to funnel in toward Europe. In other words, the centring activity of metropolitan powers was being considerably extended; this is the point in history that dependency theorists take as the beginning of the world system.

With the fifteenth century dawned the age of discovery, and Portugal took the lead. The Portuguese explored farther and farther down the west coast of Africa, where they encountered African natives. They brought home some in 1442, fifty years before the discovery of America. Prior to his voyage to the New World, Columbus acquired a "personal experience of the slave trade" as a sailor in the Portuguese merchant marine (Williams 1970, 31). The Portuguese continued to venture southward in Africa until Bartholomew Diaz rounded the Cape of Good Hope in 1486, opening a potential trade route to India. Spain was determined to compete with Portugal, its adventurous rival, and wanted legitimate claim to a territorial passage to the Indies. Columbus became part of this strategy.

Spanish discovery of the Caribbean was therefore part of a European competitive quest for trade routes to the East, and Columbus was the harbinger of the "modern age of commerce and imperialism" in this respect (Williams 1970, 20). Trade was of such concern to Columbus, when he set sail for the New World, that, some would say, it led him to completely misrepresent the lands he discovered. He clearly thought that his first landfall was on one of the 7,448 islands that Marco Polo had said were located in the Sea of China, for the day after he landed he was in a hurry to move on, to find the reputedly rich island of Cipango. But as evidence for this location dwindled, he claimed, somewhat vaguely, that he was somewhere in "the Indies." Although it was a desire for trade and commerce that led Spain to sponsor Columbus, it was the discovery of gold in the New World that particularly whetted Spanish appetites. In his report to Ferdinand and Isabella of the Second Voyage, Columbus writes, he found "a great number of rivers whose sands contained this precious metal in such quantity, that each man took up a sample of it in his hand; so that our two messengers returned so joyous, and boasted so much of the abundance of gold, that I feel a hesitation in speaking and writing of it to their Highnesses" (quoted in Major 1870, 74). The Spanish established colonies with government administrators on the northern coast of South and Central America and the larger Caribbean islands in order to mine for gold using Amerindian labour.

This extension of the known world led to rivalry over territorial claims between Spain and Portugal. The usual method of resolving such potential conflicts between European Catholic rivals was to appeal to the pope.[1] Spain and Portugal proceeded to do this, and Pope Alexander VI issued a bull in 1493 confirming Portugal's existing rights to all territories east of an imaginary north–south line drawn one hundred leagues west of the Azores and the Cape Verde Islands. Spain was unhappy with this; it appealed the decision and was formally given rights to all territories to the west of this line as far as India. Now it was Portugal's turn to be dissatisfied. The two parties finally resolved their claims through the Treaty of Tordesillas, of 7 July 1494, which fixed the line a farther 270 leagues west of the original line and gave Brazil to Portugal.

The settlement of such matters by the papacy was not acceptable to all European nations, particularly Britain, France, Denmark, and Holland. After the Treaty of Tordesillas, Henry VII of England issued a patent to another sailor, John Cabot, to undertake a voyage of discovery (Williams 1970, 71). This was a momentous event, for it signified that England did not recognize the papal partition of the entire world-to-be-discovered between Spain and Portugal and was seeking to claim territory for itself. Francis I of France went further, explicitly rejecting the papal partition in a protest to the pope; he was told by Pope Leo XII in 1535 that he was not bound by Pope Alexander VI's bulls of donation. England, France, and, later, Hol-

MAP 4   The New World: Detail of the "Cantino" World Map, 1502

Source: Columbus 1960, 49.

land thus considered themselves "free" to compete with Spain. After Henry VIII broke his ties with Rome, England increasingly became the nation that spoke "for the newcomers against Spanish pretensions to a monopoly" (Williams 1970, 72).

The newcomers employed three centring strategies in their competition with Spain. First, there was piracy, initiated originally by individuals, but developed by Britain into something of a national policy. The epitome of this activity was embodied in Sir Francis Drake, whose daring exploits at sea led to his being summoned from a game of bowls to defeat the Spanish Armada. Second, contraband trade was used to undermine Spanish monopoly. The exploits of Sir John Hawkins of Britain exemplify this strategy: he initiated the English slave trade by obtaining a cargo of slaves from Africa and selling them clandestinely to eager planters on Hispaniola. The nation that was to obtain a reputation as the scourge of the Spanish in this regard, however, was Holland. The third strategy was a policy of territorial settlement whereby land was claimed through occupation. In Dominica, it was primarily the French who used this strategy. This centring process was strengthened as profit became more firmly institutionalized as a primary organizing value in European societies and labour became increasingly objectified and "rationalized." In sum, effective centres emerged in Europe to compete with each other and to pull in to themselves increasingly vast and varied amounts of non-European, but increasingly colonized, resources.

The entropic, disordering effects of these developments were already being felt in Europe. There was a plague of epidemic diseases caused by "the crowded condition and bad sanitation of the walled medieval towns, the squalor, misrule and gross immorality occasioned by the many wars, by the fact that Europe was overrun with wandering soldiers, students and other vagabond characters, and by the general superstition, ignorance and uncleanliness of the masses" (Garrison 1929, 186).[2] These matters were compounded by very regular continent-wide famines, themselves a product of massive deforestation of Europe's countryside to make way for agriculture, and then the overuse of land and consequent infertility and soil erosion. As well, there was pervasive violence, first at the level of the everyday exploits of bands of thieves, murderers, and violators of wives, virgins, and nuns; then at the level of sanctioned violence by local authorities in terms of torture and executions; finally, there was the church-sponsored violence of the Inquisition and that of the nation states, principalities, duchies, seigneuries, earldoms, and the like, who pressed their subjects into continual war (see Sale 1990, 31–4).

The discovery of the West Indies, including Dominica, was part of this larger context of centring the world's surplus in Europe, where European countries competed with each other over control of the nation-building process. Columbus was trying to discover a western route to the Orient for the explicit purpose of extending trade and importing riches. The Europeans who arrived in the Caribbean, unlike earlier Amerindian migrants to the region, were not looking for a home, but for resources they could exploit for a profit – in particular, gold, minerals, and slaves – and funnel back into Europe to further enrich the wealthy. The impact on the periphery, in terms of entropy, social disorganization, and change, was immense. This, then, is the context for understanding the European contact with and settlement of Dominica, which played a role in each of the above European anti-Spanish strategies. The island provided a refuge and resources to buccaneers, privateers, pirates, and smugglers, and a home to would-be settlers. Thus, the competition and conflict, the control and power plays on the island were part of a larger game being played in Europe. That game is all-important for our understanding of the next phase of Dominica's history.

DISCOVERY OF DOMINICA AND EARLY EUROPEAN ACTIVITY IN THE CARIBBEAN

The Spanish discovery of the West Indies was the start of the first gold rush of modern times, and it had devastating consequences for the Amerindians. The very day after his discovery of the Bahamas on his first voyage of discovery, Columbus records in his journal, "I was attentive and took trouble to ascertain if there was gold" (quoted in Williams 1970, 23). In fact, a specific gold-and-silver clause had been written into his contract with the Spanish sovereigns before he sailed. His attentiveness paid off: he found gold in Hispaniola. He returned from his first voyage convinced that he was on the threshold of a gold bonanza.

The discovery of gold in Hispaniola was followed by a very brief period of high gold production there, the cost of which was extermination of the natives. Within a short time, tens of thousands of Amerindians had died of disease brought over by the Europeans, or had been massacred or enslaved. By the time Sir Francis Drake visited Hispaniola, in 1585, less than a hundred years after Columbus's first contact with them, the island's Arawaks had been exterminated (Rouse 1963a, 517–18).

Columbus had noted, ominously, in his diary during his first voyage that the Indians "should be good servants and intelligent ... good to be ordered about, to work and sow, and to do all that may be necessary" (quoted in Williams 1970, 31). He also mentioned that they were a compliant people: "They are very gentle and do not know what it is to be wicked, or to kill others, or to steal, and are unwarlike and so timorous that a hundred of them would run from one of our people" (quoted in Jane 1960b, 58). Here, then, lay a second source of riches: slaves, a social category well established in Spain by the time Columbus sailed from Lisbon, and embedded in "the thirteenth century code of *Las Siete Partidas* ... which recognized slavery as an integral part of the Spanish economy" (Williams 1970,

30).[3] An African slave trade was already thriving in the eastern Atlantic, and as gold production quickly started to fail and the gold mines dwindled in importance, Columbus increasingly adopted the view that the real riches of the West Indies lay in their Amerindian populations (see Williams 1970, 31).[4]

At the very outset, then, the West Indies were perceived by Europeans in terms of their exploitable resources. The overriding interest of the newcomers was what could be used to benefit the home country – or, more accurately, what could be used to benefit them in their home country. So the Caribbean was discovered *as a periphery*, a territory that was thought of in relation to the metrople. What linked the periphery to the centre was a narrow spectrum of features considered valuable by and profitable at the latter – first, gold, and then slave labour.

The ensuing plight of the "peaceful" Taíno and Arawak on the larger islands created a humanitarian backlash in Spain, which led to the cessation of slavery in those islands. On Columbus's first voyage of discovery, however, the Arawak had told him of another group of Amerindians called "Caribs." In his journal entry for Sunday, 13 January 1493, Columbus noted, "Of these islands, the admiral says that he had been told some days before by many persons. The admiral says further that in the islands which he had passed they were in great terror of Carib: in some islands they call it 'Caniba,' but in Española 'Carib'; and they must be a daring people, since they go through all the islands and eat the people they can take" (quoted in Jane 1960a, 147).

Columbus probably mistranslated the term "caniba" to mean "man-eater."[5] Taylor (1958, 157) argues that the term actually meant "manioc people."[6] The confusion was politically useful: the image of a bellicose and cannibalistic tribe began to feature in Spanish accounts of their travels, and they proceeded to identify them as fierce man-eaters,[7] bestial and animalistic, with little potential for Christianizing and civilizing. This provided Columbus with the necessary justification for enslaving them. Besides their political usefulness, such descriptions heightened the sense of adventure and enlivened story-telling at a time when this was an important form of entertainment.

The Carib thus became part of Columbus's plans to develop the colonies: "Their Highnesses might authorize a suitable number of caravels to come here every year to bring over the said cattle, and provisions, and other articles; these cattle etc., might be sold at moderate prices for account of the bearers, and the latter might be paid with slaves, taken from among the Caribbees, who are a wild people, fit for any work, well proportioned and very intelligent, and who, when they have got rid of the cruel habits to which they have become accustomed, *will be better than any other kind of slaves"* (quoted in Major 1870, 88, my italics). As part of his grand scheme, slaves were to be taken from among the cannibals to be traded for cattle, the cattle were to provide food to support settlement of the islands, and wealth generated on the islands was to enrich Spain and pay for the Crusades (Williams 1963, 50). To pique the interest of the Spanish sovereigns, from whom he sought support for his venture, Columbus shipped home some six hundred Amerindians in 1498. His plan succeeded. In 1503, the Spanish sovereign proclaimed, "Being as they are hardened in their bad habits of idolatry and cannibalism ... I hereby give license and permission ... to capture them ... paying us the share that belongs to us, and to sell them and utilize their services, without incurring any penalty thereby, because if the Christians bring them to these lands and make use of their services, they will be more easily converted and attracted to our Holy Faith" (quoted in Williams 1963, 63).

Permission to enslave "cannibals" was strengthened in 1511 by "A Royal Decree Authorizing the Taking as Slaves of the Caribs," which commanded the armadas "to make war on the 'Caribs of the islands of Trynidad, Paris, and *Domynica*, and *Mantenino*, and *Santa Lucia*, and *Saint Vincente*, and *Concebcion*, and *Barbados*, and *Cabaca* and *Mayo*, and they may make prisoners of them, and profit from them without on that account incurring penalty, and without having to pay Us any part, provided they do not sell them or take them outside the aforesaid *Indies*" (quoted in Jesse 1963, 29). There followed ten years or so of appalling brutality meted out to the Amerindians and the murder of thousands of indigenous people in the region (Moore 1973, 125).[8]

Thus, Columbus sought out the Carib not out of curiosity, nor because he liked a good fight, but because they were part of a larger plan. He was convinced that a fierce, conquering people was likely to be a robust people, and a robust people could provide a productive, lucrative work force. Reports of the Taíno and Arawak describing the Carib as a fierce, warlike people who attacked from the south, killed their men, and carried off their women led Columbus to develop a stereotype of these people which was well established before he ever set eyes on them.[9] And it was in order to set eyes on them that he headed farther south on his second voyage of discovery, a well-manned, well-equipped expedition that left Cadiz on 25 September 1493, which took him to Dominica.

Sailing by way of the Canary Islands, to avoid the Portuguese, Columbus enjoyed a perfect passage with only one piece of bad weather, on the night of 26 October. It was twenty days since he had left the Canaries, and the members of his crew were longing for land: the sea seemed boundless and ship life was uncomfortable (Edwards 1819, 1:431). On the evening of Saturday, 2 November "Columbus was convinced from the color of the sea, the nature of the waves, and the variable winds and frequent showers, that they must be near to land; he gave orders, therefore, to take in sail, and to maintain a vigilant watch throughout the night" (Irving 1973, 370–1). It was with great joy that they sighted land at dawn on Sunday, 3 November. They sailed for three miles up the island's wind-dashed eastern coast in search of a harbour, but could find none. Columbus left a caravel to search further for a suitable landing while he took his men on to Marie Galante. In honour of the day, Columbus named the island Dominica.

The rugged nature of Dominica's coastline and the hostility of its Amerindian inhabitants discouraged Spanish settlement. In 1514, Pedro Arias de Avila stayed for four days, was attacked, but took on wood and water. In 1526, Ovjedo called for the same purpose. In 1565, the fleet of Menendez stopped at the island. In 1567, his son's ship was wrecked off the coast; most of the crew made it to shore, but they were all massacred by the Carib. Although the Spanish dropped anchor there to take on wood and water, and the Board of Trade in Seville designated it officially for such purposes for all west-bound voyages, the Spanish called there "only in dire emergencies" (Boromé 1966, 33, 38). In the words of one commentator, "Except for putting a few hogs upon it, the Spaniards did little more than give it a name" (Campbell 1763, 82).[10]

Spain's European rivals also wanted access to resources in the New World. With this in mind, the French began to counter Spain's monopoly on the West Indies by pirating Spanish ships. Columbus had to change tack on his third voyage of discovery in order to avoid a French fleet. To contain this international conflict, France signed a treaty with Spain in 1559, which enshrined the phrase "no peace beyond the line," thereby legitimating New World skirmishes and preventing them from becoming European disputes. The English, too, sent a series of adventurers to seek peaceful trade in the West Indies or, if this failed, to privateer. They began successfully to challenge the Spanish claim to monopoly in the Americas with the doctrine of effective occupation. They attempted to colonize Newfoundland in 1583 and Roanoke Island, off the Virginia coast, in 1585 and 1587. The first English colonies, in the Lesser Antilles, however, were composed of very small numbers of men with limited resources (see Hamshere 1972, 20). Except for very sporadic attempts, they did not try to settle Dominica at this time. In fact, no

European nation attempted to settle the island in the sixteenth century (see Coke 1971, 333).

Early attempts to settle other islands in the Lesser Antilles also failed. The *Olive Branch*, sent out from Britain by Sir Oliph Leigh in 1607 with seventy men to reinforce Charles Leigh's colony on the South American mainland, overshot the mouth of the Wiapoco river and was forced by the prevailing winds and currents to set down on the island of St Lucia, where most of the people aboard were killed by the Carib (see Hamshere 1972, 22). A venture to Grenada, in 1609, also foundered. British colonization of the area really began when Thomas Warner settled St Christopher, in 1624. Three years later, in 1627, some eighty British colonists settled in Barbados. These early British efforts were soon followed by French ones: they started to settle Guadeloupe in 1632, and Martinique in 1635 (Goodridge 1972, 151).

In the early seventeenth century, neither England nor France was anxious to colonize the severely mountainous, heavily forested island of Dominica, which had little obvious agricultural potential. However, each realized its strategic significance and took the view that the other should not have it. As one early commentator observed, "This valuable colony is peculiarly advantageous to Great Britain in a political point of view. This arises from its position, which is midway between Martinique and Guadeloupe" (Coke 1972, vol. 2, 332). Another remarked, "Dominica lies ... in the very center of their [France's] possessions, so as to command and to distress the navigations equally of Martinico and Guadeloupe" (Campbell 1763, 211).[11]

Thus, early settlement of Dominica was part of the strategy of European countries to funnel resources toward themselves. But the competition, at this early stage, centred on other island territories; the major effect on Dominica was to people it with refugee Amerindian people and provide an image of a somewhat mysterious, inhospitable place beyond the reaches of civilization.

EARLY SETTLEMENT: COMPETITION
BETWEEN FRENCH AND ENGLISH

The second decade of the seventeenth century saw Spain's Caribbean influence decline and the interest of other European powers in the region increase. Britain and France, in particular, competed "for the Spanish inheritance" – a conflict in which Dominica was repeatedly an important pawn. As attempts were being made to settle some of the smaller Caribbean islands, a grand gamesmanship was being played out in Europe. In 1627, Charles I granted the Earl of Carlisle "all the Caribees" – all twenty-one Caribbean territories, including Dominica. Cardinal Richelieu promptly responded by claiming Martinique, Guadeloupe, Dominica, St Lucia, St Vincent, and Grenada for France.

The French settled Dominica first. They planted the French flag on the island in 1635, made a treaty with the Amerindians in 1640, sent a missionary there in 1643, and simultaneously ordered that no strangers should settle on the island (see Boromé 1966, 40). But the English continued to call. Each side actively sought support from the Carib, and fights between the two nations and between each nation and the Carib occurred chronically. In 1660, largely on the advice of Father Philippe de Beaumont, who had lived in Dominica for five years, sympathized with the Amerindians' plight, and argued that the island belonged to the Carib (see Boromé 1967, 9), the French and British governments decided to grant them exclusive rights to Dominica and St Vincent "in perpetuity" (Bogat 1967, 83).

Despite this rhetoric, the French refused to quit the island. Instead, more settlers, mostly from Martinique, continued to arrive. By 1632, the population of Dominica had increased from a few families to 349 whites, 23 free coloureds, and 338 African slaves, "who had been imported to assist ... in the cultivation of those small portions of land which they occupied" (Coke 1971, 2: 334). Most of the settlers were poor and unable to compete in the other rapidly occupied sugar islands, adventurers seeking another frontier, or persons fleeing from justice.[12] Many of them were what Mintz (1974a, 148–9) describes as a second category of peasant in the region – "the early Yeomen." They were "landholders who produce[d] much or most of their own consumption, while also producing items for sale." Intermingled with them were representatives of the system from which many of them were fleeing – plantation agriculturists who increasingly used slave labour. The French in Guadeloupe and Martinique had embarked early on sugar production. Like English sugar producers in Barbados, they received a considerable boost when Dutch Jews, expelled from Brazil, introduced their production methods in 1654. They encouraged plantation production, tried to push out the small producers, and imported large numbers of slaves.

This motley crew of Dominican settlers worked hard for small rewards. "The whole of their time was engaged in breeding poultry, and in supplying Martinico with such articles of provision as industrious poverty enabled them to raise ... They bartered at that island for various necessaries and conveniences of life, particularly tools for husbandry, and such materials for building as the place of their residence did not produce" (Coke 1971, 334). Despite the peace treaty of 1640, however, their industry was curtailed somewhat by Carib belligerence. Bell (1937, 22) observes of the latter, "The savages seemed eager to take up the gauntlet against any intruder from any part of the world, and they redoubled their attacks on the growing colonies of their enemies. Without a sign of warning their crowded canoes would suddenly round a headland and swarm into the harbour of a peaceful settlement."

The French settlers in Dominica had not only the Carib to contend with, but also the British, who continued to try to lay claim to the island and sent in settlers to curry favour with the Carib. This transitory Carib allegiance to Britain was, at least in part, the work of "Indian" Warner, the son of Sir Thomas Warner, the first governor of St Kitts, by his second marriage to a beautiful Carib woman. After his father died, Indian Warner was treated as a slave by his step-mother, so he escaped and joined his mother's people in Dominica, where he attained considerable influence over the Carib. The French tried to use him to win Carib allegiance by bestowing upon him the title of governor of the island. But, in the typical logic of the time, they then imprisoned him in Guadeloupe during the war of 1666–7. He was released by the English, through the intercession of Lord Francis Willowby, and returned to Dominica, this time to win the Carib over to English interests (see Allfrey 1972, 24–5; Burns 1954, 343). Evidently, he remained somewhat of a problem to both sides, because "neither nation was quite sure of his allegiance" (Nicole 1965, 125). Nor, it seemed, were the Carib sure. He died somewhat mysteriously in 1674, aboard his half-brother Phillip's ship, during celebrations following a successful punitive attack on the Carib in which he had helped Phillip's invasionary force.[13]

The deterioration in the relationship between England and France regarding Dominica was ostensibly halted by a neutrality agreement signed on 7 February 1686, under which Dominica was formally redesignated a Carib territory. However, this changed nothing on the island: the French settlers ignored the agreement and remained where they were, and the British continued to try to gain a foothold there. In the Treaty of Ryswick (1697), following another war with France, Britain again laid a claim to Dominica, this time based upon the patent granted to James Hay, the Earl of Carlisle (see Boromé 1967, 10). In 1700, the British sent an expeditionary force to Dominica, under the leadership of Colonel Tobias Frere from Barbados, supposedly to hew wood. Frere signed a peace treaty with some of the Carib. This angered other Carib, who were loyal to the French, who called a conference in Dominica and informed French officials in Martinique. Concerned, the French administration discussed expelling the English, but it could find insufficient formal grounds to do so. In any case, the English, stricken by a sudden bout of sickness and the arrival and attack of a French pirate ship, decided to retreat and to abandon, for the time being, their attempt to settle Dominica.

The formal prohibition against settlement in Dominica was continued by the Treaty of Utrecht, in 1713. French colonists continued, nonetheless, to settle on Dominica, and, to the consternation of the French officials in Martinique and Guadeloupe, they began to show an unsavoury spirit of independence. They consorted with and supported pirates in the area and "were so much for themselves that all of them were equal to siding with the enemy in war emergencies" (Boromé 1967, 13). To protect French interests on the island French officials appointed a commandant – a Martiniquan emigrant, Le Grand, who had settled there in 1727, and had been chosen by the locals to act as their leader. The choice was a good one: he fulfilled his role of protecting the king's subjects on the island with great skill.

As Dominica's population increased, France attempted to exert greater administrative control over the fledgling colony, and Britain became increasingly concerned over France's success. Le Grand saw the Anglo-Carib alliance as a major threat to the French settlers' interests, and with good reason. Carib who supported the British contacted Gros François, leader of the St Vincent Carib, with a view to running the French off the island. A decisive armed intervention by Le Grand broke up the anti-French alliance. He developed lasting good relations with the Carib and referred their problems with French settlers to the governor and the intendant of Martinique. This appeared to work so well that, "when troubled by French colonists, the Indians did not turn to the British or go on the warpath. They went in their pirogues to complain to the Governor of Martinique" (Boromé 1967, 15). They even sought him out as an arbitrator for their own domestic disputes.

The Carib gradually came to settle for peace, which permitted the French hold on Dominica to strengthen. As they did so, they acquired a taste for French products, which had increased in number as the French population on the island had grown. They sold land to the French, they promised to return runaway slaves, and they gradually retreated to the deep forests on the inaccessible east coast of the island, where they have continued to live into the present.

We can see these events as ripple effects from metropolitan efforts to funnel resources to the centre. Sometimes the effects were indirect, as in the case of the small-scale French producers being unable to compete in the French-dominated market in Martinique and seeking a refuge in Dominica. Nevertheless, they maintained contact with Martinique and, through it, with the French metropolitan centring strategy of primary production and trade. At other times the effects were more direct, as in the case of Britain's foreign policy of piracy on the high seas.

In this period, several categories of player were caught up in the developing periphery of Dominica – each trying to centre its world in its particular way. The Carib, fighting a rearguard action, caught between strategies of belligerence and retreat, isolated themselves from the encroaching metropole. Pirates and buccaneers, based on the island, worked the margins of the metropolitan enterprise, trading their booty for supplies. Although they had initially been an important element in the British and French strategy to erode the Spanish monopoly in the region, they were now an unofficial and increasingly unwanted element in the metropolitan mercantile enterprise. The island also came to be occupied by a small but growing number of independent settlers. Their informal encouragement by the metropole was part of a European centring strategy for the region as a whole, but they survived by small-scale production and trade with the neighbouring French islands. At the far edge of the European mercantile invasion of the world, their activities contributed little to the funneling back to Europe, but they attempted to establish the rudiments of a fragile order on the periphery of empire, an attempt that was designed to be continuously eroded. Finally, there were representatives of the French administration, who carried out the wishes of their island administrations and, ultimately, of the metropole. They did this by identifying clearly with the centre's colonizing-peripheralizing process.

DEVELOPMENT OF A FRANCOPHONE
FRONTIER AND "COLONY"

The alliance between the French and the Carib encouraged more and more Frenchmen to leave Martinique and Guadeloupe to settle in Dominica. They were joined by French buccaneers, who had been invited to settle there to increase the size of the community, to effectively occupy the territory, and to claim Dominica for France. Within a thirty-year period, from 1730 to 1763, the population of Dominica grew from 776 to 7,890 (see table 1).

Table 1
Immigrant Population, 1730–63

	Europeans		Free Coloureds		Slaves		
Year	Number	% Total	Number	% Total	Number	% Total	Total
1730	351	45.0	30	3.9	425	54.8	776
1731	432	42.0	36	3.5	565	54.6	1,033
1743	717	23.7			1,114	36.8	3,030
1745	1,152	38.0			1,880	62.0	3,032
1749	1,023	31.0			2,263	68.9	3,286
1753	1,260	26.3			3,530	73.7	4,790
1763	1,718	21.8	300	3.8	5,872	74.4	7,890

Source: Boromé 1967, 16. Boromé notes that the census totals for the 1730–53 census are mis-totalled (n. 17).

The number of Europeans increased by nearly 400 per cent, the number of "free Negroes" by 900 per cent, and the number of slaves by nearly 1,300 per cent. Obviously, a new social structure was being built in Dominica, despite the fact that, in negotiations with Britain in 1751, France had described the people living there as simply adventurers. A frontier society was emerging that reflected to some extent, in microcosm, the colonial societies of Martinique and Guadeloupe from which the settlers had come. There were the free and the unfree, the white and the non-white, the planters and the administrators, all found in somewhat similar proportions to populations on the colonizing islands – all trying to make a life for themselves, trying to centre their world.

Membership in these categories was, however, fairly transitory. Individuals and families came and went between Dominica and the two neighbouring islands. Those who returned to Martinique were replaced by new migrants. Settlers were a mix of the good and the bad: "Not all were debtors fleeing their creditors, nor individuals seeking to live as they chose, though there was a fair share of ne'er-do-wells to give the colony a bad name. The majority were poor souls unable to compete in the rapidly occupied sugar producing isles, or younger sons of good family (many with names of colonial nobility) who could find no property there available to purchase. Some were men of substance like Le Grand and the planter who re-portedly settled down with forty slaves" (Boromé 1967, 16–17). But while the major social categories of the neighbouring islands were reproduced in Dominica, the economic base supporting them was not.

The mountainous terrain, official discouragement, and uncertain title to the island inhibited people from investing the considerable sums necessary to develop sugar plantations on the island. The settlers were therefore an individualistic, entrepreneurial bunch who produced cotton, cacao, bananas, garden produce, and coffee for sale to Martinique. They cut timber for export at such a rate that "the woods near the shore had been denuded and it became necessary to build roads into the interior and use conveyances with animals to haul the drywoods and hardwoods to the coast" (Boromé 1967, 18). They imported horses, cattle, mules, goats, and slaves, and the island became a secret conduit for English trade with the French islands. They also engaged in illicit trade of smuggled goods, from slaves to sugar.[14] In the process, they gave Dominica a reputation for smuggling, an activity that is institutionalized to this day (see Beck 1976, 44). Father Guillaume Martel, a missionary to Dominica at the time, was "appalled at the crime and vice that flourished in a community as yet without laws or judges" (Boromé 1967, 23).

Initially, then, the European settlers created a frontier society in which behaviour was largely dictated by individual strategy and interest within the social categories recognized in the islands from which individuals came. As in most colonial situations, there was the implicit belief that the colonizers had a natural right to exploit whatever resources they found and to displace and even exterminate native peoples in order to settle the territory. While "law and order" was yet to be fully established, the majority of settlers were linked to local markets in Martinique and Guadeloupe, and production for these markets created certain standardized behaviours and expectations. The centring activity of these various categories of individuals increasingly tied them into the periphery of the metropolitan centring system and reinforced the value of the profit motive. Thus, their efforts to create order out of chaos in the frontier context laid the groundwork for the new order that was to emerge as Dominica became a colony, that was clearly tied to the metropolitan centre.

To control this growing population, in which "an honest man lived in peril," as well as to add to the French presence on the island, Caylus, the governor-general of Martinique, appointed a military man, Descasseaux Bontemps, as commandant to replace Le Grand, and sent militia (three hundred in 1735, five hundred in 1744). By 1759, Dominica had become a "colony," with a commandant, judge, customs officer, prison, missionaries, and the like. Caylus wanted to see Dominica fully settled. To encourage this, he worked to impose the rule of law and order on the island and to protect the population against British attacks by building up fortifications. He divided the island into eight military districts and curbed foreign commerce and the smuggling and manumission of slaves. All the while, as a backdrop to this, France and Britain kept

up appearances regarding the 1727 agreement by periodically pro-
claiming the island to be Carib. Both countries issued eviction
notices to their subjects, which either seemed to get lost in administration or were repudiated on the grounds that the people in
Dominica were not settlers.

In 1733, there were only 1.2 slaves per white person and an
almost equal number of slaves and free persons (1.1:1) in Dominica,
indicating that most of the first settlers had been small-scale, self-
employed pioneers who used a few slaves to help work their gardens. By 1763, there were 3.4 slaves per white person and 2.9 slaves
per free person. This indicates an influx to the island of more prosperous persons who wished to set up larger economic enterprises,
which depended more on slave labour.[15] Although Dominica did
not become a sugar island at this time, cotton cultivation increased
from 98,000 *pieds*, in 1730, to 261,400, in 1753; cacao from 4,272 *pieds*
to 952,200; bananas from 30,000 *pieds* to 235,000; and coffee from
584,700 *pieds* to probably over 1,585,400 *pieds*, which was the figure
for 1749 (see Boromé 1967, 17–18).[16]

The increase in Dominica's population and productivity led to
British fears that the French were setting up a colonial "regime"
there, despite the island's technical neutrality. In 1753, Commodore
Thomas Pye, commander in chief of the Barbados station, ordered
Lieutenant Rose to visit Roseau to verify the existence of a commandant on the island. He was horrified to learn not only that there was
a commandant, but that he lived "in a well-built house set amid
cultivated land on a hill overlooking the town and that on a plat-
form before the house, facing the sea, lay four new nine-pounders
and ammunition" (Boromé 1967, 31–2).

Sixteen years later, the commandant of Dominica is described as
having "a flock of officers commissioned by the Governor-General
in Martinique and batteries with mounted cannons to ward off
privateers at Roseau and Grand Bay" (Boromé 1967, 22). There were
a judge to settle disputes, a "Council of Twelve Notables," and a
few priests. By 1773, there were two priests on the island: Father
Massey, a Franciscan in Roseau, and Father Sigismond, a Capuchin
based in Pointe Michel. Proesman mentions missionary work in
Dominica by the Jesuits and the Dominicans (Proesmans 1972,
166–70).[17] There was also the celebrated Father Antoine La Valette,
SJ, whose commercial exploits in Dominica and elsewhere led to the
suppression of the Jesuit Order in France, and finally to its expul-
sion from that country.

As Dominica was increasingly and more effectively occupied
during the eighteenth century, it evolved from a typical frontier

society, whose settlers were small-scale entrepreneurs with little fealty to their country of origin, into a more stable, ordered society. This process involved the extension of French administrative control and the attempt to draw Dominica into the ambit of French colonial administration and law, and the island became significantly more embedded in the periphery of a metropolitan centre. Before considering what this closer tie to the centre would bring to Dominica, a significant feature of the emerging society must be mentioned – its free coloured members.

THE FREE COLOURED IN DOMINICA

The free coloured from the French islands, particularly Martinique, were an important category of early settler in Dominica. In order to understand their significance, it is necessary to retrace a few steps in the history of Martinique and Guadeloupe. They were discovered by Columbus on 4 November 1493, on his second voyage, and on 15 June 1502, on his fourth voyage, respectively. They remained uncolonized by Spain and attracted French interest early in the seventeenth century. A French expedition led by L'Olive and Du Plessis landed in Guadeloupe, and another led by Pierre D'Esnambuc landed in Martinique in 1635. The islands have remained French, except for a brief period of military occupation by the British between 1756 and 1763 (see Murch 1971, 12).

In the early days of colonization and slavery, French settlers did not worry about the effect of creating a mixed race of people: "In the French islands, the white colonists had no singular or common attitude toward their coloured subjects" (Elizabeth 1972, 135). Nor were there the discriminatory policies against them that characterized the later colonial period: "As late as 1713, the administrators were remarkably free from preoccupation with *le mélange des sangs* typical of the late colony" (Hall 1972, 186). Rather, the economic position of white and coloured peasant proprietors and cultivators of small holdings meant that "free colored peasant farmers had much in common with poor white farmers" (Elizabeth 1972, 136).

The *Code Noir*, promulgated in France by Colbert in 1685, "guaranteed in unequivocal language full citizenship rights to slaves emancipated in the French islands, considering them as native-born French citizens, regardless of where the slaves had been born" (Hall 1972, 185). It also exerted pressure on the master to marry his slave concubine, thereby freeing her and legitimizing their children. Even before the *Code Noir*, it was accepted practice for the offspring of the unions of white men and black women to be automatically emancipated when they reached the age of twenty-one (see Hall 1972, 185).

This policy enabled France to count a majority of heads at a time when the principle of effective occupation determined the control of the islands and it was difficult to obtain white colonists. The strategy had important implications for altering the social structure and demographic composition of the islands, and created a significant element in the population with the potential for further alterations. "A judgment rendered by the Council of Martinique in 1698 declared the *Code Noir* aimed only at the vice of concubinage. Far from preventing racial mixture, *le mélange des sangs*, it was concerned only with augmenting the colony" (Hall 1972, 186). Thus, emancipation was encouraged and freedmen enjoyed a relatively high status among the colonizers, who used them as a major source of military strength.

The growth of the plantation economy starting in the early eighteenth century and the introduction of sugar in the French islands changed this situation dramatically. It put pressure on land and increased competition, and this generated new colour and class distinctions. Sugar production enabled an individual to amass a fortune in a way that could be achieved by no other colonial activity. It also accelerated a process of land concentration in the hands of a planter class that brooked no competition from the free coloured population, and promoted strong interest in preserving the slave system intact. As far as the social structure was concerned, therefore, there emerged an economically powerful group of large landowners who persuaded the legislatures to pass laws that restricted the numbers of free coloureds and made them an "intermediate class," although "class" is a misnomer for the multiplex social position of free coloureds (see Elizabeth 1972, 153).[18] Impediments were created to coloured manumission, to whites making bequests to coloureds, and to free coloureds marrying slaves. Rigorous prohibitions were introduced on mixed marriages, on coloured people adopting white names, and so on.

One result of these strictures was the emergence of a category somewhat "between" freedmen and slaves, composed of people who, having been unable to obtain *de jure* liberty in the islands, had obtained deeds of liberty abroad. "This group was referred to as the *soi-disant libres* (nominally free), a term used by the administrators of the Lesser Antilles as early as 1723" (Elizabeth 1972, 145). Other results were the establishment of colonies of maroons, escaped slaves, and the flight of coloureds from the colony to other territories.

Free coloureds in the French islands could escape some of the social barriers that were being erected against them by moving into rural areas, or by migrating to Dominica. It is likely that the coloured population that emigrated to Dominica as free persons of colour actually included the *soi-disant libres* and escaped slaves as well as legally free people of colour.

There were only thirty free coloured settlers in Dominica in 1730, comprising 7.9 per cent of the settler population, but this category was to grow and become a significant force in the island. By 1763, there were three hundred, comprising 14 per cent of the settler population. They had little reason to return to Martinique. Their interests were focused on Dominica, and, as they increased in numbers, they added an important dimension to the French individualism that characterized the nascent community. Some of them owned slaves themselves and saw their interests as bound to those of the whites. Speaking of their role in the post-revolutionary French Antilles, Elizabeth (1972, 171) observes, "They did not seek the help of slaves, nor did they offer much succour to them. The free coloured advocated equality, but only vis-à-vis themselves and the white ruling class. They sought alliances, but primarily with the white ruling class." And they set the stage for the emergence of a mulatto élite whose values reflected those of the white ruling class. They were, in embryo, a community of settlers whose "home" was Dominica.[19]

The centring strategy of free coloureds, therefore, was to migrate from Martinique and Guadeloupe and attempt to establish themselves in Dominica on a par with their white and free-coloured neighbours back home. Their attempt to centre their world in a peripheral situation created a second "indigenous" group on the island. As they increased in numbers, the groundwork was laid for a distinct mulatto identity and collective action to further their interests.

BRITISH ATTEMPTS TO WREST THE ISLAND FROM THE FRENCH

Despite the French settlement of Dominica, Britain was not prepared to yield the island to France, nor to accept France's colonizing of it. Much of the Anglo-French war of 1744 centred on the neutral islands of the Caribbean. Britain periodically decided to occupy the islands so that the French would not use them as bases from which to attack British shipping in the area. During this war, British ships visited Dominica, and there were military skirmishes between the French and the British. Peace was restored by the Treaty of Aix-la-Chapelle (1748), and Dominica was again declared neutral and as "belonging to the Caribs" (Boromé 1967, 30). There were more eviction notices, and representatives of both nations visited to see how eviction was progressing. But nothing changed. The French returned and further consolidated their presence on Dominica.

The Seven Years War (1756–63) between England and France saw heavy fighting in the West Indies.[20] Commodore Moore, of Britain, arrived off Dominica and forced the French to respect neutrality and not harass British shipping. Nevertheless, Dominica increasingly became a haven for French privateers. The British retaliated with raids on towns and the confiscation of ships. By 1761, however, the French had become so strong in Dominica "that a special expedition had to be sent to eradicate this danger point to the British arms and these waters, and on 8 June, Commodore Sir James Douglas ... [with] troops from 'North America' under Lord Andrew Rollo, attacked and captured the island" (St Johnston 1932, 3). It was the arrival of Lord (Admiral) Rollo in 1761 that turned the tide. He captured and plundered Roseau, summoned the population to lay down their arms, and made them take an oath of submission. British control was formalized by the ninth article of the Treaty of Paris, 1763, which ceded Dominica to Britain. This ended the French era of Dominican history, except for a couple of transitory French occupations of the island in 1795 and 1805.

THIS EARLY PERIOD of Dominica's history involved the first direct attempt to make the island a periphery to Europe. The metropolitan centre comprised a series of newly emerged European nation-states that were vying with one another for trade and territorial influence in the region. As Spanish influence in the Caribbean declined and islands became fair game for conquest by other European powers, Britain and France both took an interest in Dominica, principally for strategic and geographical reasons. There were no concerted attempts to exploit the territory, but a watchful eye was kept over who might be trying to lay claim to it. At this stage, Dominica was only loosely tied to the metropole, but its existence was acknowledged and its strategic importance appreciated.

What was evident, even in this early stage of European contact, was a new, modern, dimension to categorization – domination, and a new dimension to differentiation – exploitation. Whereas the Carib and the Taíno and Arawak distinguished between "them" and "us,"

Columbus made not only this distinction, but also one between good natives (Taíno and Arawak) and bad (Carib) and one between civilized and "bestial" people. Racial stereotypes were created, and racism was initiated as part of the centring strategy of the Spanish metropole. As part of the Columbian legacy, it developed, as an ideological concomitant to economic exploitation, to encompass native peoples beyond the scope of this chapter. As competition for land grew with the introduction of sugar, colour became an impediment to its access. The human face of the slave disappeared and the body of the slave came into view as something to be used. Some free coloureds and slaves escaped Martinique and Guadeloupe and fled to Dominica, where the seeds for using racial distinctions to assist in funneling resources back to the centre were already being transplanted.

At this time, Dominica was a frontier where law and order had yet to be established and where the forces to draw resources back to the metropole were weak. No major economic enterprises were undertaken by the metropole at this time, and the most significant metropolitan initiative was the attempt by the French to create a rudimentary administration on the island. The scale of operation was small: some privateers, some settlers, a handful of administrators, followed by a few more settlers. The settlers created a tenuous social order within the context of metropolitan competition for control of the region. Many were not from the metropole, however, but from other Caribbean islands. In contrast to European settlers, their interests were centred in the region. In trying to start anew in Dominica, they brought with them expectations, values, behaviours, and technology that they had learned in what were formerly French colonies. To this extent, they were extensions of metropolitan influence and interest. But in undertaking local, small-scale trading, they produced for regional markets and attempted to centre a small-scale world.

The Dominican context in which this activity occurred was, nonetheless, already affected by the disordering affects of metropolitan peripheralizing. The Carib were now permanently resident on the island because of the chaos created by Europeans elsewhere in the Caribbean. The island was also semi-permanently populated by the non-Amerindian settlers from neighbouring islands, who had come in response to disorder created by metropolitan centring strategies there – specifically, the development of a sugar industry in Martinique and Guadeloupe. These settlers, mostly small-scale operators, pushed out by the land-grabbing strategies of a budding sugar plantocracy, were trying to escape mounting economic and social pressures. They, in turn, had a further entropic effect on Dominica: they pushed the Carib into still remoter regions, and they devastated the timber stands on the east coast, which, to this day, bear the scars of this initial deforestation. (Soil erosion is difficult to reverse on a volcanic island whose soil depth, overall, is shallow.)

The nature of the society being created on the periphery was not envisioned by the metropole to be a replica of itself. It was viewed as an extension of metropolitan control over a foreign territory *as* a foreign territory. In fact, the metropole actively tried to create a different form of society than that at the centre. Its major interest in the Caribbean region was narrowly conceived: it was a source for a very limited range of resources, such as gold, labour, and monocrop agriculture, or, as initially in the case of Dominica, a strategically useful location for protection and furthering of metropolitan economic interests in other parts of the Caribbean.

Those who represented metropolitan interests on the periphery reflected diverse elements of its social structure and diverse motivations for the metropolitan centring activity in which they engaged. There were privateers and pirates prompted by the bleak chances of obtaining wealth at home, planters and merchants drawn by the new opportunities for wealth of an emerging planter class, and administrators and military personnel associated with the career possibilities of their positions. Attempts to bring Dominica into a more developed peripheral relationship with the centre occurred when the island was formally ceded to Britain in 1763. What this entailed for the island is the subject of the next chapter.

4 Formal Colonization: British Annexation, French Conquest, and Slave Revolts

Thus it was sugar which excluded the white labourer from Caribbean agriculture and which made the Caribbean in the eighteenth century even more an image or effigy of Ethiopia.

Williams 1970, 109

Up to this point in its history, Dominica may be thought of as a periphery on the periphery. There was no direct, formal contact between it and the metropolitan centre, which, indeed, disavowed any controlling interest in the island. Even the slaves who had accompanied French masters to the island were more like the feudal dependents of the small-scale producers who owned them than the anonymous work units of an opulent plantocracy. However, this picture of Dominica changed dramatically in 1763, when Britain annexed the island and implemented its colonial policies.

THE BROADER CARIBBEAN: THE METROPOLITAN CONTEXT

Britain had a strategic interest in laying claim to Dominica. Were France to obtain Dominica, it would possess three large islands in the middle of the Antillean arc from which it could exercise considerable control of the region. Thus, a British colony there would be a major obstacle to French hegemony in the region. To achieve this, Britain wanted to populate the island as quickly as possible; territorial occupation, after all, translated into possession. The centring strategy adopted by the government, therefore, was to entice would-be planters to settle there with the promise of land which could be used for the planting of sugar. This also would contribute to a second British interest in Dominica, the bolstering of Caribbean production and trade.

As early as 1660, "the value of sugar imports exceeded that of all other colonial produce combined" (Solow 1987, 70). Europeans had been producing increasing amounts of sugar in the Caribbean since the time of Columbus, who had written in his report to Ferdinand and Isabella, "There are also sugar-canes, of which the small quantity that we have planted has taken root" (quoted in Major 1870, 81). When Britain acquired Dominica, in 1763, the poorest English housewife was accustomed to taking sugar in her tea and West Indies rum was supplied to the navy.

With the increase in economic importance of sugar, Britain experienced the emergence of a new political influence on its government – the sugar barons, planters who had made a fortune in the West Indies and returned to England to live an opulent life and protect their economic interests abroad through lobbying government. They were a particularly myopic, self-interested group. Among other things, they persuaded the British government, at the Treaty of Paris, to annex the non-sugar islands in the Caribbean, such as Dominica, in order to minimize competition with their own plantations in the West Indies and thus keep the price of sugar high. Niddrie (1966, 76) describes the island's unsuitableness for sugar in these terms: "Of all the British Ceded Islands, Dominica presented the greatest environmental hindrances to rapid development. Its relief, inaccessibility, its mantle of gloomy cloudiness, together with the absence of suitable beaches from which cargoes could be lifted, did not encourage pioneering ventures into the interior, with the result that much of the island remained under dense rain-forest for another 150 years." French planters in Dominica, who cultivated cotton, coffee, cacao, and bananas, had been an exception to the regional trend to sugar production, already well established in Martinique and Guadeloupe by 1664. Elsewhere in the Caribbean, sugar was king. Notwithstanding the fact, then, that the island had been singled out by the sugar lobby for its unsuitableness for this purpose, the British government, with some duplicity, attempted to lure settlers to Dominica with the promise of sugar plantations.

Initially, the Dutch were the masters of transatlantic trade; by 1763, however, Britain and France had successfully loosened Holland's hold. Mercantilism was the favoured economic theory of the period, and monopoly was the national British policy that translated it into practice.[1] From this perspective, a colony existed to promote metropolitan interests, both as a market for the metropole's products and as a source of primary resources. In the Caribbean, this produced the infamous triangular trade and the "factory in the field," the plantation (Sheridan 1969, 8). The former linked Africa, Europe, and the West Indies in a particularly exploitative but lucrative trading network that generated profits at each leg of the triangle: "A viable Atlantic trading area depended in large measure on the performance of the slave triangle, whereby European and East Indian goods were exchanged for African slaves; slaves for bills of exchange, specie, and plantation produce; and plantation produce for manufactures, intermediate goods, and services" (Sheridan 1969, 14). As far as plantation development was concerned, Hall (1962, 305) has summed it up well: "Of the three classical factors of production, land to be paid for in rent, labour to be paid for in wages, and capital to be paid for in interest, the least important on the slave-estates was labour ... The slaves were not accounted as labourers. They were the most important part of the capital equipment of the estate."

There were, then, two dominant eighteenth-century metropolitan centring strategies in the Caribbean – the first was to produce sugar. Indeed, for the British, the West Indies had become synonymous with sugar production, and this was such a preoccupation that the islands did not even grow their own food, but were forced to import it. The second was to promote trade, and here Britain and France had emerged as the two major players in a competition that Sheridan (1969, 13) describes in these terms: "From the vantage point of the Caribbean plantations this was a struggle to expand the area of tropical staple production, to augment supplies of manufactures and services from the metropolis, to control and develop outlying regions capable of supplying forced labour and intermediate products, to build sea power to keep open the lifelines of trade in the formal empire and to expand trade with the informal empires." An indication of the importance of this to the metropole is that, when Britain annexed Dominica, it seriously debated whether it was better to return Canada or Guadeloupe to France. It decided on Guadeloupe, and France considered this a significant coup.

Sugar

Sugar production demanded a large labour force. Initially, poor indentured labourers from Europe were the solution for the labour shortages on the small farmsteads of the early colonizers in the Caribbean. However, as farmsteads became estates, the labour supply from Europe could not meet the demand; furthermore, planters found it too costly. They sought another source of labour, and they found it in Africa.

The need for and discovery of cheap, plentiful labour in Africa precipitated one of the greatest human migrations in recorded history and the growth of "one of the most important businesses of the seventeenth century" – the slave trade (Williams 1970, 137). This trade, according to some, was instrumental in the rise of metropolitan mercantilism and came to account, in the eighteenth century, for at least 36 per cent of Britain's commercial profits. "The slave trade kept the wheels of metropolitan industry turning; it stimulated navigation and ship-building and employed seamen; it raised fishing villages to flourishing cities; it gave substance to new industries based on the processing of colonial raw materials; it yielded large profits which were ploughed back into metropolitan industry; and finally it gave rise to an unprecedented commerce in the West Indies and made the Caribbean territories among the most valuable colonies the world has ever known" (Williams 1970, 148).

Subsequent research has questioned Williams's claims. Richardson has argued that slave trading, sugar production, and metropolitan economic growth are interrelated in a more complex way than Williams indicated. "In particular, the slave trade and slavery should be viewed not as some peculiar promoter of industrial expansion and change in Britain, but rather as integral though subordinate components of a growing north Atlantic economy" (Richardson 1987, 105). Recent evidence suggests that Williams exaggerated the importance of the West Indies to the imperial economy before 1775 and the diminution of its importance to Britain after 1783. Either way, however, the trade was important.

Sugar production and the slave trade escalated the centre-periphery dynamic that had emerged in earlier times. The energy expended to bring sugar to Europe was enormous and extended the periphery to Africa; resources from both Africa and the Caribbean were funnelled to the metropolitan centre. People were removed from Africa, and crops from the Caribbean, in return for investment in terms of cash, commodities, and the like. Although some diversification accompanied sugar production in the Caribbean colonies, as the profits from sugar grew, so did a monocrop agriculture. Sugar came to be seen as synonymous with economic growth and the only intelligent investment.

These views and the consequent practices resulted in the creation of a narrow monocrop enterprise in the Caribbean, at enormous human cost and detriment to the environment. Planters made no attempts to improve techniques for sugar production or to experiment with alternatives. Their focus was narrowly avaricious and rapacious and can be summed up as: Get as much as possible out of the land and the slave for nothing. The results were increasing soil erosion, dropping yields, and a horrendous slaughter of slaves from neglect, overwork, and punishment.

The inhumane treatment of slaves by Caribbean planters and overseers was bolstered in a most vicious racism and resulted in a high slave-mortality rate that itself strengthened the triangular trade by making more slave imports necessary.[2] Dunn (1987, 165) observes, for example, that on Mesopotamia Estate in Jamaica, "nearly twice as many deaths as births were recorded between 1762 and 1831. In order to maintain a viable work force at Mesopotamia (as also at Worthy Park and most other Jamaican sugar estates), the owners had to purchase a great many new slaves." As the lucrative African slave trade progressed, an inter-island slave trade developed to distribute the "goods" more efficiently. Supplying slaves to foreign nations became an integral part of British economic policy (see Williams 1970, 155).[3]

The operation of this system made some people very wealthy. They returned home to form a powerful lobby to protect and further their interests. The sugar lobby not only succeeded in getting Britain to annex the non-sugar-producing Caribbean islands and return the sugar-producing islands to France and Spain, they also persuaded the British government to limit the size of lots for sale in Dominica to three hundred acres. Furthermore, they were behind "a curious shortage of capital for these new territories" (Williams 1970, 130–1).[4] The contradictory colonizing policies in Dominica reflected conflicting centring tactics emanating from the metropole. On the one hand, the sugar lobby did not want sugar plantations in Dominica; on the other hand, the government wanted to settle the island for strategic purposes.

Trade

The interest in trade produced a further contradiction in British government policy. The colonies were not only producers, but also consumers, and provided a means of generating profit from an intra-regional trade. To this end, the government passed the British Freeports Act, in 1766, which opened up four ports in Jamaica (Kingston, Lucca, Montego Bay, and Savannah-la-Mar) and two in Dominica (Roseau and Portsmouth, in Prince Rupert's Bay) to foreign shipping. This actually prejudiced the interests of the British metropolitan sugar lobby, for it allowed sugar both to be imported from the two French islands and to be re-exported to Britain. "By providing French sugar with this market, Britain was encouraging sugar production in the French islands, and by permitting the sale and export of slaves to non British colonies like Cuba, she was enabling them to keep down their sugar production costs. In this respect the policy ran contrary to West Indian sugar plantation interests" (Sherlock 1973, 167). It also allowed slaves to be sold to competing non-British sugar islands such as Cuba. But, while it had these negative repercussions, it increased trade – and increasing trade was a major British goal. It was in this regional context of a triangular trade, in which the Caribbean leg was dominated by trading in sugar and slaves, that the British era of Dominican history began.

BRITISH ANNEXATION:
SUGAR, TRADE, AND SLAVES

Almost immediately following annexation, Britain decided that, to develop and stabilize trade with Dominica, there was a "need for a bigger population to stave off the constant menace of both the French and the Caribs" (St Johnston 1932, 4), and it used the general belief in the economic potential of sugar to lure settlers there. Commissioners were sent out to ascertain what land was available, to possess it in the name of the Crown, and then to sell it in "lots not exceeding 100 acres in size, and no one applicant being allowed to buy more than 300 acres" to Englishmen only (Cracknell 1973, 60).[5] The commissioners, in the process of completing their survey, set aside three chains (there are sixty-six feet in a chain) from the high-water mark around the perimeter of the island (the Queen's Three Chains) for defence purposes and sold about half the island (94,346 acres for £312,092 sterling). White settlers were expected to have one white servant and two white women for every hundred acres.

This settlement strategy was minimally successful. Ownership did not translate into settlement, and many of the persons whose names were appended to land titles never set foot on the island. As Byers's map (1776) shows, there was at least one buyer who circumvented the three-hundred-acres-only rule and owned four hundred acres, which he probably never saw. It is quite likely that some individuals bought up continuous three-hundred-acre plots, or had someone else purchase land for them. Almost all those who went to Dominica tried to take up sugar production, but, given the topography of the island, their prosperity was far from assured, and many returned home in short order. Clearly, some of those who purchased land in Dominica were speculating and never intended to settle there, as evidenced by the number of absentee-owned estates.

How, then, could Britain claim the territory by possession? One solution was to try to get the French to stay, on the premise that "experience shows that the possession of property is the best security for a due obedience and submission to Government" (Acts of the Privy Council, Colonial Series 1745–66, 590). To foster their allegiance, the British government allowed the French to retain their estates and property, and granted them leases of between fourteen and forty-two years for the lands they had purchased or inherited. Nonetheless, it also required that they pay a rent of two shillings per acre per annum, that they take an oath of allegiance to the British Crown, and that they agree not to dispose of lands without the governor's prior permission (see Coke 1971, 336). The majority of the French took the oath and remained on the island; some of the wealthier, older families sold out and left for Trinidad.

According to Cracknell (1973, 60), there were some 343 French-men who owned 6,054 acres and cultivated coffee, cotton, and cacao at the time. These figures contrast with those on Byers's (1776) map, which listed the land owned in Dominica between 1765 and 1773; according to his figures, there were 498 individuals owning land on the island and 1,965 leasing land.[6] Byers's map gives some interesting information on the type and size of holding according to nationality. Eighty-six of the names he records are French, accounting for 17.3 per cent of those owning land on the island. Sixty-five per cent of the French owned less than one hundred acres each, and over half of them (53 per cent) owned less than fifty acres. Interestingly, there were eighteen Frenchmen (21 per cent) who each owned between 200 and 299 acres. No Frenchman owned over three hundred acres. In contrast, 65 per cent of the 412 English names listed owned over one hundred acres, and 22 Englishmen owned over three hundred acres, with one owning over four hundred acres! Some 10,541 acres were rented to the French under the new arrangement. Again according to Byers's map, 72 per cent of the French who leased land leased less than fifty acres. Thirteen French-men leased over 100 acres, two leasing from 200 to 299 acres. Only four Englishmen leased land, two leasing less than fifty acres and two fifty to ninety-nine acres (see table 2).

Thus, the majority of the "French" who remained in Dominica when the island was annexed by Britain were resident small holders, many of them likely to have been free Negroes or coloureds.[7] Although Britain granted all French-speaking settlers access to land and an enticement to stay, they denied them civil and political franchise (see Goodridge 1972, 155). This was later to create a political opposition which would become a thorn in the side of the British island administration.

The measures taken to encourage French planters to remain in Dominica suited the powerful metropolitan sugar lobby perfectly,

Table 2
Number of Land Holdings in 1773 by Ethnicity

	Freehold Acreages						
	Numbers of Acres						
	Under 50	50–99	100–199	200–299	300–399	400+	Total
English	76	71	138	105	21	1	412
French	46	10	12	18			86
	Percentage of Holdings						
	Under 50	50–99	100–199	200–299	300–399	400+	Total
English	18.0	17.3	33.6	25.6	5.0	0.2	100
French	53.4	11.6	14.0	21.0	0.0	0.0	100
% French of Total	37.7	12.0	8.0	14.6	0.0	0.0	21
	Leasehold Acreages						
	Numbers of Acres						
	Under 50	50–99	100–199	200–299	300–399	400–	Total
English	2	2	0	0	0	0	4
French	140	41	11	2	0	0	194
	Percentage of Holdings						
	Under 50	50–99	100–199	200–299	300–399	400–	Total
English	50.0	50.0	0	0	0	0	100
French	72.1	21.2	5.6	1	0	0	100
% French of Total	98	95	100	100	0	0	98

Source: Byers 1776.

because they were primarily producers of coffee and cacao. In fact, Trouillot (1988, 54) observes, "France essentially ceded a coffee-producing island to Britain ... [and] at the time of the abolition of slavery ... coffee production still contributed to about half of Dominica's export revenues." The greater the number of French settlers who remained on the island, the less land would be available for sugar production to compete with the metropolitan sugar-lobby interests on the domestic market.

The hopes of British absentee owners and settlers who purchased land in Dominica was to create sugar plantations, making Dominica a sugar island. They were successful: "Within the next ten years the British established a sugar industry and a slave society with a population of 3,850 and 15,753 slaves" (Marshall 1965, 26). Cracknell states that in 1774 "Dominica exported 2,673 tons of sugar, which compares not unfavourably with 2,379 for Monserrat, 3,129 for St Vincent, and 3,320 for Nevis. These figures," he comments, "are worth noting because it is sometimes asserted that Dominica was never a sugar island. This is false. Sugar was grown on Dominica for over a century and for much of that time was the major crop. In fact, although Dominica never produced a significant proportion of the sugar output of the West Indies, its cultivation was a big source of employment and, when the industry collapsed, there was much hardship" (Cracknell 1973, 69). There was even, according to some, a short period of sugar-related prosperity in Dominica. Coke, an English patriot, paints a positive economic picture of this time in the island's history: "The rapid progress of the colony to a degree of prosperity unknown before it came into our possession, is acknowledged by the French writers, though denied by Edwards, who asserts, in perhaps a little partiality for *Jamaica*, that 'it does not appear, that the purchases made by British subjects have answered the expectations of the buyers.' Indeed, it was very perceptible, in a few years, by its exports to Great Britain, of coffee, cotton, and sugar, and by its increased imports of British manufactures" (Coke 1971, 336).

However, the conversion of the island to sugar was accomplished with a great deal of difficulty. New settlers underestimated the difficulties of clearing land there. Furthermore, they were inexperienced in managing plantations in such terrain and planted cane in unsuitable mountainous locations. As a result, failures were common and many settlers quit the island. By 1790, there were fifty estates, with only two thousand acres combined under cane production, producing cane at half the yield obtained in other British islands (Atwood 1791, 78, 85). Atwood, at one time a chief judge on Dominica, records, less than thirty years after Britain annexed Dominica, that "at the time of writing, 30 estates had been abandoned recently because of poor management, trouble with escaped slaves and British–French confrontations" (Atwood 1791, 74). And by 1815, for example, Dominica produced only 2,205 tons, whereas St Vincent produced 11,590 tons (Knight 1978, 240).

The British government's strategy to encourage sugar production in order to settle Dominica paved the way for failures. It was costly in terms of the energy expended by the would-be planters in trying to create a plantocracy in an evidently unsuitable environment, and in terms of the labour and lives of slaves. Unlike the small-scale French producers preceding them, the British settlers tried to centre their world by accommodating themselves to the mercantile goals of the metropole. Many were local attorneys and overseers managing the estates of absentee owners, seeking to maximize profits through monocrop cultivation. Their activity supported the triangular trade, and they were ruthless in their efforts to generate profits.

The entropic effects of this strategy will be pursued further in the next chapter, where slavery is discussed in greater detail. It is noteworthy, however, that, as the increase in flow of resources, personnel, and goods and services expanded under British annexation, as part of the centring policy to incorporate Dominica as a periphery to Britain's colonial empire, the disordering impact in Dominica was considerable. It created a social category of nakedly and brutally exploited slaves, whose interests was diametrically opposed to that of their masters and who therefore required increasing efforts and energies to control. This dehumanization would feed back to the metropole and stir up the conscience of persons such as William Wilberforce. It also created the social category of French white and free-coloured political opposition, whose members were disenfranchised and whose interests would later generate a strong spirit of Dominican independence. Finally, it created an atmosphere of greater general uncertainty in which major decisions concerning the price of sugar, the acceptable productivity of managers, and the continuance of estates were made outside the island, frequently with no reference to those in the territory.

There was another side to the British economic-development policy for Dominica: the funnelling home of the profits of commercial exchanges as well as primary produce. Dominica's strategic location between the French sugar islands of Martinique and Guadeloupe made it ideal for entrepôt trade. The use of Dominica for the trade of slaves and sugar with French Caribbean colonies was probably more the reason for the brief period of prosperity mentioned above than was the production of sugar. Edwards observes of this period,

At the commencement of the hapless and destructive war between Great Britain and her colonies in North America, the island of Dominica was in a flourishing situation. The port of Roseau, having been declared a freeport by act of parliament, was resorted to by trading vessels from most parts of the foreign West Indies as well as America. The French and the Spaniards purchased great numbers of Negroes there for the supply of their settlements, together with vast quantities of merchandise and manufactures of Great Britain, payment for all of which was made chiefly in bullion, indigo, and cotton, and completed in mules and cattle; articles of prime necessity to the planter. (Edwards 1819, 1: 433–4)

Davey (1854, 498–9) describes the period between 1763 and 1778 as "an interval ... of much prosperity, numerous allotments of land having been sold, and estates formed, and sugar plantations commenced, Rousseau [sic], moreover, having been made a free port in

1766, and having become a great mart of commerce, especially in slaves."

Boromé (1967, 37) gives the population of the island in 1763 as 1,718 whites, 500 free Negroes and 5,872 slaves, of whom 3,145 were working adults. For 1778, he records 1,574 whites (two-thirds of them French), 574 free coloured (mulattos and blacks), and 14,309 slaves (Boromé 1969a, 41); some 1,194 whites were without land at this time.[8] This indicates that a sizeable number of island residents were managers, overseers, or people involved in trade. Thus, the mercantile economy accounted not only for an increase in prosperity but also for a sudden increase in population.

Many of the slaves would have been in transit to other islands. Curtin (1969, 69) observes that Dominica's "principal function in the late eighteenth century [was] as an entrepot for the illicit British slave trade to Guadeloupe and Martinique."[9] Williams (1970, 244) points out that "in Dominica, from 1784 to 1788, total imports [of slaves] amounted to 27,533; re-exported to 15,781, or more than one half." In two specimen years, 1788 and 1792, a total of 6,035 Africans were exported from Dominica (Armytage 1953, 151). The slave population of Dominica, then, increased overall, but it also fluctuated because of the island's slave entrepôt trade (see table 3).[10]

This trade in humans commoditized people and enabled them to be treated as less than human. Craft was employed to present the best face on the slave being sold and to conceal undesirable qualities such as poor health and age. The good of the slave was lost in the good of the deal. The transportation, barracking, and the sale of such individuals were "rationalized" responses to what was considered a business enterprise and justified by a racist ideology.

DOMINICA HAD BECOME a much more thorough periphery and consequently was paying much greater costs, and the order being created was highly unstable and generated a high level of ongoing turbulence in its wake. Before we consider what this meant for those on the periphery, and how they responded to their peripheralization, we must turn again briefly to France, for that country was not yet completely done with Dominica.

FRENCH CONQUEST AND MILITARY FORTIFICATION

France had not relinquished the hope of possessing three large territories in the middle of the Antillean arc. Britain inadvertently aided France in this quest, for, as we have seen, it put all its ener-

Table 3
Reported Slave Populations of the Smaller Territories in the British West Indies

Grenada		St Vincent		Dominica	
Year	Population	Year	Population	Year	Population
1700	500	1763	3,400	1763	5,900
1753	12,000	1764	7,400	1766	8,500
1771	26,200	1787	11,900	1773	18,800
1779	35,000	1805	16,500	1780	12,700
1785	23,900	1834	22,300	1787	15,000
1788	26,800			1805	22,100
1834	23,600			1834	14,200

Trinidad		Tobago		St Lucia	
Year	Population	Year	Population	Year	Population
1776	10,800	1797	10,000	1776	1,000
1800	15,800	1787	10,500	1834	13,300
1802	19,700	1805	14,900		
1811	21,100	1834	11,600		
1834	20,700				

Virgin Islands		Bermuda		Bahamas	
Year	Population	Year	Population	Year	Population
1756	6,100	1773	2,200	1787	2,200
1787	9,000	1787	4,900	1834	10,100
1834	5,100	1834	4,000		

British Honduras	
Year	Population
1834	1,900

Source: Curtin 1969, 65.

gies into promoting trade and establishing plantations rather than developing the military fortification of the island, although it had established some coastal defences. Fort Young and Melville's Battery at Roseau were linked by signals to the small fort (Cacharou) at Scotts Head, on the southern tip of the island. This fort, though small, was important, since assaults on the island "always came from the south, where the wind bore ships swiftly up from the French island of Martinique" (Buisseret 1973, 62). But the entire regular British force on the island in 1778 "amounted to no more than six officers, ninety-four privates, and about one hundred and twenty militia" (Coke 1971, 337). This overall failure to develop fortifications laid Dominica open to recapture by the French.[11]

In 1778, war broke out between France and England, when France joined forces with the thirteen American colonies in their fight for independence from Britain. "For the next five years the two most powerful naval fleets in the world were concentrated along the eastern coast of North America and in the Caribbean" (Honychurch 1983, 15). The West Indies became a theatre of action because a number of islands were vulnerable to re-conquest by the French. Dominica was one of them.

The French acted promptly at the outbreak of war so that "no reinforcements might arrive from England" (Coke 1971, 337).[12] De Bouille, a military general from Martinique who was already well informed on the Dominican situation, landed on the island at dawn on 7 September 1778, with eighteen hundred soldiers and a thousand Creole (white and free coloured) volunteers. He took Fort Cachacrou easily; its guns had been spiked by local French patriots who had inveigled their way in on the pretext of regaling the soldiers. Though de Bouille found surprising resistance from the small number of British military personnel on his march to Roseau, he forced a surrender from the inhabitants by five o'clock that evening, and his troops marched triumphantly into Roseau.[13]

Britain was stunned by the swift seizure of the island, but could do little about the *fait accompli*. De Bouille set about making Dominica militarily impregnable and establishing a communication link with Guadeloupe and Martinique. Unconcerned with retaliating against the English, expropriating their property, or denying them civil rights, he set up a new government within a few days, made up of Englishmen but headed by Commandant Duchilleau. He left a garrison of 700 regular and one hundred free coloured men and returned to Martinique.

Duchilleau was faced with the difficult task of disarming the Englishmen and preventing them from assembling, while promoting the general contentment of the island's population and developing its agriculture and commerce.[14] The British had built upon the early French efforts to create an administration on the island, and had an Island Council. Duchilleau tried to work through this assembly. Initially, things went well. He introduced the first Frenchman, de Belligny, to the Council without incident in October of 1778. Hoping to inhibit the growing number of escaped slaves, he issued a pardon for them all, which appeared acceptable to the largely English Council. But he was also bent on fortifying the island, and in this he came unstuck. He incurred enormous financial expenses; he requested more troops; he took slaves away from agricultural work and put them on corvée work building roads and fortifications; he demanded more cattle from the island inhabitants to feed his troops. On one occasion, in 1779, he demanded cattle to feed twelve hundred sick men who had been landed in Dominica from a Spanish fleet allied with the French.

To make matters worse, with the outbreak of the American Revolution, commerce stagnated as trading ships were intercepted by the British and direct trade with Britain and France was forbidden. Carrington (1987, 138) argues that "the impact of the American Revolution on the British West Indies was traumatic and permanently devastating; the islands never recovered their earlier productive capacity." Prices of provisions soared. In the words of one observer, "Most planters gave their slaves dry salt for cooking instead of salt provisions which cost dear, while encouraging them to feed on local resources like hogs and *crapauds* (frogs); with crop production crippled by the steady furnishing of slaves for public works; with livestock decreasing to supply French troops; with coffee, the only produce in demand, selling as low as 7 to 8 sols a pound, every Englishmen who could leave the island began to do so, once he had obtained the required written permission of Duchilleau" (Boromé 1969, 48). By January 1780, many English residents, both white and coloured, had left the island. The population fell to 1,066 whites (three quarters of them French), 543 free Negroes, and 12,713 slaves (Boromé 1969a, 50; Cracknell 1973, 63).

Relations between Duchilleau and the English deteriorated progressively. They disliked the equal treatment he granted free Negroes, most of whom were French, the praise he lavished on their militia, the cavalier way he and his officers addressed the English women, and the fact that the slapping of an English chief justice by a French free Negro went unpunished. They became incensed when, on the grounds that there were more French inhabitants than English on the island, Duchilleau revised the Registers Act to make all documents, including deeds and conveyances, written in French equally valid to those written in English. Moreover, a Frenchman had had the temerity to threaten "a respectable English merchant" with a drawn sword in a tavern. Duchilleau then aggravated the situation by refusing to grant arms to English planters, who were being increasingly attacked not only by other citizens but by maroons. In fact, some British settlers suspected that Duchilleau had gone so far as to encourage the maroons to attack, and had even armed them. Atwood (1791, 230) observes that at that time "they [the maroons] often came in the same manner, with conch shells blowing and French colours flying, close to the town of Roseau."

The English were also perturbed by the sudden appearance of many French Catholic missionaries and Franciscan, Capuchin, and secular priests, who settled along the leeward coast and in the old Jesuit parish at Grand Bay, in the south. All frustration was focused on Duchilleau. To make matters worse, two dreadful hurricanes, in

1778 and 1780, severely damaged crops and housing on the island. The last straw was a fire that broke out on 16 April 1781, in Roseau, which quickly burned six hundred houses to the ground, including the main buildings and stores. Duchilleau had often threatened to burn the town, and many English were convinced that he was responsible for the disaster. They said that during the conflagration he would allow soldiers to assist only French merchants and did not punish the looting of English stores.

Duchilleau left the island permanently two months later. He was replaced for a very short period by Bourgon, who returned to France and was replaced by de Beaupré in January 1782. Dominica was in such a pitiful state that Martinique and Guadeloupe were moved to send food and wood to its people, and to lift import and export taxes and restrictions on trade. But commerce did not recover. As a further aggravation, the Americans captured and sold two heavily laden ships, the *Resolution*, bound for Amsterdam from Dominica, and the *Ersten*, bound from Ostend with plantation supplies. De Beaupré tried to introduce some measures that would placate the English: he allowed planters to have guns to defend their plantations and levied five hundred johannes from planters and inhabitants for suppression of the maroons. But life still looked very bleak to the English.

Then, in April of 1782, Admiral Rodney appeared in the channel between Dominica and Les Saintes and took on the thirty French ships of Admiral de Grasse in what the French call "the Battle of Dominica." Rodney's victory ended French naval influence in the Caribbean and the French occupation of Dominica. In August of that year, Lord Shelburn was told in London by Admiral de Grasse, an honoured prisoner of war on his way to Paris, that France intended to keep Dominica (see Boromé 1969, 56). The island became an important part of the ensuing negotiations with France, which reluctantly ceded it to Britain in 1783 by the Treaty of Versailles in return for Tobago.[15]

The French authorities in the West Indies found this decision hard to take, and French residents in Dominica were appalled at the restoration of the island to Britain. They exhibited their disagreement by refusing to leave the island. The local governor initially refused to relinquish his post. He then allowed British soldiers to land but forbade them to enter Roseau. Finally, he ordered his men to demolish the fortifications they had built and to damage those they had found on their arrival on the island. Besides restoring the island to Britain, the Treaty of Versailles also returned Roseau to its previous status as a free port.

There were three further French attempts to capture the island. In 1789, the French Revolution erupted in Paris, and by 1793 Britain was again at war with France. The French West Indies were involved, of course, and in 1793 between five and six thousand white and coloured French royalist refugees arrived in Dominica from the neighbouring islands. Victor Hugues, the new French West Indian commissioner, hoping for the support of the French in Dominica, sponsored unsuccessful invasions of the island in 1795 and 1797.[16] The English responded by deporting six hundred French inhabitants who had shown support for the enemy. A third attempt was ordered by Napoleon in 1805, and a French fleet with some thirty-five hundred French soldiers, under the leadership of General La Grange, arrived at Roseau flying British colours. In the ensuing fight, Roseau caught fire and General Prévost decided to surrender the town. He retreated to Portsmouth to carry on the battle from the well-protected Cabrits fort. General La Grange stayed for six days, during which he made a cursory attempt to pry Prévost from the Cabrits, levied a ransom of £12,000 on Roseau, and then "immediately left the island in order to tackle a bigger target – St Kitts" (Cracknell 1973, 65).[17] Dominica was not invaded again.[18] In fact, it was the base from which the British invaded and captured Guadeloupe in 1810.

The end of the French Revolution, in 1815, ended the official French hope for a restoration of Dominica, "though rumours of possible cession occasionally circulated in Dominica itself throughout the nineteenth century" (Boromé 1969, 57–8). The protracted interest by the French in possessing the island had led to almost fifty years of war, and this had greatly damaged the island's economy. "In point of trade, the English and French inhabitants were partners in calamity ... The impenetrable gloom that hovered over them had relaxed the springs of industry; their hopes were frozen, and the expectations had almost formed an alliance with despair. Many of the planters were absolutely ruined" (Coke 1971, 342).

The period of British attempts to centre their world by creating colonies – in this case, by settling and "developing" Dominica – was punctuated, therefore, by counter-strategies by other European powers to use the same territory or practice to centre their world. In this case, the "progress" of Dominica was halted and even reversed, through the centring activities of the French rival.

SICKNESS AND DISEASE

As if there were not enough difficulties already, these events occurred against a background of disease and sickness. "When death was stalking around, sparing few, and sweeping hundreds away with unrelenting hand, the effect on the minds of the inhabitants and garrisons was such as may be supposed – dejection – sometimes bordering on despair ... Respecting deaths – indeed, such is the nature of the climate, so fatal are its diseases, and so rapid are they in their course, that the friend, or neighbour, whom yesterday you may have met, may today be ill and tomorrow you may be summoned to perform the last sad duties to his remains" (Anonymous 1828).

Endemic diseases such as the dry belly ache, dysentery, and malaria were compounded by epidemics of yellow fever (the black vomit). Malaria was so prevalent in the Portsmouth area that Prince Rupert had the reputation of being the least healthy place in the entire Caribbean region. The black population, however, appeared to be far less susceptible to the pernicious fevers than the white (see Clyde 1980, 23). Statistics from a later period support this: in 1804, one out of every two white soldiers died of disease, while one out of every forty-three black soldiers did so. During the twenty-year period 1816–1836, a total of 4,723 white and 2,454 black soldiers served in Dominica. The mortality rate per thousand for whites was 137.4, and for blacks it was 39.9 (see Clyde 1980, 24–5). Dysentery was a particular menace for white troops, and was much more widespread in Dominica than in other islands. The year 1793 saw the first major epidemic of yellow fever, brought by the French royalist refugees from Martinique. It killed some eight hundred refugees and two hundred British, including soldiers and sailors (Clyde 1980, 27). The general trend in causes of slave deaths in the new sugar colonies was "diarrhea and dysentery, dropsy, fevers (malaria and yellow fever), tuberculosis, nervous system diseases, and digestive system diseases" (Higman 1984, 341).

Even among slaves, there were variations in morbidity and mortality, in terms not only of the type and scale of enterprise for which they worked but of what work they did. Higman (1984, 333) indicates that "the most important occupational mortality differential was that between field laborers and 'privileged' drivers, skilled tradespeople, and domestics ... In the case of Creole males attached to sugar estates, the death-rates of field laborers were more than double those of the privileged group at all ages over 30 years, and 50 percent higher among younger slaves. On plantations producing the minor staples – coffee, cocoa, cotton, and provision – the differential was less consistent." Moreover, the specific tasks that slaves were expected to do as the seasons passed also had an impact of morbidity and mortality, with the greatest mortality occurring at harvesting. In Dominica, this meant that slave mortality on the sugar plantations increased quite steadily through the calendar year, peaking in December, whereas on the coffee plantations mortality peaked between July and September, when coffee was harvested (see Higman 1984, 338).

SLAVE REVOLTS: *MARRONAGE*

In the face of the dehumanizing and marginalizing effects of metro-politan centring in Dominica, there were attempts to create order on the periphery and to centre the local world. French settlers stayed away from sugar, which was not suited to Dominica, and traded more locally in coffee. Amerindians survived on the isolated cliffs of the east coast and had little contact with the new settlers. As well, slaves sometimes revolted and often slipped away from the planta-tions into the interior to form what Mintz (1974a, 152) describes as "runaway peasantries," attempting to create a new and free kind of community outside of, and in opposition to, the slave-based planta-tion-oriented society. These maroons, as they were called, were minimally economically integrated into the wider society and were therefore not typical peasantries.

Marronage was the ultimate form of slave resistance: slaves would escape from their owners into the interior, whence they would return to plunder plantations and rob citizens.[19] *Marronage* differed in kind between what the French called *petit marronage* – in which individuals ran away more as a form of protest, for shorter periods, subsisting in the bush through the help of fellow slaves – and true *marronage*, which consisted of bands of escaped slaves, able to subsist, defend themselves, and sustain their numbers in the face of white resistance (see Craton 1982, 61). It varied, too, from territory to territory according to geographical, political, and demographic differences. In some cases, as in St Vincent and Dominica, maroon communities were formed in alliance with Amerindian people, whereas in others they were the product exclusively of African or Creole runaways. In Jamaica at one time, runaways occupied a town, whereas in Dominica they dwelt in the bush (see Hart 1977). In Jamaica, Hart argues, "the blacks conceived of the white popula-tion as being both the oppressor class and the oppressor nation" (Hart 1977, 21). In Dominica, slaves and maroons distinguished between British and French whites. Slaves ran away most often from the former, and, as maroons, returned to attack them most frequent-ly, sometimes aided by the French in this enterprise. Their camps, given Dominica's "virgin jungle, as dense as that of the Cameroons, its mountains and defiles" (Craton 1982, 141), were almost inaccessible. Initially, they were in contact with local Amerindians, from whom they learned certain survival strategies in the bush, but "so numerous did the fugitives become, and so large were the areas to which they could flee to become independent maroons, that cooperation was no longer attractive to the Caribs or necessary for the African runaways" (Craton 1982, 142).

Throughout the West Indies, the maroons represented a strong challenge to white authority and the plantation system. Fitting carefully into the specific contexts they found, they varied in their organization and response from area to area. They were militarily ahead of their time, being quite expert in guerrilla warfare and in exploiting their environments. Yet, like guerrillas, they were a product of the society they were fighting and relied on it for munitions, hardware, clothes, and the like. They were therefore unavoidably dependent on the very plantation societies from which they were trying to free themselves, and "this inability to disengage themselves freely from their enemy was the Achilles heel of maroon societies throughout the Americas" (Price 1973, 12). For the colonial administrations, the maroons were a "chronic plague" on New World plantation societies, and local governments, charged with protecting the plantation system, defined them as enemies (see Peytraud 1897, quoted in Price 1973, 4).

Although *marronage* existed prior to British annexation of Dominica, it escalated dramatically afterward. Atwood (1791, 26) records, for instance, that when the Jesuits left Grand Bay and disposed of their sugar plantation and slaves, the slaves ran away from their new masters into the woods, "where they were joined from time to time by others from different estates." As the British established or took over estates and imported more slaves, their reputation as hard taskmasters grew and the number of slave runaways increased. The governor of the island at the time, Ainslie, described them as "an internal enemy of the most alarming kind" (Ainslie to Bathurst, 1814, quoted in Marshall 1982, 36). The actual number of maroons cannot be accurately established; Marshall (1976, 27; 1982, 34) cites a figure of 300 in 1785, and 578 in 1814, when they were defeated. In 1778, they took advantage of the French capture of the island and, armed with bayonets, cutlasses, and pistols, swept down from their fortified camps and raided plantations for stores, cattle, and recruits.

This surge of maroon activity against British plantations reflects a clear difference in the relationship that the French and the British maintained with their slaves. Some fifty years after British annexation, Sturge and Harvey (1838, 103) observed, "The coffee estates in this island ... are mostly small properties in the hands of the old French residents ... the Negroes on many of them ... will not emigrate or suffer themselves to be transferred to sugar estates." They noted of one estate,

This benevolent old [French] gentleman seemed to live in patriarchal style in the midst of his people. Some of the young children almost lived in his house, and served to amuse him with their play; one who was present, received his supper from the table. The Negroes on this property, we were told, have doubled their numbers within the last twenty years. Nothing can be a greater contrast, than the condition, appearance, and manners of the people on some of these properties of the old French residents, and of those, on even the well managed English estates. On the former, there has generally been an increase, and the latter a striking decrease of numbers. (Sturge and Harvey 1838, 106–7)

Not only were the French less prejudiced toward their slaves but, as we have seen, the alliance between the French and maroons was suspected to extend to support from the French governor, Duchilleau (see Atwood 1791, 145, 228). Boromé, however, remarking on the role of the maroons in the French possession, cautions against this interpretation. He notes that the French sometimes sent militia against the maroons and refers to a letter Duchilleau sent to the legislature in 1778 stating that no Negro should be allowed to bear arms (Boromé 1969a, 55). Moreover, Atwood (1791, 255) observes in a post-manuscript footnote that maroons, "having been joined by a number of other negro slaves, from different plantations of the French inhabitants, have again commenced depredations of a most serious nature." Elsewhere, however, Boromé (1972c, 112) seems to support Atwood's observation: "These slaves who had fled into the rugged interior mainly from British masters, were emboldened by the French capture of the island." Craton supports this view:

In May 1795 some francophone smallholders and their slaves took part in a smaller version of Fédon's rebellion at Colihaut, in St Peter's parish. The uprising was planned to coincide with a major landing of French troops sent by Victor Hugues to Pagua Bay, on the opposite side of Dominica, once the British had evacuated St Lucia. Elements of the Colihaut rebels joined up with the "Brigands" landed at Pagua Bay, having found a route over the supposedly trackless Morne Diablotin. A French proclamation held out the prospect of freedom for friendly slaves but death for those who would not join the republican cause. (Craton 1982, 227)

BRITAIN USED THE SLAVE TRADE to develop a more complex society at home, centring its world around industry and mercantilism in increasingly large urban complexes. The slave trade was part of a triangular network that transformed English villages into towns, towns into cities, and crafts into industries. It fostered monocrop sugar production in the West Indies, and it made the West Indian territories into exploiter colonies. Britain's interest in the West Indies included trade as well as sugar production. As a result, in Dominica, where the potential for large-scale sugar production was limited, the island's two towns were designated free ports with a view to entrepôt trade. The military fortification and defence of the island were a low priority. In contrast, the French centring strategy was to incorporate Dominica into France for military reasons to protect other French islands, and its strategy was to set up strong local administrations and to fortify the island.

Dominica was increasingly drawn into a high-entropy society's "gravitational" orbit during this period, and considerable energy was used to further metropolitan interests. The consequence was an increase in the entropy and disorder produced by the nature of the order established on the island. At the physical level, soil erosion limited the ability for the land to carry its usual flora and fauna. This meant that harvests were increasingly unpredictable, which, in turn, affected the human population and its activities. High death rates, from disease and misuse of slaves, was another entropic effect of the metropole's centring strategy, which led to further unpredictability in the social order. The French decision to increase the fortification of Dominica took a high toll on local settlers and their resources and generated further turbulence. In sum, the order established by Britain and France to exert control over the island and to extract produce and profits from it generated unpredictability in its wake as settlers, merchants, and administrators found themselves in a context in which major decisions were made by influential players back in the metropole, in which slaves were daily faced with brutality and starvation, and in which land was quickly deforested, overgrazed, and overworked.

Those who found themselves on this periphery tried to manage the situation, centre their world, and shape some sort of order for themselves. Sugar planters attempted to develop a plantation society, a strategy that had been financially successful in other islands and contributed to metropolitan centring. In Dominica, however, the size of their operation was limited both by edict and by the natural topography of the island. The disorder generated meant that considerable effort had to go into maintaining the fragile order.

Managers and overseers of estates centred their world by distancing themselves from their slaves, perceiving them as less than human, and seeking as much short-term gain from them as they could. They were very much part of the order established to funnel resources back to Britain, who centred their world by trying to realize the dictates of a distant metropolitan government on the periphery.

The slaves used several strategies to create order for themselves. Some accepted their lot of hopelessness and were worked to death, sometimes hastening it by their own hand. Others attempted to improve their position within the slave system by obtaining "better" roles within it. And some rebelled against it, both within the system by working slowly, sabotaging work, poisoning animals, committing acts of arson, miscommunicating information, and the like, and without the system, by escaping and leading armed resistance and pillaging planter property. The maroons adopted the last strategy, and, like the Amerindians, created an order that removed itself as far as possible from any contact with metropolitan centripetal forces.

In sum, the institutions developed by France and Britain in Dominica were designed to serve their respective interests – the plantation system, fortresses, a militia to hunt maroons, and new forms of social control. Metropolitan centres thus established a social order in Dominica in order to draw resources from it. They created Dominica as a periphery using considerable energy in the process. This, in turn, generated entropy and considerable turbulence in the system. Slaves were a particularly important and vulnerable element in both the plantation and mercantile aspects of the centring strategy of Britain, and the next chapter will consider slavery more fully and what followed its demise.

5 Slavery and Emancipation

The British West Indies were developed as exploitation colonies.
Tropical heat, the flocking out of adventurers, and easy credit in Great
Britain combined to that end. Climatic conditions made an economic
system based on free European workers impossible. Hence arose a
regime of forced labor, resting first on the native Indian and, following
his virtual extinction, upon the more sturdy transatlantic black.

Ragatz 1963, 3

The history of the Caribbean can be defined as the history of labour.

Cross and Heuman 1988, 1

SLAVERY AND SOCIETY

Civilizations emerged as populations and politics centred on cities.
This centring of power in urban concentrations and peripheraliza-
tions of rural populations was accompanied by an increasing reliance on unfree labour. (The terms *free* and *unfree*, as used here, do
not refer to the cost of the labour, but to the independence of the
worker. In free labour, the worker is free to work or not, while in
unfree labour the worker has no choice in the matter.) Greece and
Rome flourished as a result of their dependence on slave labour; it
was the rural slave economy that enabled landowners in these societies to live "free," luxurious lives in cities. Slavery accentuated the
meaning of citizen, providing it with degrees of liberation from the
productive, subsistence process unheard of in earlier forms of society. This detachment from work enabled intellectual activity to be
directed away from mundane problems of food production and distribution toward a concern with questions of "truth" and "beauty"
and those phenomena that Kroeber (1952; 1963) defined as "value
culture."[1]

These civilizations obtained their slaves largely through a second
indispensable component of "civilized" society – warfare. Slaves
were, in large measure, imported inhabitants from conquered
territories. It was wars and colonies, and the slaves they produced,
that funnelled resources and production in toward the centre and
enriched the Greco-Roman city-state. There is therefore a direct

relationship between the emergence of early civilizations, the creation of urban centres, the invasion and subjugation of foreign territories, and the exploitation of unfree labour. The countryside was essentially the working region that supplied the city with its needed resources, and the use of imported slaves reinforced peripheralization of the former and the centring of the latter. The production of surplus in these societies was tied to a whole set of mutual obligations and encumbrances.

The period of European dominance emerges with the "liberation" of surplus from tributary and obligatory relationships, giving rise to the possibility of naked profit – a surplus with which one could do what one liked. As war and trade became tied to colonization, new arms and strategies in warfare, new forms of transportation, and a new colonial thrust by Europe produced unprecedentedly effective means of transferring surplus from the conquered territories to the metropolitan centres. Taken together, these developments spelled the beginnings of capitalism. In this context, slaves not only enabled the acquisition of surplus through unpaid labour, but represented capital in economic enterprises. The productive areas were no longer the rural hinterland of the city, but the conquered territories themselves. Slaves were not brought home to rural employment near the centre, but were transported and used in colonial territories to further production. The aggrandizement of the centre and the use of unfree labour on the periphery were closely linked to one another.

In the West Indies, slavery appeared on a large scale with the Spanish enslavement of indigenous people to mine gold and silver, although the Amerindians themselves indulged to some extent in unfree labour. But with the decimation of the Amerindian population, metropolitan centres began to look for new sources of labour to import into the region. As Europe became increasingly interested in the profit potential of the West Indies, it transported "captives" from one part of the world to another to labour in its interests. It sent out its own nationals to control the process, with the overall purpose of amassing the resources and profits generated in the colony. The whole enterprise was supported by an ideology of domination, translated particularly into racism and exploitation in the Caribbean.[2] Here we find a far wider centring activity than occurred in Rome and Greece, with a much greater entropic and chaotic effect.

The African population that provided the slaves was not large enough to accommodate easily the European demand. Nevertheless, Africa was able "to sustain a large-scale trade in people" (Wolf 1982a, 204). The African delivery system that emerged in response to European demands instigated a series of political upheavals on the African west coast, where "big men" emerged – such individuals as the Akrosan brothers and Johnny Kabbes of Komenda – whose considerable power was augmented by the support of European firearms. These new opportunities for trade and warfare "prompted the emergence of small states, all of them based ... on firearms" (Wolf 1982a, 210).

The influence of powerful individuals, however, was cut short by the Asante, who expanded rapidly in the eighteenth and nineteenth centuries and dominated the Gold Coast slave trade, as well as the Yoruba, Dahomey, and Benin, who had satellite kingdoms close to the coast. Slave trading polarized African peoples into slave-hunters and slave-providers; the former (*olu*), a riverine people, controlled the trading routes, and the latter (*igbo*) were the upland peoples (see Wolf 1982a, 217).[3] Slave trading created major centres of exchange on the coast (Kalabari, Adoni, Bonny, Okrika, Brass, and Old Calabar). As local population resources dwindled, new sources of slaves were sought farther inland, until, "by the end of the 18th century a major transcontinental trade route linked the Atlantic shore with the littoral of the Indian Ocean" and "the demand for slaves had reshaped the political economy of the entire continent. It gave rise to one common process, to new tributary states and to specialized organizations of slave hunters, and it turned societies described by anthropologists as 'acephalous, segmented, lineage based' into the predelict target population of slavers" (Wolf 1982a, 227, 230).

Again, we see the centring strategies of the metropole drawing a territory, this time in Africa, into a peripheral relationship in order to achieve its goals. And, as its human resources were funnelled out of the continent to satisfy metropolitan interests, Africa was shattered and transformed. Some individuals and groups attempted to centre and order this newly disorganized, peripheral situation by identifying with the peripheralizing force and helping to funnel out resources. What remained were truncated lineages, depopulated villages, and traditional beliefs and behaviours that no longer fitted the new situation – the entropic effect of an order created to transfer energy for use at the centre.

SLAVERY IN THE BRITISH WEST INDIES

Earlier European attempts to develop settler colonies in the Caribbean failed dismally, because "an acute labor shortage jeopardized the success of a viable agricultural economy" (Knight 1978, 41). White indentured servants, convicts, and nonconformists were shipped out from the metropole (another dimension of the peripheralizing process – the dumping of the unwanted) to provide a labour force for planters in the seventeenth century. By the eighteenth century, however, many of them had served their terms, and had gone on to form a category of poor whites. A solution to the problems of developing settler colonies in the West Indies was to turn them into exploitation colonies. As early as 1650, "Barbados and the Leewards forsook their settler destinies to pursue the lucrative path of the tropical plantation society" (Knight 1978, 61).

Under the catalyst of mercantilism, the exploitation colony arose in response to metropolitan demand for staple commodities of high value and small bulk. Effort swung from transferring and perpetuating European values in new lands to making as large and as quick a profit from them as possible.[4] Carrington (1987, 135) observes, "The plantation system in the British West Indies cannot be viewed only in the light of the monocultural production of sugar by exploited black slave labor. It was also the social, political, economic, cultural and psychological lifeline of British mercantilism." Thus, slavery in the Caribbean "stemmed from the growing demand of Europeans for a wider range of food stuffs and raw materials, the large scale production of which was only feasible in humid tropical and semi-tropical regions of open resources" (Sheridan 1977, 7). In the Caribbean, slavery differed qualitatively from its forebears, for it was intrinsically linked not only to labour, but to profit – a profit that could be realized from sugar production. To facilitate the realization of this profit, the entire edifice of the slave trade was shot through with racist beliefs that justified, to the believers, their exploitative brutality. Thus, "Slave exports from Africa quintupled to an estimated total of 1,341,000, primarily in response to the development of sugar cane cultivation on the islands of the Caribbean" (Wolf 1982a, 195).

Certain characteristics of sugar production significantly influenced the social organization that accompanied it. Sugar cane could be grown extensively with little expertise, but it was perishable and had to be processed immediately. Sugar factories were needed, which meant heavy investments in buildings, machinery, and labour, and a continuous substantial supply of raw cane. Sugar therefore required a large initial capital outlay – it was a rich man's crop (see Lowenthal 1972, 27). Furthermore, it took a large labour force to keep up the supply of raw cane necessary to make the sugar factory cost-effective. There was something different about the Caribbean "factory." While metropolitan factories relied on free labour, this was unpredictable and scarce in the Caribbean, and so unfree, slave labour was sought. African slaves had already been used to produce sugar in Madeira, the Canaries, and the West African islands (see Solow 1987, 57–8) – why not the Caribbean? Sugar therefore lent itself to a unique power relationship between master and worker.

To meet factory demand for a large, regular quantity of cane, a new agricultural institution emerged – the plantation, a unit of land in a tropical or subtropical region on which a commercial crop or crops were grown for sale in European markets for a profit. The labour was supplied by slaves of non-European – primarily African – origin. The slaves, along with the land and the other means of production, were owned and managed by Europeans, who were in turn subject to the sovereignty of a European nation-state (see Greenfield 1979, 87–8).

These developing centring patterns emphasized a newfound rationality that abstracted, calculated, and specialized. Their underpinnings were epitomized in the Newtonian world view, with its vision of a mechanical universe of parts, forces, and effects, all of which could be measured and, more importantly, used. It was a world that prompted new quests for technologies and techniques. Thus, the notion of "factory," as a local, rationalized, specialized edifice for production, and "plantation," as a local, rationalized, specialized territory for production, were products of the growing modernism in Europe. Ideology, technique, and social organization worked together to funnel resources in an effort to maximize control and, thereby, profits.

The advantage of the slave-based plantation system for the metropolitan-oriented planter was its impersonal organization, which allowed it to respond to market fluctuations. Slaves were "capable of being organized, concentrated, combined and directed towards profit making activities" in the most calculating, impersonal way (Sheridan 1977, 8). The sociological implications were profound. The defining characteristics of this emerging social system were the overwhelming imbalance of power that existed between its parts and the dehumanizing racism that was used to justify it. By linking notions of productivity and profit with human exploitation and degradation, it created two rigidly separate worlds: that of the master and that of the slave. The law, that guardian of rights, applied quite differently to each. While slavery brutalized Africans, it had a reciprocal effect. As Mintz (1974a, 81) observed, "one cannot degrade another without degrading oneself."

Although it in no way mitigates its atrociousness, Caribbean slavery occurred in a social context that was already extremely cruel and insensible. At least one observer has maintained that European indentured labourers were dealt with more severely than were the

African slaves who succeeded them in the Caribbean (see Cross and Heuman 1988, 1). Harsh treatment of sailors was the order of the day, and not only on slave ships. Hughes (1987, 72) writes of the first shipload of convicts sent out to Australia, "All were [for] crimes against property, some forced by pitiful necessity. Elizabeth Beckford, the second oldest woman on the First Fleet, was seventy. Her crime, for which she got seven years 'transportation,' was to have stolen twelve pounds of Gloucester cheese ... Fifteen-year-old John Wisehammer grabbed a packet of snuff from an apothecary's counter in Gloucester. They all went down for seven years." Transportation to Australia was truly horrendous:

The bilges were foul in all of the ships. Even those whose guts have heaved at the whiff from the boat's head at sea can have little idea of the anguish of eighteenth-century bilge stink: a fermenting, sloshing broth of sea water mixed with urine, puke, dung, rotting food, dead rats and the hundred other attars of the Great Age of Sail ... When tropical rainstorms whipped the fleet, the convicts – who had no change of dry clothes – could not exercise on deck. They stayed below under battened hatches, and conditions in their steaming, stinking holds were extreme. (Hughes 1987, 79)

However, there was a dimension to the ill-treatment of slaves that surpassed the widespread brutishness of the period. The very acquisition of slaves in Africa entailed treachery and violence. Slaves were kept in damp, dark, airless dungeons on the West African coast in castles such as Cape Coast and Elmina. They wore heavy fetters or a cannonball chained to one ankle, so that movement was painful and difficult. This did not compare to the brutality of the middle passage. Shelves in ships' holds were built one above the other, and the slaves were packed onto them and remained chained to them for days with no food, no drink, no exercise – unable even to sit up. More cruelty was meted out by the slavers, who used shackles, thumbscrews, and instruments for force-feeding. The celebrated case of captain Luke Collingwood shows how slavers depersonalized their captive Africans: he had 133 slaves thrown overboard because they were sick and there was a shortage of water. He regarded this as a legal "jettison" – a normal practice for a ship carrying horses (see Halcrow 1982, 31). Occasionally, the entire cargo died from food or water shortages or disease, although this could not have occurred regularly, as it would have been too unprofitable. Williams (1970, 139) posits that there was a 32 per cent death rate on the middle passage, although Anstey (1975, 31) calculated a mean mortality of 8.5 per cent from a large random sample taken from 1769 to 1787. One account given to the British Parliament by James Penny, Esq., on three voyages between 1775 and 1778, states that between 531 and 560 Africans were purchased, of whom between twenty-four and thirty-one died during the middle passage. On these voyages, between thirty-eight and forty-eight seamen manned the ships, and between three and six of them died (see Craton, Walvin, and Wright 1976, 34). The crew were often treated little better than the slaves, many of them having been press-ganged into service. In fact, Halcrow (1982, 31) argues that "by the eighteenth century the death rate among the crew tended to be higher than the death rate among slaves. Slavers had learned how to reduce the death rate among slaves, frequently the result of dysentery or lung disease, by reducing over-crowding and improving sanitation. They did not discover how to prevent or cure malaria and yellow fever, the killer diseases responsible for the death of so many of the sailors."

As for slavery itself, gruesome stories from this period abound. Anstey (1975, 32) records the acts of a certain Captain Williams, who would "personally flog slaves who refused to eat, delighting in such operations, and severely beat women slaves who refused to sleep with him." James recounts that a Mr Le Jeune, suspecting that the mortality among his Negroes was due to poison, murdered four of them and then tried to extort confessions from two women. "He roasted their feet, legs and elbows, while alternately gagging them thoroughly and then withdrawing the gag" (James 1980, 22). In 1811, Arthur Hodge, of Tortola, was found guilty and executed for murdering "sixty of his slaves by excessive punishment"; the year before, a Nevis planter named Edward Huggins had had thirty of his men and women slaves "whipped in the public market place to the tune of 240 lashes each" (Hamshere 1972, 132). M'Mahan describes how a white proprietor, who had been trying to seduce the fourteen-year-old daughter of his coloured mistress, overheard his mistress threatening the girl. In a fit of pique, he took a chair onto the terrace, sat down, and ordered that the girl be brought out, stretched out, and her body laid bare. He then had her flogged for two and a half hours. M'Mahan says, "The driver had to stop three times to put lashes to his whip ... Her appearance was aweful – I thought she was dying" (quoted in Craton, Walvin, and Wright 1976, 129). The girl died shortly afterwards. Such examples abound.

The brutality of this system was probably furthered by the quality of early settlers in these territories and the cultural climate they created. Ragatz (1963, 3) portrays the original settlers of the Caribbean islands in a way that suggests that the degradation had already set in: "The islands became the goal of spendthrift bank-rupts eager to recoup their wasted fortunes, of penniless younger sons of gentility desirous of amassing means sufficient to become landed proprietors in the homeland, and the dumping-ground for the riffraff of the parent country."[5] Ironically, many of those who arrived in the Caribbean from the metropole had been brutalized themselves. But just as we must be careful in stereotyping all slave owners as excessively cruel, we must be careful in generalizing all early settlers as ne'er-do-wells. Among the greedy, the poor, and the criminals were those, for instance, who had been deported from the metropole for their political and religious non-conformists views (see Williams 1970, 100 ff).

Nevertheless, cruelty, supported by a sinister racial ideology and fuelled by a repressed rage, pervaded Caribbean culture. A major factor in the harsh treatment of slaves was their masters' belief that they were a different species: Africans were viewed as less than human and therefore could be justifiably treated as animals. As Craton (1974, 158) observes, "In ancient times slavery rarely had a connotation of race or color, and in the earliest days of the British Empire 'servants' could be white as well as black. But this did not last, and as soon as the need was strong enough, tendencies to equate black with slave and white with free triumphed – distinc-tions that have affected West Indian (and Southern American) social attitudes ever since."

Racist beliefs were instrumental, for they permitted maximal manipulation of slaves by their masters. Besides being a product of racism, it is possible to argue that the cruelty of Caribbean slave masters was a product of their own experience of violence, which socialized them into a set of attitudes that led them to enjoy owning and torturing slaves. Finally, cruelty was also probably the product of the fear-inducing situation itself:[6]

The difficulty was that though one could trap them like animals, transport them in pens, work them alongside an ass or a horse and beat both with the same stick, stable them, and starve them, they remained, despite their black skins and curly hair, quite invincibly human beings; with the intelligence and resentments of human beings. To cow them into the necessary docility and acceptance necessitated a regime of calculated brutality and terrorism, and it is this that explains the unusual spectacle of property-owners apparently careless for preserving their property: they had first to ensure their own safety. (James 1989, 4)

Whatever its causes, slavery was a horrendous institution in itself. Sherrard (1959, 53) observes, "Slavery is not made bad by cruel masters, nor good by tolerant masters; it is an insufferable wrong in itself, and betrays its true nature by its fruits – the perpetually recurrent unhappiness of the slave, the inevitable brutalization of the master. It is not the trappings of slavery, but slavery itself which is wrong."

Not all slave owners, of course, were sadistic extortionists; some even cared for and helped their slaves. Christopher Codrington felt a special relationship with his Coromantee slaves, and saw their murder of a neighbouring planter as an indication of his failure. Sir Charles Price customarily freed his most faithful slaves annually (see Craton 1982, 37). Ransford (1971, 123) observes, "We must accept ... that some planters were genuinely fond of their black domestics and showed tolerance to the men and women who made up the field gangs." Nevertheless, this was unusual, and was more likely to be the case where the plantation owner was resident and the size of the operation was small. "The slaves in the British West Indies preferred to be bought be small farmers rather than by wealthy planters; for they worked with the former in the fields, readily identified themselves with their master's interests and to some extent became part of a family" (Ransford 1971, 112). In general, the whites played "a brutalizing role, in which the whip and gun were ineffectual antidotes for isolation, disease, and the fear of slave uprisings. Overeating, drunkenness, and degraded sex were common anodynes" (Craton 1982, 38).

As for the slaves, "Quite apart from the fact of unfreedom (which planters claimed was an abstract notion, beyond the slaves' intellectual grasp), their common experience was poverty, undernourishment, and ill health as well as drudgery and repression ... an existence that was essentially 'nasty, brutish and short' " (Craton 1982, 52). There existed "a small privileged caste, the foremen of the gangs, coachmen, cooks, butlers, maids, nurses, female companions and other house servants" (James 1980, 19), many of whom repaid their masters for their easy life with strong attachment and despised the slaves in the field. However, even these slaves could rebel against their status, could dislike their masters, and, when opportunity provided, escaped: "Domestic and urban slaves displayed an equal dislike of slavery and an equal proneness to flee the system as did the field slaves" (Knight 1978, 102–3). On the whole, reading reports of the slave system in the West Indies, one is struck by the Europeans' unrelenting antipathy for the Africans, and by their reciprocal distrust and hatred of the white man.

The impersonal harshness of the plantation usually had two symbiotic effects: it impoverished the slave as it enriched the planter. The overwork, underfeeding, poor housing, and physical brutality meted out to slaves resulted in a high mortality rate in, and a low natural increase of, the slave population. In the words of Henry Coor, a millwright who serviced sugar estates in four parishes in Jamaica, speaking to a parliamentary inquiry in Britain in 1791, "It was more the object of the Overseer to work the slaves out, and trust for supplies from Africa ... I have heard many overseers say, 'I have made my employer 20, 30 or 40 more hogsheads per year than any of my predecessors ever did; and though I have killed 30 or 40 Negroes per year or more, yet the produce has been more than adequate to the loss' " (quoted in Hart 1977, 3). As a result of this strategy, slaves on Antiguan plantations "seldom lived more than nine years after importation" (Hart 1977, 4). Together, these factors meant a continual dwindling in the slave population, necessitating regular inputs from outside, perpetuating a demand for slaves that nourished the transatlantic slave trade and kept slave traders in business.[7] This squeezing of work out of slaves with the starkest of support for them made many Caribbean landowners rapidly wealthy. As their wealth increased, they would follow their money back to the metropole. First, a planter would send his children "home" for education. Then he and his wife would follow, and he would direct his plantations from a newly acquired mansion. He would then bequeath his estates to his children, now established in the metropole. Finally, his heirs would pass their estates on to metropolitan creditors or speculators. In this process, control of and profits from the plantations were constantly moving from the Caribbean to the metropole, where the plantation owners and merchant companies were located (see Ragatz 1931, 7).

The effect of this tendency toward absenteeism was to compound the harshness of the slave experience, for the owner was replaced by managers and overseers who were even more concerned with short-run returns.[8] They were apt to be more demanding, and more pernicious, than resident owners in the West Indies. "Attorneys and overseers were primarily interested in the quantity of produce grown, the former because their compensation rested on a percentage basis, the latter because the test of success was the ability to win the agents' favor ... Many of the inhumanities towards the Negroes can be traced to a desire on the part of those directing tropical agricultural enterprises to increase production or at least to maintain it in the face of growing soil exhaustion" (Ragatz 1931, 22). To make matters worse, offices were often concentrated in a few hands, thus enabling the owner to avoid paying several salaries.

As the wealthy returned to Europe, the calibre of whites who were left in the islands to fill local offices and manage estates dropped. "Men of little or no education in law held judicial posts; truly remarkable concentrations of governmental functions in given local worthies, without the slightest regard for incompatibilities, were to be found" (Ragatz 1931, 16).[9] These people lived lavishly off the estates and lined their own coffers, with no thought of consolidating the enterprise; they had no knowledge of agriculture and no capital of their own at stake. Such persons were privileged to occupy the great house, to be served by the owner's slaves, to use his horses and carriage, to live off plantation produce, to pasture livestock on their own account, and, without expense of any kind, to receive their compensation as the first charge against the season's crop. "In truth, to occupy such a post was frequently better than enjoying title to the land" (Ragatz 1931, 20).

The results were disastrous. With no checks upon them, attorneys

commonly purchased excessive quantities of stores from themselves in the names of the proprietors, met obligations thus incurred out of the produce remaining after having drawn their commissions, and shipped the balance to Great Britain ... No attention was paid to safeguarding the money originally laid out. The present alone was thought of. So long as the owner received a regular and steady income, he was content. Improvements were seldom made because they temporarily reduced net returns. Buildings were allowed to fall into ruins, fields were tilled until exhausted and then left to grow up in weeds; properties bore the ungenteel signs of general neglect, new lands were opened only at rare intervals because of the large initial expenditure and great amount of supervision required. *Thus the actual value of Caribbean investments progressively declined.* (Ragatz 1931, 20–22, my italics)

These matters were compounded further when any natural disaster, such as fire, blight, or hurricanes struck.

Besides using punishments to extract maximum work from their slaves, masters also wanted to create ties of dependency among them. This, however, proved a more difficult task. There were areas of slaves' lives over which the master had no control: what they thought, what they did and said when not being overseen, and what other resources they managed for themselves, most importantly in their own gardens. Moreover, it was clear to both parties that there was a reciprocal dependence: the slaves were quite aware that the master needed them. Masters therefore had to resort to a combination of strategies, including fear, coercion, and negotiation. One important result "was that masters failed to stifle the sense of injustice or hostile feelings that slaves could act upon from time to time, in one form or another ... Ultimately, whatever techniques of control masters used to establish supremacy over partly dependent slaves did not make slave resistance impossible" (Gaspar 1985, 171).

The entropic effects of this energy-hungry system, centred on metropolitan power and peripheral exploitation, resulted in exhausted land, dead labourers, poor yields, and increasing disorder. Moreover, because the centre and the periphery are dynamically interrelated, these effects of peripheralization fed back to the centre that had created the order. Slavery was found to be increasingly problematic, and the metropole abolished first the slave trade, and then slavery itself. These decisions did not serve the individual centring strategies of the attorneys, overseers, and planters in the West Indies. Because they were on the periphery, where it is difficult to order one's world, their attempts to resist emancipation were to no avail, and it was imposed by the metropole. The result was a particularly chaotic period in West Indian history, manifested by large-scale movements of ex-slaves off the estates, increased labour problems, and the impoverishment – sometimes destitution – of planters through reduced productivity.

SLAVERY IN DOMINICA

How did Dominica fit into this general picture? Early on, the French brought slaves to Dominica. Writing to the Father General of the Jesuits, Fr. Pierre Gombaud, SJ, records the existence of Creole and "dandas" blacks on the island in 1707. Le Grand, who landed in Dominica in 1727, "had settled his household and several Negro slaves on property given him by chief Petit Jacques" (Boromé 1967, 14). Most of these slaves came with their masters from Martinique, where there was already a sizeable slave population. Father Martell, who became the first parish priest of Roseau in 1730, describes the situation in his earlier parish in Martinique: "There are more than 50 estates in my Parish, plus a borough of some thirty houses ... Two types of people inhabit our land, the French and the Negroes ... and so among the 4000 slaves of the Basse Pointe Parish, it requires super human effort to find some 10 who are fit to receive Holy Communion" (quoted in Proesmans 1972, 171). At that time there were also three hundred free Negroes, comprising 3.8 per cent of the population.

Because, under the French, sugar cultivation never became a dominant crop in Dominica and the scale of operations tended to be small, the master-slave ratio was low compared with that in other Caribbean territories.[10] In 1730, there were 426 slaves in Dominica, who formed 52 per cent of a total population of 806.[11] This majority was to increase unevenly. By 1753, slaves formed 75.27 per cent of the total population in Dominica. This dropped slightly, to 72.8 per cent in 1763, when the British annexed the island. This large proportion of slaves may be explained partly by the fact that many slaves were employed in a non-productive capacity, as domestics, coachmen, and the like. One must conclude that although, typically, the French settlers had small holdings, some large operations must have opened up shortly before annexation by the British. Coleridge (1826, 167), for instance, observed, "Some of the French Creoles in this colony are men of considerable wealth; they live retired on their estates, but are withal hospitable and fond of a good deal of feudal display." Nevertheless, most French whites and free people of colour were involved directly in small-scale agricultural ventures at this time, and the master-slave ratio in Dominica remained lower than that in most other Caribbean territories, despite its increase during the eighteenth century.

Williams's data on compensation claims made under the British Emancipation Act of 1833, eighty years later, support the contention that a lower master-slave ratio continued in Dominica (Williams 1970, 283). By converting his figures into percentages and comparing Grenada, Dominica, Monserrat, Nevis, St Kitts, St Vincent, and Tobago, we find that Dominica had a significantly lower percentage of landowners who possessed over a hundred slaves (4.0 per cent in comparison, for example to 13.4 per cent for Tobago and 9.9 per cent for Grenada and St Vincent) (see table 4). It was the only island that did not have a single individual who owned from three to five hundred slaves. But Dominica had a significantly greater percentage of owners with twenty-six to fifty slaves than did the other islands (6.3 per cent, in comparison with 2.0 per cent for Tobago and Grenada and 2.9 per cent for St Vincent). Thus, Dominica had significantly more small plantations, on which owners probably lived. The labour-intensive nature of the sugar plantation suggests that the concentration of slaves would have occurred on the larger plantations and that these would be British-owned. Within three years of British possession, slaves comprised over 80 per cent of the population (Myers 1976, 59).

This apparent concentration of slaves in British hands also meant a concentration of slaves in absentee hands; authority over them was mediated through attorneys and managers. As a Methodist missionary observes,

Now every non-resident proprietor of a plantation must, of course, commission some gentleman in the island to act as his attorney, to whom he

Table 4
Number of Slaves Owned, by Territory, in 1833

Territory	Number of Slaves											Total
	1	2	3–5	6–10	11–25	26–50	51–100	101–150	151–200	201–300	301–500	
Grenada	301	128	222	129	76	20	27	45	30	20	4	909
Dominica	233	124	169	120	87	55	49	23	7	5	0	823
Montserrat	53	31	33	35	33	7	14	10	7	6	1	232
Nevis	54	41	67	40	34	14	15	22	9	7	0	276
St Kitts	225	113	189	82	43	15	27	29	23	18	2	659
St Vincent	211	101	153	102	73	22	31	26	21	22	7	718
Tobago	105	44	62	27	25	7	25	22	10	12	2	306
Total	1,182	582	895	535	371	140	188	177	107	90	16	3,923
Percent Dominican slaves	19.71	21.31	18.88	22.43	23.45	39.29	26.06	13.00	6.54	5.56	0	20.98
Percent of Dominican slave owners	28.31	15.07	21.00	15.00	11.00	7.00	6.00	3.00	1.00	1.00	0.00	100.00

Source: Compiled from Williams 1970, 283.

MAP 5   Comparative Slave Concentrations in the Early Nineteenth Century

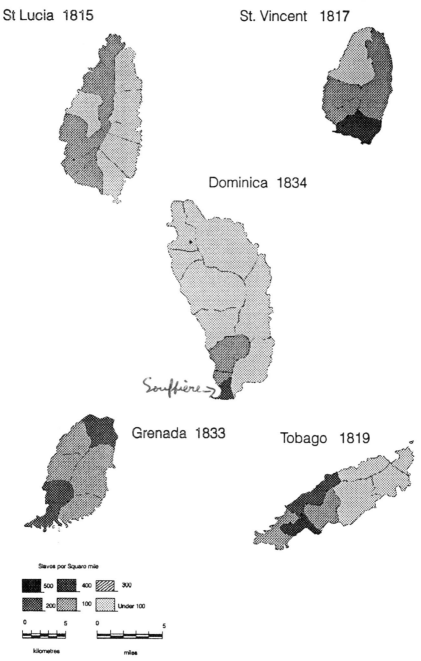

St Lucia 1815

St. Vincent   1817

Dominica 1834

Grenada 1833

Tobago 1819

Souffière →

Slaves per Square mile

500 400 300

200 100 Under 100

0   5   0   5

kilometres   miles

Source: Compiled from Higman 1984, 89.

delegates the power of superintending and controlling the whole economy of the estate. But the incomparably major part of attorneys are men of business; and it rarely happens that a person acting in that capacity has not the charge of more than one plantation; the necessary consequence of which is, these agents can obtain, in general, but very superficial information respecting the real feelings and ordinary treatment of the poor slaves; for they cannot often visit each estate, and seldom remain long on such as they occasionally visit. (Peters n.d., 59)

The day-to-day control of the slaves fell to managers, who, as noted, had a reputation for brutality. Speaking of Dominica again, the missionary comments, "There is, however, one powerful temptation to oppressive conduct peculiar to managers. It is undoubtedly the interest, and consequently the wish of every person acting in a subordinate capacity to ingratiate himself with his principal. Now, by no other means is a manager as likely to accomplish this object, as by increasing the annual revenue of the proprietor; but the produce of an estate, *caeteris paribus* must always be proportionate to the quantum of laborious exertion. The designed inference is obvious" (Peters n.d., 61). He then describes how, on the Picard estate in Dominica, which worked 160 slaves and was absentee owned, 90 slaves had died in the space of two years, a mortality rate of 281.25 per annum.

Within a few years of British annexation, a large proportion of the slave population of Dominica was clustered on a few British plantations, located in the larger river valleys. Here, they experienced not only the harsher treatment customary of the British, but the impersonal inhumanity of the plantation way of life. They tried, often successfully, to escape the system by taking to the bush. This brought them into closer contact with the French slaves, who were generally on smaller plantations, and who were more acclimatized to Dominica.

Although there were differences between the French and the British in the treatment of their slaves, many of the characteristics already described for the Caribbean at large were to be found in Dominica. Peters (n.d., 29), describing some of the cultural components of the system, speaks of "that contempt of the Negro race, which may with justice be considered as an inveterate disease, contaminating alike the moral and intellectual principles of our Colonists in (I believe) every part of the West Indies. Of the disease I could not but discover everywhere indubitable symptoms, soon after my arrival at Dominica." He suggests that these attitudes were to be found not only among whites, but also among free coloureds.

This is an important observation, for it argues that harshness toward slaves was by no means confined to situations of whites and absentee ownership. He recounts the trials of three coloured slave owners in some detail, adding, "He *does know* instances (instances too many and too well authenticated) of such inhuman acts, committed by white persons in the island of Dominica" (Peters n.d., 51).

The atrocities were not committed only by men, nor only on large-scale operations. Peters recounts "the Trial of Cordelia, A free Woman of Colour, for the Murder of her Female Slave." During the trial, Mr Brownsil, a printer in Roseau, testified that he had seen the deceased in her mistress's courtyard: "It was impossible for her not to strike him as being a most pitiable object; it being with difficulty, he observed, that could even walk across the court, and every part of her body which he saw exhibiting marks of outrage and disease ... He was daily in the habit of seeing her in nearly the same condition, for several preceding months" (Peters n.d., 39). One of the instruments that the mistress used on her slaves was "a large iron instrument, part of which she was accustomed to insert into the mouth of the deceased, and there to secure it by a lock ... The instrument, I should imagine, must weigh nearly two pounds, and it appeared to me impossible that it should be used without occasioning the most excruciating tortures" (Peters n.d., 40). A local physician, Dr Johnstone, confirmed this assertion, saying that he was present when the device was removed by order of the civil magistrate.

There was nothing idyllic about French slavery, but the small-scale nature of its operation in Dominica improved the institution and led to a certain stability of slave and ex-slave populations around the French settlements. This is not to say that master-slave relations were amicable – there were abuses of power, fear, and resentment – but more positive social relations were likely to be found in this dimension of the Dominican slave experience. This had important consequences for Dominica's subsequent identity and culture, which shows a significant French influence. Insofar as most of the French were resident, they provided an element of continuity on their plantations and farms. Their practice of *metayage*, or sharecropping, created a greater co-operative relationship between master and slave. The planter usually bequeathed his property to his coloured progeny. As a result, the Negro and coloured population increasingly adopted French cultural elements such as language, religion, names, and dance.

Thus, the attempts of the planters, then, to centre their world varied with the size of operation and the residence of the owner. The larger the plantation, the more the planter tried to organize his operation on impersonal, calculative, hierarchical, and exploitative lines. The structure of the plantation, with its division of labour and hierarchy of control, supported by overt racism, also distanced the most powerful from the most powerless. And, whenever possible, the owner created a physical distance from the situation by delegating responsibility for the actual operation of the system to others and removing himself as far as possible from the actual scene of labour – preferably back home to the metropole. In contrast, many of the French and all coloured estate owners had been born in the Caribbean and lived on their estates. They were therefore much more directly involved in the operation of the estate, and it followed that they were more concerned with the long-term outcomes of their slaves' well-being. There was less peripheralizing of the slave and greater mutual respect and co-operation between master and slave. There was also a greater investment in the land.

Just as the notion of centre logically requires that of periphery, so the concept of slave requires that of master, and vice versa. But beyond a logical requirement, slave and master were bound together in a particular type of experienced, living relationship. Each had expected behaviours that were defined in terms of the other, and the identity of each was formed as a reflection of the other, for both were, in Meadian terminology, "significant others" to one another (Mead 1962). Each was part of the environment of the other, and thus part of the resources available from which to order and centre their respective worlds. What skewed their interrelation was the access to power and the potential for self-determination of each. The master was completely free to decide the actions of the slave, while the slave was totally unfree in what he could expect of the master. What heightened and facilitated this power imbalance was that it was clearly visible from a distance, for it involved distinctions of colour – although we have to be careful with this notion, for there were poor whites and rich blacks, a class of middle-class *mulatres* and one of poor *mulatres*. In general, however, colour both expressed and grounded attitudes of racism and accounted for social status.

It is amazing how resourceful the slaves were in the face of such bleak resources. They created their own network of support relations, wealth of folk remedies, responses to disaster, and cultural world of belief, custom, art, dance, and rhetoric. In a world where uncertainty was compounded by the master/overseer's often arbitrary and vengeful demands, punishments, and decisions, the slaves, for their part, tried to centre their world as best they could given the situation in which they found themselves. Just as there were variations between white planters, attorneys, and overseers, so there were among slaves. Slaves' centring efforts ranged from a refusal to accept their role by revolting or running away, to psychologically distancing themselves from their masters, to working slowly, to sabotaging work, and for some even to identifying with the master.

In most British estates, slaves had at best an ambiguous attitude toward whites – a mixture of trust and mistrust, need and independence, love and hate. On the French estates, however, the slave was more likely to identify with the owner. Where there was sharecropping, estate productivity benefited the slave. Moreover, there was the possibility of inheriting land and property on the demise of the planter – an opportunity that did not exist on British estates. The language of the slaves became a patois developed by the French slaves, which was passed on to the British slaves, permitting them to communicate among themselves without being understood by their British rulers.

With a few exceptions, the British settlers on Dominica generated higher entropy than did the French. Besides the greater tendency for the British to demand more work of their slaves while providing them with fewer resources, much more energy was used to control, punish, organize, capture, transport, and replace slaves in their system than in the French one. The nature of the British plantation system, moreover, was fashioned along the lines of small-factory production, while the French and coloured planters created a plantation organization that was less impersonal, and more an adaptation of local experience with agriculture.

THE ABOLITION OF SLAVERY

While slavery was being practised in various forms in Dominica, the moral problems raised were being hotly debated back in the metropole, and its termination was in the wind. There are competing explanations for the abolition of slavery. Williams's two influential books on Caribbean history (1961, 1970) argue that the abolition of the slave trade and emancipation were direct results of an economic decline in the British Caribbean, competition from new tropical territories such as Mauritius, Cuba, Brazil, and the American South, and what Ragatz (1931, 12) calls "vicious fiscal legislation in the home country."[12] This thesis has been enormously popular: "What makes the case Williams presents appear compelling is not the evidence he cites, which singularly fails to support the large claims he makes, or the logic of his arguments, since these on closer examination turn out to be incompatible, but the power of the rhetoric with which it is presented" (Temperley 1987, 246).

Drescher argues, however, that "abolition came not on the heels of adverse economic trends, but in the face of propitious ones. British slavery patently declined after, not before, the abolition of its Atlantic slave trade" (Drescher 1977b, 134; see also Drescher 1977a). He states that the very year of the abolition of the slave trade "stands as a monument to mercantilism" (Drescher 1977b, 135).[13] Woolley (1938, 262) has shown that in the first reformed Parliament, when one would have expected the new merchant capitalists to show their strength, "the mercantile element was actually less." Anstey (1975, 1979) posits that it was the response of politicians to changing attitudes within the electorate that accounted for abolition. "It is beyond all reasonable doubt that without the 'popular feeling excited by religious principle' – George Stephen's explanation of Emancipation – the Government would have been borne down by the combination of West Indians and tory Ultras in the Lords, and would either have seriously qualified emancipation, or even have abandoned it altogether" (Anstey 1979, 108).[14]

Notwithstanding these criticisms, and the fact that Williams may have exaggerated the overall importance of the West Indies to the British economy, his approach focuses on a significant dimension of the historical play.[15] Economic factors may not have been sufficient in themselves to cause abolition, but they were certainly a necessary aspect. Williams's argument is important for another reason: it came from within the Caribbean and accorded with West Indians' long-term experience of exploitation, supporting a deeply ingrained suspicion of white people and the metropole. Slaves and ex-slaves had little experience of white humanitarianism; indeed, they had had a long exposure to vicious racism. It therefore seemed highly improbable to them that slavery was abolished for humanitarian reasons and much more plausible that it was abandoned because it had become economically burdensome. It may be because it struck a West Indian chord that Williams never responded to his critics or entertained revisions of his thesis set forth in *Capitalism and Slavery* (1961) in subsequent work to include new research findings that at least qualified his argument. To have done so would have been to assail what West Indians deeply felt to be true.

While pauperization of the West Indies may not have been the cause of emancipation, it was associated with – indeed, exacerbated by – it. Even during the quarter-century after the Peace of Aix-la-Chapelle, "the golden age of the planter" (Burns 1937, 22), planters, though wealthy, were seldom out of debt. As hurricanes decreased the supply of sugar on British markets, or the capture of a French colony increased it, prices rose and fell disconcertingly even in years of prosperity. Thus, "the industry was in no way prepared to withstand bad days," such as those in 1806, when sales plummeted (Burns 1937, 23).

Although abolition of the slave trade in 1807 had a negative impact on Dominica's economy – an effect worsened by the calamitous impact of hurricanes at regular intervals (for example, 23 July 1813, 3 August 1814, and 21 September 1816) – there are clear indications that planters were experiencing considerable hardship, even when production of sugar and rum was increasing, in the period before the abolition of slavery (see table 5). Many estates, despite trade with America and some good seasons, "were abandoned and the proprietors ruined; many hardly paid their contingent expenses, and the interest on their debts; and but a few compensated in any fair degree for the capital invested, the risks incurred and the labours endured" (Lovell 1818, 5).

Not only did serious hurricanes affect planters in terms of the estates' productivity, but the slaves lost their provision grounds as well; when this happened, it fell to the estate to feed them.[16] In the words of one such planter, "We are, at present, destitute of provision, our internal resources having failed; nor do the vegetables growing show their usual luxuriance, or promise the abundance they formerly gave. We shall therefore be under the necessity of assisting our Negroes for some months longer" (Lovell 1818, 15). His attorney writes, on 27 May 1817, "The provisions shipped ... are a most seasonable supply, for the Negroes are a good deal pinched for supplies and I should have been under necessity of purchasing them at four times the amount they are invoiced at" (Lovell 1818, 16). As if this were not bad enough, to recoup their own losses or to increase their profits, the Roseau merchants responded by increasing their prices for provisions exorbitantly.

In many instances, only the large estates had the resources to feed their slaves in the face of these natural disasters.[17] Where they did not do so, either because of a lack of financial resources or because of the disposition of the managers to ignore the slaves' sufferings a planter described the consequences: "the Negroes, ill-housed and ill-fed, have taken to the use of improper food and have fallen into desperate courses. Many have become weak and inefficient, many have contracted diseases, many have died, the great part have stolen at home if there was anything there to steal and abroad, if there was not. Punishments have followed and at length complete alienation from their masters and their homes and their total deprivation of character" (Lovell 1818, 23–4). This planter concluded that many of these ills were irremediable, and he saw no clear culprit.

Table 5
Dominica: Major Exports, 1826–30

Year	Sugar (h.hds)	Coffee (cwt)	Rum (pun)	Molasses (pun)
1826	3,178	13,350	326	740
1827	2,957	1,193,359	331	833
1828	3,888	2,546,635	548	1,136
1829	3,805	1,096,223	659	786
1830	4,071	1,311,473	873	254

Source: Martin 1844, vol. 2, 346

There was one other recourse for the starving slave: escape. Maroon activity, as mentioned in the last chapter, increased at this time, although the maroons remained dependent on the society from which they had escaped. Their own provision grounds were as susceptible to hurricane and wind damage as those of the slaves and planters. Much of their raiding activity was a collective solution to such shortages and, "violence between plantation slaves and marauding often hungry maroon bands ... was sometimes awesome" (Mullin 1977, 483). In Dominica, these needs were more pervasive than in other Caribbean territories, for the planters were sometimes as destitute as their slaves and the maroons.

APPRENTICESHIP

Abolition of slavery revolutionized the social order. Planters throughout the Caribbean and the local governments that protected them feared that abolition would bankrupt the Caribbean colonies through labour shortages and widespread violence by newly released slaves. Although abolition was seen as an acceptable goal, how it was to be achieved was debated extensively. In the British parliament, Taylor suggested that an interim period be set aside during which slaves would be free for certain days of the week. Howick proposed a period of semi-military slave control. But it was Edward Stanley's proposal for creation of a state of "apprenticeship" that was adopted.

Under apprenticeship, the ex-slave was to work for his or her former master, and in return would be paid for a quarter of the work. It supposedly offered important strategic advantages to the European establishment: it would allow additional time for missionaries to mould the beliefs of ex-slaves, for the preparation of a legal system to replace the slave codes, for the establishment of colonial institutions, and for planters to experiment with new techniques and methods of labour management. The advantage to the planters was that it involved the least structural change: the apprentice would continue to work on the same estate, thereby ensuring labour, while technically enjoying a new state of freedom, learning to manage cash, and the like. As well, the master would have a period to learn how to relate differently to his ex-slave.

In 1833, the British government passed the Act for the Abolition of Slavery throughout the British Colonies; for promoting the Industry of the Manumitted Slaves; and for compensating the persons hitherto entitled to the Services of such Slaves. A major problem with this hastily conceived plan emerged when it was put into practice: insufficient attention had been paid to the social and administrative context in which it would be carried out, and the Caribbean colonies lacked satisfactory judicial systems. "In many of the colonies, the commissioners reported, there was a total want of any fixed principles of jurisprudence, even of the knowledge of the extent to which English common and Statute law was in force. After that it was not surprising that the actual administration of Justice should exhibit the most glaring defects" (Burns 1937, 160). Thus, the apprenticeship system was developed by people in one social system to be transplanted and administered in another, foreign system.

The British government quickly realized this and sought a remedy. It planned to send out "stipendiaries" – officers receiving half-pay in the army or navy – who would be beyond the influence of local politics and free from local passions. The government seriously underestimated the number of officers needed to carry out the work. For Dominica it allotted three stipendiaries, of whom only one was in place by August 1834. There were other, more pervasive problems. Dominican apprentices spoke an unintelligible patois; this required hiring an interpreter, which undermined the desired "objectivity" of the magistrates. Furthermore, stipendiary magistrates tended to be integrated into white society.

In theory the S.M.s [stipendiary magistrates] were expected to walk along a knife-edge of polite aloofness in their attitude towards the planters, neither needlessly crossing them nor dependent upon them. In practice it was very hard to do so, for the pleasures which white society offered were all the more tempting to officials so ill-paid. Men would not be mortal who found no temptation to stop for a drink and a siesta in the afternoon or to prefer the offer of a dinner and bed to a weary ride through the evening damp ... The implications of the acceptance or refusal of hospitality was obvious. In all but a few cases the one meant that the S.M. was more or less a planters' magistrate, the other that he was not. (Burns 1937, 220)

This system, hastily put together, placed in the hands of largely untrained and inexperienced officers, and imposed on an already crumbling social structure, only created more injustices and the perpetuation of brutalities. Apprenticeship came to be linked, in the eyes of ex-slaves, with coercion, generating new frictions between manager and labourer. On the other hand, despite the appointment of stipendiary magistrates, whose job it was to see that ex-slaves were not exploited by their former masters, the apprenticeship system was abused by many farmers. Sturge and Harvey, on their visit to Dominica in 1836, found that the blacks gained nothing from apprenticeship: "The proprietors and attornies [sic] of the island compensate their apprentices for their own time, either by payments of fish, or by returning the time at their own convenience. They studiously avoid paying wages – a short-sighted policy, which originates in prejudice and interest" (Sturge and Harvey 1838, 93). Some planters did not have enough money to pay their ex-slaves. Many of the French planters, following the coffee blight, were almost destitute themselves and had not the wherewithal to hire labour and pay more wages, even if they wished to. In fact, their relative powerlessness led to insubordination by ex-slaves on many French estates and a complaint by the British that the French did not make much effort to keep their workers under restraint.[18]

Apprenticeship failed in Dominica, and it was ended early, on 29 June 1838. Although it was never a burning issue in Dominica, as it was elsewhere in the Caribbean, it was opposed by two important absentee proprietors and became mixed up with the political activities of a coloured stipendiary magistrate, Lynch, who gained a seat in the Assembly for a remote part of the island through the good graces of the local political manager (see Burns 1937, 357).

Once apprenticeship ended, it was very difficult to prevent ex-slaves from moving around and abandoning estates en masse, for, in this new situation, freedom and independence became dominant values in their centring strategies. Trouillot observes, "In their efforts to quantify the flight from the estates, scholars have generally relied on evidence going back only to the 1840s, but our data for 1838 document a very sharp decline in the labour force immediately after Emancipation," and the majority of these left at a time when they were still protected legally from eviction from the estate (Trouillot 1984c, 77–8). Some ex-slaves were enticed off the island by recruiting agents; others went into pre-existing settlements; still others went onto new lands, where they established villages. This was easy for them to do, for there was a substantial amount of uncultivated land in the interior and around the perimeter of the island. The British Commissioners, in their 1773 survey of the island, had designated that the Queen's Three Chains be left uninhabited and unused for defence purposes. Even though rigorous laws were introduced to this effect in the Dominica Legislative Assembly in August 1838, it was largely onto this peri-island land that most of the ex-slaves moved and squatted illegally. To circumvent the new laws, most squatters joined an unsuccessful petition to Queen Victoria requesting permission to remain on their land (CO 71/109, Cunningham to Gladstone, 7 April 1846).[19] They were joined by several thousand slaves who had fled from Martinique and, particularly, Guadeloupe, where slavery was not abolished until 1848 (Bogat 1969, 149).

Riviere (1972, 14) asserts that in Dominica "conciliatory management evidently achieved the adequacy of labour sought." In fact, within a year, the negative effects of emancipation on labour were being seriously felt, and some estates had been abandoned. The Dominican Assembly attempted, unsuccessfully, to recruit labour from Anguilla. It then suggested that planters adopt *metayage* as a temporary recourse. In this share-cropping system, the planter retained ownership of the land and paid his labourers wages in kind rather than in cash. The labourer was thus in "partnership" with the planter and could use his cart, horse, and machinery, in exchange for labour. The British planters in Dominica saw this as a last resort – and when they did resort to it, they made it clear that it was a temporary expedient. Their suspiciousness of the newly freed slaves prevented *metayage* from developing into a permanent type of land tenure, with the enduring feudal social relations of landlord and serf. It was adopted on smaller estates, where, to this day, the agricultural tenancy of small plots is paid in kind and *metayage* has endured as a popular form of land tenure.

Emancipation thus had a major impact on land tenure and occupancy patterns in Dominica, and these, in turn, had important implications for the economic and social development of the island. Estates began to dwindle in size and in cultivation. Some were sold off; some were parcelled off into lots; others were held in name but were little more than country residences; still others were abandoned. Ownership of many estates tended to pass out of the hands of whites and into the hands of coloured Dominicans. By 1854, all but two of the English proprietors were absentee and most of the resident French proprietors were "in straightened [sic] and reduced circumstances" (Davey 1854, 504).

A peasant-based agricultural economy emerged. "The exodus from the plantations was largely in the direction of subsistence

farming. Labourers acquired plots of land and used them in growing ground-provisions, vegetables, fruit and the occasional small
cash crop" (Riviere 1972, 15). Given the availability of land, a
majority of Dominican ex-slaves chose to fend for themselves rather
than to work for others. Yet the influence of a French co-operative
ethic was pervasive, so that, even today, there exists among banana
producers the custom of *coup de main*, in which labour is recipro-
cated between friends and neighbours. Although a recent map of
Dominica suggests a generous smattering of estate names over the
island, there are barely a handful of productive estates, and even
these are dwindling in number. The origins of today's agricultural
economy, a peasant-based banana industry with attempts to diversify into other peasant-based agricultural production, lie in this post-
emancipation period of the island's history.

Emancipation in Dominica generated a pattern of peripheral island settlement. Slaves settled on the coast, whence they went up-
and inland to work their gardens. This pattern of peri-island settlement created communities that were isolated from one another and
from Roseau, the capital.[20] Community members were largely self-
sufficient subsistence farmers who could pursue several crop-
production strategies: they could continue growing the subsistence
crops that they had grown on their provision grounds during slavery; they could adopt the plantation crops; or they could cultivate
new crops. Some peasants grew provision crops both for domestic
consumption and for sale, while others grew some of the production crops, sugar and cacao. Some worked part-time on estates or on
the roads, while managing their gardens on the side. Some were
sharecroppers. Others set themselves up as small shopkeepers,
seamstresses, and tradespeople. All of these activities required hard
work for relatively meagre rewards and very little cash.

The opportunity to work for oneself in the context of plentiful
land created a strong spirit of independence among Dominicans.
Strengthening this was the institution of family land and the security of subsistence gardening established by the freed slaves. Garden
land owned by an individual would be passed on to *all* his family
members, who were given equal access to it. Families tried to diversify their economic activities, with members doing a little of this and
a little of that. The strategy of diversification extended to subsistence
gardening itself, where a variety of plant species were intercropped.
Caililous, as it is called in patois, was an enduring component of the
Dominican economic structure, and it remained unmodified until
well into the twentieth century. It is interesting to note that while
access to land gave emancipated slaves a degree of independence

from estate owners, cereals had to be imported and bought with cash, and meat was beyond the reach of the majority. On the whole, however, they were successful. A medical doctor in Dominica in the nineteenth century, who was renowned for his work on yaws, observed, "The working population of this island are probably better fed than in most countries. Vegetable food of great variety is abundant, and fish almost everywhere can be easily and cheaply obtained; and those who are inclined to labour for wages can always find employment" (Imray 1873, quoted in Clyde 1980, 82).

While many ex-slaves in Dominica adapted well to the new situation, and a few even prospered, some clearly suffered, particularly those in Roseau. For those who migrated to or found themselves in the town, there was no obvious means to afford them subsistence apart from casual labour, where this was available. These persons were far less successful in their adaptive strategies. Poverty was not a new problem. In 1773, Governor Ainslie had referred to "the miserable objects daily seen in the streets of the town without support or resource," and in 1789 Governor Orde told the Assembly, "The number of sick and dying that are daily found lying about the streets ... leads me strongly to recommend to you to take some steps to remedy those mischiefs as soon as possible" (quoted in Clyde 1980, 56). After emancipation, the situation deteriorated further. Lieutenant-Governor McPhail complained that there were no provisions for the poor in Roseau. In the same year, the Act for the Relief of the Poor of the Island, and for Regulating the Distribution of Such Relief, 1840 was passed, and within five years 286 persons (1.3 per cent of the population) were receiving relief (see Clyde 1980, 59). A poor house was built on Morne Bruce, and a Poor Law Act was passed in the House of Assembly in 1858. These solutions only created further problems. As the local newspaper, *The Dominican*, observed on 14 August 1880, "Another nuisance is the paupers who are allowed to quit their resident on Morne Bruce, to prowl about the Town, in quest of 'little coppers'. These mendicants are daily seen (in Town), with large sore-legs (*gros malengres*) begging alms of those very persons who pay taxes for their maintenance" (quoted in Clyde 1980, 63).

Emancipation, at a stroke, undercut the foundation on which the plantocracy was based – the legitimated oppressive domination of slaves – and provided a new resource for ex-slaves to centre their world. Both sets of actors were too entrenched in their ways to enable apprenticeship to work. The planters wanted control, and the ex-slaves wanted freedom. Neither trusted the other sufficiently to make a co-operative transition work. Planters were left bereft of labour and of a creative ordering response, and they suffered considerably. In contrast, the oppressed slaves developed a new order out of the periphery that was relatively independent of the metropole.

SLAVERY WAS THE cornerstone of the profit-driven metropolitan centring strategy in the West Indies. Considerable energy was used by the system to funnel profits from sugar and trade into European industrial, urban centres. The effects of such energy transformation were entropic – the uprooting of people, in both Africa and the Caribbean, and the creation of brutalizing relationships, in which there was a high degree of unpredictability (chaos) – all in order to obtain resources from the periphery. Despite its disordering impact, profits grew from enslaving people. Slavers made lucrative deals in both acquiring and disposing of their merchandise. Once purchased, the slave was viewed as a source of virtually "free" labour in that maintenance costs could legally be minimized and the most work extracted for the least cost.

If slavery was a centring strategy designed to extract maximum labour from a role, the plantation was a centring strategy designed to extract maximum produce from an organization. The plantation mirrored the profit-structured factory organization of production developing in the metropole. The toil of the periphery channeled goods and wealth to the centre, and the entire system was geared to maximizing returns on the metropolitan market. Thus plantations tended to grow, and as they did so their entropic costs became enormous. There was the waste of African lives occasioned by the wars and the kidnapping raids in which the slaves were obtained, the losses of life on the Atlantic crossing, and the early deaths on the Caribbean plantations themselves (see Hart 1980, 70).

From the viewpoint of those in Dominica itself, this peripheral territory of a metropolitan centre was their world. Whether one was a slave, an owner, a manager, a merchant, or a judge, this was the "world" to be centred. The slaves had limited resources with which to do this. They could identify with and support, sabotage, rebel against, or escape from their masters. They centred their worlds most fully when they ran away and formed maroon communities. Plantation owners and managers were the instruments of metropolitan centring and attempted to order their world by participating in the metropolitan mercantile market economy. Their prime interest was in producing sugar and produce for the market and, thus, in making a profit for themselves or their clients. They refused to reinvest in the well-being of their labourers and in developing new techniques to improve productivity.

Such a social, economic system is clearly far-from-equilibrium. Held together by force, using more and more energy, and highly entropic, it has a particularly high potential to dissipate completely. The entropy created by the plantation system created chronic disorder – labour shortages, slave revolts, harassment, murders of planters and managers. Finally, it fed back into the metropolitan system and resulted in abolition and emancipation.

Abolition and emancipation were decisions made at the centre and exported to the colony. The slaves, whose experience of the plantation had been so brutal, saw emancipation as an opportunity to distance themselves from whites and more freely create their own way of life. This accounts for their widespread abandonment of the plantation upon emancipation, and for their setting up of dwellings and gardens in non-plantation localities. In contrast, the local planters considered it a threat to their own ability to centre their world and tried to maintain the old order. Thus the fragile system created by the metropole to extract profits collapsed, and the freed slaves followed the maroons and Amerindians in trying to remove themselves as much as possible from the orbit of metropolitan centring by establishing subsistence-gardening communities. The characteristics of these communities and the way of life the ex-slaves created is the topic of the next chapter.

6 A Dominican Peasantry

By and large, Caribbean peasantries have been "interstitial" groupings, living on the margins of Western enterprise. But reflection on these "interstices" tells us something about the direction and intent of imperial strategy in the islands, and allows us to discern more clearly how the peasantries responded to such strategy. If the emphasis seems to rest unduly on conflict, on resistance, this is because only rarely and briefly have European powers or even local governments viewed the peasantry as more than an "obstacle" to development; and the reason for this negativism, as well as the negativism itself, still persists.

Mintz 1974a, 146–7

The effect of the metropolitan centring strategy on plantation-slave sugar production was to create a social world of managers and slaves that was largely based on force and fear. These two elements created a slave experience of the world that accentuated the roles of arbitrary violence associated with racial stereotyping. Thus, an important element in the centring strategy of slaves and ex-slaves was a healthy suspicion and distrust of white people and of those members of the coloured élite who espoused white values, attitudes that continue to run in Caribbean culture. They have given rise to a counter-movement in which Caribbeans attempt to wrest back the world and distance themselves from the white dominating metropole. In the idiom of the present work, Dominicans have tried to centre the periphery. We shall see how this worked itself out in the post-emancipation period.

The new, post-emancipation order of largely squatter settlements consisted of villages that were, to varying degrees, independent of outsiders for supplying subsistence resources. The villages developed a fluid structure that allowed families and villages to move back and forth from degrees of independence to degrees of dependence on the cash-based economic system of their former masters. The important feature of the new emerging peasant order was that it had removed itself to a large extent from the peripheralization of the metropole and its entropic centring effects. Thus, peasants increased their ability to be self-determining. Their order was less energy-hungry and, therefore, less entropic.

Several factors led ex-slaves to leave the plantations on which they had worked and to establish themselves as independent cultivators of their own gardens. Some wanted personal freedom and a chance to own their own land, others wished to escape the oppressive regimen of the plantation itself, still others were not secure in their estate arrangements and found rents too high. As well, the great majority of ex-slaves had a knowledge and experience of agriculture, and of where land was available. The peasantry grew as plantations were abandoned, but not uniformly or equally. The mode of peasant land acquisition was affected by the restraints placed upon it by existing land ownership and the legal codes passed by local legislatures, many of which were aimed at preventing ex-slaves from obtaining land.[1] Some peasants acquired land by purchase, others through lease-hold agreement, and others simply by squatting on Crown lands. The land varied in quality, but it was mostly marginal, with poor access to the market, often unsurveyed and uncleared (see Dookhan 1975, 12).

The exodus of ex-slaves created the considerable labour problems that planters and managers had envisaged. To minimize this, the colonial plantocracy tried to inhibit it through government regulations. It introduced new, burdensome ordinances concerning the acquisition of Crown lands, levied heavy taxes on small-holdings, tried to restrict the physical movement of ex-slaves, and introduced apprenticeship as an intermediary step to complete freedom.

The ex-slaves, with their warranted strong mistrust of planters, saw through these strategies and simply ignored them. They sought independence from their former masters and chose to create a separate and marginal identity for themselves. Land had a different value for them than it had for their former masters: they thought of it as an expression of freedom and identity rather than as an economic resource to exploit to exhaustion. Besson (1987, 14–15) captures this perspective when she observes, "Firstly, the short-term economic aspects of such land are subordinated to its long-term symbolic role. For the land serves primarily as a symbol of personhood, security, and freedom for descendants of former slaves in the face of plantation-engendered land scarcity." They also regarded money and goods differently from their masters. They viewed them much more particularistically – to be used for this or that specific purpose. Work was seen in the same way: one worked to attain this or that goal. They therefore found it easy to resist any long-term commitment to operators of the market system and frustrated efforts to embroil them in dependent relationship. As a result, local administrators and planters often considered them lazy and unproductive.

Peasants varied in the extent to which they produced for the market, but over time the trend was for market production to increase. The market was considered to be a resource that could be accessed in an *ad hoc* manner, something one could move into and out of as circumstances dictated, and not as something wholly requisite for any economic activity. The more the peasants involved themselves in market activity over time, however, the more dependent they became on it, and the more they came under metropolitan influence again, the more they experienced its entropic effects – monocrop agriculture, with the dangers inherent in such a narrowly based economic resource.

Peasants used mutual self-help, *coup de main* strategies within communities and tended to minimize co-operation and support between communities. This led to the emergence of isolated and inward-looking villages, and, over time, generated stereotypes associated with each community. As peasants gradually returned to the metropolitan-dominated market system, the emergence of a strong collective class-identity within the peasantry was inhibited, although there was a deep shared tradition of opposition to and suspicion of whites in particular and of *gwans gens* (important people) in general.

As I have suggested, the peasant way of life created by many of the ex-slaves significantly shaped Dominica's evolving cultural identity. Prior to emancipation, slaves had engaged in what Mintz describes as "proto-peasantry." They provided for themselves through their gardens and the markets they ran themselves, but they controlled neither the land nor their time and labour (Mintz 1974a, 151). This slave experience of garden work was often curtailed and truncated by outside forces, including owner decisions to resell and deport slaves (see Silverman 1979). Runaway maroons had established something of a peasantry, but their guerrilla warfare and their way of life were illegal, and there was often concerted military activity to eradicate them.[2] Their efforts were often interrupted and cut short. Therefore, the " 'peasant way of life' fully blossomed only upon the ruins of the plantations, amid the remains of the developed technology and the highly stratified social structure that King Sugar had fostered" (Trouillot 1984a, 38). Within this system, the type of land tenure that emerged was "a reflection in some measure of the relative importance of the two antecedents of the peasant farmer: the slave with the provision ground on the plantation; and the runaway or manumitted slave living outside the plantation economy" (Momsen 1987, 48). What were the characteristics of this peasant phenomenon in Dominica?

DOMINICAN PEASANT COMMUNITY FORMATION

Dominican peasant formation followed the classic pattern observed by Marshall (1972, 31): "The West Indian peasantry started its existence after the complete emancipation of the slaves in 1838. It was composed of those slaves who started small farms on the periphery of plantation areas, wherever they could find land, on abandoned estates, on Crown land and in the mountainous interior." This process occurred within a mountainous terrain with considerable amounts of available Crown land both in the interior and around the periphery of the island, on the Queen's Three Chains. The latter were used by the ex-slaves for settlements, while the former were used for cultivation. There emerged relatively isolated village communities dotted around the periphery of the island. Because the road network was so poor, most peasant communities were forced to become self-reliant to an important degree, although they occasionally worked for cash on neighbouring estates. Villages varied in the extent of their isolation. On the east coast, for instance, communities were very much on their own, whereas villages in the south were linked by regular contact with Roseau and with communities across the channel in Martinique, and in the north with Quadeloupe and Marie Galante (see Myers 1976). The nature of the intervening terrain, rather than distance, was the important variable in accounting for the degrees of isolation. There was some contact between each community and Roseau by road, trail, or boat.

There was sufficient separation between communities throughout the island that specific stereotypes developed for people in the different "regions" of Dominica and for certain family names to become associated with certain communities. Names such as Scotland, Stephenson, and Bannis, for instance, are associated with Castle Bruce, on the windward side of the island; Leblanc, Royer, and Seaman with Vieille Case, in the north; Henderson and St Luce with Grand Bay, in the south; and so on (see Honychurch 1982, 8). Genealogical differences between villages became associated with the socially significant category of colour. For instance, Delice, La Plaine, Bagatelle, and Vieille Case are associated with lighter-skinned people. Common names for certain things, such as plants, also varied from place to place: "*Bonavis* in Giraudel would be *Boucousou* in Pennville, *Ma Visou* in Citroniere would be *Mai Visou* in Sylvania" (Honychurch 1982, 15).

The village communities became the foundation of Dominican society and developed characteristic patterns of land occupancy, subsistence farming, family structure, religious practice, and the like.

Many communities appear to have changed little until after the Second World War, and even today they show cultural practices that have a long history. A description of the characteristics of these communities follows.[3]

A methodological observation must be made at this point. The peasant villages were not the object of metropolitan or élite "study" or documentation. Thus the following observations are based on more recent anthropological studies that used participant observation and fieldwork. The findings of these studies are presumed to correspond to the period under discussion. Although the data for the following description were obtained at a later period, I would argue that the principles of organization that they illustrate emerged at emancipation and provide a fair picture of the new peasant way of life at that time.

LAND-USE PATTERNS

The peasants' centring strategy was clearly affected by the availability of land, which affected their ability to produce. Access to land could be obtained through individual or collective ownership, or through some share-cropping agreement. A pervasive feature of Dominican landholding was "family land." While this was developed as a strategy that protected family members against alienation from access to land, it affected productivity negatively, for all family members had rights to usufruct, and this discouraged individual agricultural effort.[4] Individuals and nuclear families were loath to toil in their gardens only to have the harvest taken by some other members of the extended family. While individual ownership might have appeared therefore to be the most "rewarding" strategy, the practice of working land collectively tended to qualify individual "success," for each individual would be expected to work on someone else's plot.

The nature of land in different areas of Dominica encouraged different settlement patterns. It also influenced the extent to which the peasant was involved in estate labour. The eastern, windward coast is the most rugged and so accommodated fewer estates and led to a more scattered, *strassendorf* form of village community. This coast, which Columbus had first encountered, was where the Carib finally retreated. The western, leeward coast, in contrast, had land that was suitable for estate agriculture, particularly up the river valleys. This coast had been occupied by French settlers, who had deforested the slopes, grown coffee and cacao, and overused the land. Nevertheless, this side of the island was more fully settled and led to the formation of more nucleated, tightly packed villages.

Various methods of acquiring access to agricultural land emerged, and these varied from community to community. Some peasants squatted on Crown land, some purchased land from plantations or from the Crown, some rented land from plantation owners or from other individuals. In each case, the plots tended to be scattered and at some distance from the peasant's place of residence, often "up in the heights." Together with "family land," this accounts for a saying in Dominica today that "everyone have land." There is the feeling that land is not a finite phenomenon; there is always more that one can use.

The best and most accessible land was in the river valleys, and this had been claimed by the estate owners. The contiguous ridges and the "heights" were left for peasant cultivation. The difficulty of accessing and working this land prevented the peasants from producing cash crops to any significant degree. An important characteristic of Dominica, in comparison with other Caribbean territories, was therefore, on the one hand, a much greater accessibility to land, and on the other, less reliance on markets.

The peasants' use of land was influenced by Carib and Arawak horticultural strategies learned by maroons prior to emancipation. The Arawak form of swidden horticulture entailing frequent relocation, similar to such practices in Africa and thus also imported to the Caribbean with slavery, was initially adopted, although this gave way to more permanent sites for *jardins nou* (gardens). Clearing land was valuable in itself, for the cutting down and burning of trees yielded the fuel *chebon* (charcoal) as a by-product of clearing. This is still widely practised. What was grown in the gardens was also both learned from the Indians and brought from Africa. Typical of what was produced in *jardins nou* were various types of manioc (*blue, beurre, blanc, violet, noir, cent liv, doux, camanioc*), tanya (*chou*), varieties of yams (*blanc, de l'eau, batard, marron, a piquants noir, couche-couche, jaune, yam bonda, ba-ba-oulay*), dasheen, sweet potatoes (*rouge, jaune, blanc*), plantain, bananas, cacao, arrowroot (*toloman*), papaya, *pomme canelle*, pineapples (*zazana*), *corosol, cachiman, roucou*, calabash (for water collection and consumption), sugar cane, ginger, peppers (*bonda ma Jacques, piment cafe, piment taytay, negwess, piment lai, piment zwozio*), white and black cotton, and a variety of tree fruits including citrus, coffee, guava, sappodilla, and mango (see Honychurch 1982, 13–14). The staples were plantain and cassava, processed into farine from manioc according to methods reminiscent of the Arawak, and made into bread, pancakes, and sweet dump-lings called *canqui*. Oils were obtained from various sources: "shark," snake, turtle, certain fish, coconut, and bay leaves. Variety in the diet was obtained with spices, the production of cane syrup (*siwo*), the distillation of illicit rum, called "mountain dew" (*wabio* or *zayida*), and the use of herbs. The major sources of protein were wild pigs, "mountain chicken" (*crapaud*), a local variety of large frog, occasionally an agouti or a pig, and fish. There were both river fish – mullet, pike, eels, suck-fish, and crayfish – and sea fish – grouper, cavallies, snappers, kingfish, Spanish mackerel, jacks and sprats, "shark," and lobsters. There were also both sea and land crabs and, occasionally, turtles (see Atwood 1791, 36, 41, 49).

Peasants working land on steep slopes discovered ways to im-prove the yield of their land. They noted that the leaves from trees provided natural fertilization, and so large trees on one's land were considered an asset. They also tried to nourish the soil by practising *U ba te ya di fe* or "firing the ground," whereby they set fire to a plot of land, or *bukan*, in which shrubs and weeds were cleared, piled, and burned two to three weeks later. The nature of this activity tended to restrict it to the dry season. They would also dig pits on the slopes, bury weeds, garbage, or animal dung, and cover it with soil for a period, although this yielded only patches of fertilized land.

PEASANT VILLAGE SOCIAL STRUCTURE

As villages developed, access to land holdings and the nature of the land became important in the intra- and inter-organization of communities. Heredity became important in this respect, and both matrilateral and patrilateral inheritance patterns were recognized, except in cases where parents had only a daughter or were not prosperous enough to give land to their children. In such cases, a woman might have access to land through a fictive kinship relation (see Eguchi 1984, 109). One of the results of inheritance practices was the creation, as already noted, of considerable quantities of "family land" – ancestral land that remains, to this day, undivided – held jointly by an individual's descendants. In principle, any descendant may use it, especially for housing purposes. All descen-dants must agree before the land may be partitioned and sold. While it provides a resource in time of need for family members, family land is often not used to the fullest. Either all family mem-bers consent to division of the land, in which case any one indi-vidual is likely to obtain only a small piece, thus limiting the land's production potential, or, as already noted, if a individual decides to plant on family land, all family members have an equal right to harvest what has been planted.

The ideal production unit in the village was the household made up of an adult of each sex and their children, who often "jobbed" for the unit – that is, they performed a task for a specific, short-term goal. The division of labour between "husband" and "wife" depended on the age of children. Friends, kin, and neighbours helped in co-operative groups.[5] The ideal domestic strategy was democratic agreement between husband and wife, but this was determined and modified by factors associated with the developmental cycle. A man advanced to social maturity by demonstrating both sexual and social competence. The former was measured by his ability to sire children, the latter by his ability to assume responsibility for them. He thus moved from being a boy (*ti garso*) to a man (*nom*) to a "big man" (*gwoh nom*), and in the process from being responsible to himself (*weskonsab ko-y*) to being responsible for a house (*weskonsab kay-li*) to being responsible for a family (*weskonsab famli-li*). Proven virility was thus the requisite for manhood, but responsible paternity was required for the acquisition of the ideal adult male role, at which stage he would be accorded the title of *musje*. Because the *gwoh nom* role hinges on regular, adequate economic support for a man's family, "marriage was the precondition rather than the validation of a mature adult status" (Spens 1969, 133). A father who failed in this responsibility was called an old vagabond (*vye vagabon*).

There were similar criteria for development of the female role. Giving birth transformed a girl (*ti fi*) into a woman (*yo fem*), and this transition occurred for the majority of girls before they became wives. Unlike men, women obtained mature status through motherhood; indeed, the term "wife" might be used for someone who was, in fact, not married but cohabiting. Nevertheless, marriage provided an added status, particularly if it was the state in which the first pregnancy occurred. It transformed a woman into a *gwah fem*, or "big woman." However, a woman was expected to demonstrate independence and an ability in business affairs (*wekonsab zafa-yo*). Thus marriage was not absolutely necessary for full female status; in fact, a single woman could lower her status by marrying below herself. A consequence of this set of values was a tendency to find respected spinsters in a community.

The three types of sexual association typical in the Caribbean – marriage, consensual union, and extra-residential visiting unions – were also found in Dominica. The statistical prevalence of one over the other, however, varied from community to community and over time.[6] Extra-residential visiting unions are the hardest to define in terms of reciprocal rights, for they can vary greatly and be difficult to designate as casual as opposed to a more permanent relationship. Recognition of paternity in this relationship tended to determine whether the man would be allowed further access to the woman, or whether the relationship would be terminated. Recognition of paternity also tended to transform a visiting relationship into a consensual union. This recognition by the father had important ramifications for the child, giving it a superior social status that benefited it for life. Spens (1969, 60–8) suggests that in the communities where marriage was more common than consensual unions, the institution had existed in the area before emancipation.

Locally, families were defined in terms of a mother and her children and her daughters' children. Households changed their pattern of membership over time according to the membership of former relatives present. A woman might have her first children as a member of her mother's household. If her mother died or she moved out, her household would then consist of her own children. Later her daughter might give birth to a child but remain part of the household. Subjectively, a girl tended to see future relationships in terms of herself and her children, with the husband–father relation being apart. Headship of the household was determined by who owned the house; although a man was expected to own a house before he married, Spens (1969) indicates that in the village she studied over half the household heads were female.[7] This had important implications for the children. Illegitimate children could legally inherit from their mother but not from their father, even if he "recognized" them. On the other hand, the father could grant illegitimate children land as a favour. A woman could assume independent headship and expand her household by extra-residential mating, absorbing collateral kin and unrelated persons, and so on. Finally, although a woman lost status if her daughter bore an illegitimate child, if the father of the child recognized and supported it, his economic contribution could be used to defray costs within the domestic unit – a practice that was common but that frequently led to conflict between cohabitants in consensual unions.

Ranking within peasant communities was primarily according to how individuals fulfilled roles associated with being an adult member of a family. There was probably, however, some economic ranking based on the nature of families' landholding, their horticultural practices, their possession or part possession of cattle, goats, or sheep, their access to wage labour, and the size of the household labour unit. Eguchi (1984, 168ff) identified three ranks in a recent study of a Dominican community, and argued that land was the most important variable in accounting for middle over lower rank in the village, while income was the most important variable in accounting for upper rank in the village. Income was a product of whether individuals in households had permanent salaried positions or relied on jobbing for income. Cattle were more prevalent among higher-ranked villagers because they require flat pastures for grazing. Lower-ranked people owned fowl, which require no special land set aside for them. A larger proportion of middle-rank people owned pigs and goats, which require some, but not necessarily flat, land. It is likely that a limited type of economic differentiation of this nature has existed in the peasant villages since their inception, although it probably increased as peasants increased their participation in a cash economy.[8]

Rankings reflected not only differences in role performances and economic management within the village, but also another set of criteria – education. The French-speaking Catholic priest, who either resided in or regularly visited the community, was traditionally the pinnacle of social status. The village teacher was also highly respected. More recently, the policeman was added to this list. None of these personages necessarily owned land in the community. They derived their prestige, instead, from the knowledge that they possessed and the financial security this established.

The peasant culture that emerged allowed for a variety of responses to environmental conditions, be they natural or cultural. Even in the sphere of religion, peasants held an array of beliefs, borrowed from Christian, African, and probably autochthonous sources, which could be used to explain and control any eventuality. Along with the belief in God, the Virgin Mary, and the efficacy of the sacraments were beliefs in *obeah* and *loups garroux* and *jumbi* and *cockmar*, and forms of contagious and sympathetic magic such as love potions, "make-sick" potions, and the like. These provided peasants with an arsenal of remedies that could be used singly or in combination in response to "environmental" pressures and the need for explanations.

The centring that promoted the peasants' world order was created through a series of small-scale and eclectic strategies. The approach, on the whole, was energy-efficient. Nature, in the form of disease, hurricanes, or rain storms, could "waste" the peasants' efforts by ruining their crops, but otherwise the effort they put into production they later reaped. Similarly, the custom of jobbing was a response that minimized wastage. It used energy to meet a specific, limited need, and thus inhibited the creation of new needs which are often the by-product of excess cash; it also inhibited exploitation by employers.

PEASANT VILLAGES AND
THE DOMINANT SOCIETY

As we have seen, peasants used two conflicting methods of managing their lives and their environments. On the one hand, they created order for themselves by removing themselves from the peripheralizing effects of the metropole and reverting to an essentially subsistence horticulture – a strategy associated with their maroon antecedents, who, in turn, had learned how to survive in the interior from the Amerindians.[9] On the other hand, they grew crops for the market. In both cases, the centring strategy involved important symbolic elements, not the least of which were colour-class distinctions and the existence of a wider society. Special significance was attached to the white man's world, which for a majority of peasants presented a paradox: it contained desired resources, but at the same time it was a constant threat to their self-determination. At times, peasants availed themselves of opportunities in and profited from contact with the metropolitan-dominated market system, while at other times they consciously rejected and opposed that system.

These strategies were exercised within the context of an exploitative, dominating society. Patterns of village structure emerged in an environment in which domination or fear of domination by the white and coloured élite remained a key component. The existence of white or coloured estate owners and merchants was always on the horizon of the ex-slaves' environment. For some peasants, the local estate continued to be an occasional economic resource when they needed access to cash – in fact, it was their major source of cash. Others had as little as possible to do with the local estates. Some used this cash source to purchase land that the estate was willing to sell. Many peasants, however, were reluctant to work for estates, and some categorically refused to work for them, a reaction that Marshall (1968, 252) characterizes as "a negative reflex to enslavement, mass production, monocrop dependence and metropolitan control."

"What the whiteman doin" became an important element of information and a major source of rumour, gossip, and innuendo. In the days following emancipation, the ex-slaves saw the British government financially compensating planters for the abolition of slavery, but providing them, the ex-slaves, with no materials, resources, or monetary recompense to make a successful transition to a new way of life. Nor can it have been missed that the estate owners in general were unhappy with the new turn of events. The result was a continuation of the attitudes of suspicion and mistrust generated under slavery. These were sometimes expressed overtly in peasant behaviour and gave rise to public events that became part of Dominican history.

In 1844, the government's centring concerns led it to carry out a census of the island, so it dispatched enumerators into the country areas to identify the population. The peasants thought that the enumeration was part of a white plot to re-enslave them; in several regions, villagers abandoned their houses when they saw enumerators approaching. Occasionally, they armed themselves, congregated in the streets, and threatened enumerators with physical harm. In some of these instances, the enumerators managed to flee, but at Canefield, Colihaut, Point Michel, and around Roseau itself, enumerators were attacked and beaten and a white magistrate just managed to escape with his life (see Minutes of the House of Assembly, 29 July 1844, Minutes of the Privy Council, 4 June 1844 *Official Gazette, 1844*). The villagers' resistance spread rapidly, becoming more generalized, and was directed in some cases at local planters.[10] The events have been variously referred to as *la guerre nègre* (Honychurch 1984, 105) or "The Black Rebellion in 1844" (Grell 1976, 143).

The Dominican villagers' reaction thwarted the administration's centring strategy. The government became alarmed and responded by declaring martial law. It dispatched soldiers and police to the troubled areas, and it issued a proclamation on 4 June 1844, stating that the census was designed purely to provide the administration with necessary accurate statistical data and was in no way related to any plan to re-enslave the population. It urged Dominicans to end their protest and assured them that they would never be enslaved again. A week later, Sir Charles Fitzroy, the governor-in-chief of the Leeward Islands, arrived in Dominica and issued another proclamation, offering a pardon to all involved in the incidents, except the leaders, if they would surrender. A detachment of troops of the Royal Regiment arrived from Barbados to join the local militia, and this show of force quashed the uprising. Hundreds of rebellious villagers were captured, and several of their leaders were hanged. At Grand Bay, a villager captured by the militia was beheaded and his head was impaled on a pole. The pro-planter *Colonist* reported, "The Aweful beacon now exhibited on the high road to Grandbay will, we trust, act as a solemn, docile monitor of these misguided people that the laws of the land are not to be set at defiance nor her Majesty's peaceful and loyal subjects threatened with death and destruction of property. The head of the rebel now blanches upon a pole erected at the junction of three roads" (*Dominica Colonist* 8 June 1844, quoted in Grell 1976, 145). By 13 June 1844, President Stewart Laidlaw could report that the rebellion had been suppressed, and the state of martial law was terminated.

Ten years later, peasants were again worried about what the dominant society might be doing. This time, it concerned land ownership. As mentioned earlier, in the original allocation of island land in 1763, Britain had reserved three chains of land around the island as Crown land for "defence purposes." The military judged that it had sufficient defences at Roseau, Scotts Head, and Fort Shirley and did not use these lands to increase its fortifications. Estate owners were reluctant to risk developing areas that might be commandeered for military purposes. However, as we have seen, ex-slaves did not hesitate to settle on these lands. Some estate owners suddenly saw that fertile land in the mouth of the valleys, often the flattest and broadest part, was being squatted on by ex-slaves and yet was formally beyond estate possession. They sought a redefinition of Crown lands from the metropolitan government, and "were eventually allowed to make 'legal' claim to the crown lands inhabited by black Dominicans" (Grell 1976, 148–9).

One group of planters who were given legal title were the owners of the Batalie estate, in 1853.[11] Ex-slaves were squatting on the Crown lands to which Batalie now had title, and had brought them under garden cultivation. When the Batalie estate owners sought to evict the peasants, the latter saw this as another attempt to curtail their freedom and economic development. They remembered how planters and administrators had tried to tie them to estate labour, and they now thought that they were trying to force them off the land. They refused to budge. A magistrate was appointed to settle the dispute, and the peasant-squatters were given the choice of land leases, for which they would have to pay a small rent, or else of quitting the land. They rejected the offer. The Crown surveyor and three policemen arrived to eject them, but the peasants forced them to beat a hasty retreat. The following day, Lieutenant Governor Blackhall made a show of force, making a personal appearance with eight policemen and four sailors "who had been sworn in an special constables" (Honychurch 1984, 107). After making a speech on the shore, Blackhall sent the policemen to work, but the villagers met them with strong physical resistance. Blackhall and his men were forced to return to Roseau defeated.[12]

Blackhall interpreted the situation as a crisis confronting estates, and he sought troops from Governor-in-Chief McIntosh in Antigua. Detachments of the 2nd West India and 67th regiments were immediately dispatched to Dominica, where they arrived on 5 February 1854. In the interim, Blackhall tried another tack: he ordered the arrest of the alleged black leaders, hoping thereby to cave in the resistance. But support for the peasants' cause had spread, and boatmen in Roseau refused to sail the marshal and his crew to Batalie; he was forced to use a European ship that happened to be in harbour. This delay enabled the squatters to prepare their defence, with the result that the authorities were able to arrest only three women.[13]

This defeat prompted the administration to use military force. Blackhall sailed to Batalie with the magistrate, the inspector of police, twenty-four soldiers, ten officers, and eight constables. At the sight of such a force, the peasants' ringleaders took refuge in the hills and the remainder were forced to come to terms with the legal situation, either agreeing to pay rent on their property or removing themselves.[14] By 14 March 1854, things had quieted down enough for the military support to return to Antigua.

These incidents indicate that while, on the one hand, ex-slaves had distanced themselves from metropolitan control, they still lived within a broader societal context that was threatening to them. Their attitudes toward the wider society were suspicious, defensive, and at times aggressive.[15] One last incident of peasant reaction to the dominant society illustrates both their attitudes toward it and how they attempted to distance themselves from it.

The taxation of peasants was a particularly inflammatory issue. In 1886, Governor Gormanston, responding to clear inequities in the existing taxation system, sought to extend taxation throughout the society.[16] Land tax was set at one-half per cent, and a general income tax was imposed on those earning over £50 a year.[17] In at least one case, these measures led to a confrontation with the authorities which one author has dubbed the Revolt at La Plaine (Grell 1976, 152). It concerned Pierre Collard, who, in 1893, found that he was unable to pay the tax on his house lot in La Plaine, a village situated in the poorest region of Dominica, where sugar cultivation had dwindled to nothing and the only products, arrowroot and farine, had to be carried overland to Roseau, eight hours away, where they were bought by merchants at pitifully low prices (Hamilton 1894, 98–9). Collard's house lot was ordered sold, but when the bailiff, "an active and rampant smuggler in the region" (Haynes-Smith to Ripon, 17 April 1893, C.O. 152/186), and the police inspector arrived to take possession, an angry mob gathered and the two men had to flee, first to the police station and then across the river.

Governor Haynes-Smith arrived aboard the *Mohawk*, with at least twenty-five armed soldiers and additional police. Accompanied by Commander Bayley, he proceeded to the presbytery, where he heard the people's complaints and interviewed Collard privately. When Collard still refused to vacate his property, Haynes-Smith ordered him ejected. On their way to Collard's house to carry out the eviction, the police and soldiers were stoned by the villagers. They opened fire, disbanding the mob, but left four men dead and two women wounded (Honychurch 1984, 110).[18]

Thus, while the peasants were ready to centre their world with minimal reference to the authorities, the authorities were not prepared to leave the peasants alone, for they still viewed them and their lands as an exploitable resource. They frequently complained that they could not get them to work; they sought to reclaim some of the lands taken by the peasants; and they imposed taxes which forced peasants to seek some sort of cash-recompensed labour.

THE EX-SLAVES' response to the chaos generated by the metropole's decision to emancipate slaves in the wake of the high entropy produced by plantation sugar production was to create peasant communities. The metropole and its local representatives sided with the planters and tried to tie the ex-slaves into the periphery, by making them work for wages and become dependent on the market system. But the ex-slaves created a series of low-entropy communities, mainly around the coast of Dominica, and a way of life that was remarkably stable and resilient. This was in marked contrast to the unstable, high-entropy market-dominated system of the estate owners, who were now faced with serious labour shortages and potential collapse.

The peasant centring strategy focused on self-sufficiency and provided an identity in opposition to the white planter and manager and their like. It peripheralized the peasants from the centre, which is what they wanted. It also tended to peripheralize each community from the others. The communities lacked complex, hierarchical, bureaucratic, formal organization and operated on a simple technology based on a low-energy use. But, being on the margin of the periphery, when their interests conflicted with the dominant society, they were often forced to yield.

Administrators and power interests in the island saw the peasants as a barrier to progress and used various strategies to minimize their "negative" influence, ranging from attempting to dupe or persuade ex-slaves to remain working on plantations, to taxing peasants and evicting them from their properties, to buying off their resistance, and even to physically crushing them. Frequently, they backed up these actions with legal enforcements – the use of stipen-diary magistrates, police, and military personnel. In all these cases, the decision makers were outsiders to the peasant communities.

The formation of the peasantry created certain characteristics in Dominica – inadequate flow of information throughout the society, creating uncertainties, and a severe cleavage in the social fabric based on the coexistence of two economic systems – a peasant subsistence economy and a struggling but politically dominant colonial plantation market society. As we shall see, peasants later moved toward a growing reliance on the market, becoming more embedded in and dependent upon the centre. However, before con-sidering these events, what happened to those at the other end of the social scale – the local planters and merchants? They too had experienced the peripheralization of the centre and the disorder of emancipation. In contrast to the peasants, they tried to centre the periphery while remaining in the wider system. They will be the topic of discussion in the next chapter.

7 The Rise of the Mulatto Élite

With a white population which amounted to only about 5% of the
whole and with so much of that population widely scattered and very
imperfectly assimilated to the British tradition, public life in the island
could be nothing much better than the farce it was. Its main feature
just before and just after emancipation, was the attempt of coloured
voters to gain political control. In few of the colonies was the influence
of white upon black less and slavery probably bore as easily upon the
slavery there [Dominica] as anywhere in the West Indies.

Burns 1937, 68[1]

Out of the remnant planters and managers left in Dominica, there
emerged a group who wanted to exert control over their destiny,
not by retreating, as the ex-slaves had done, nor by acting as
instruments for the metropole, as the immigrant settlers and managers had done, but by increasing their influence on the periphery
while remaining in the wider system. Thus, not only did emancipation produce a new peasant social class, it also resulted in the
emergence of the mulatto élite, which adopted a centring strategy of
competition for control at the local centre and tried to direct administrative decisions toward local mulatto interests. The rise of this
group was a stormy, fractious affair, which dominated the politics of
the nineteenth century on the island.

The activities of the metropole had led white entrepreneurs,
usually male, to come to the Caribbean as owners, managers of
estates, or merchants in the towns. Their sexual liaisons with local
slaves, and ex-slaves created a new category of coloured person
whose members variably benefited, in terms of status or economic
resources or both, from their white ancestry. In some cases, whites
recognized their coloured progeny and supported them financially;
in cases in which they did not, the coloured person differed from
other ex-slaves only in colour, though this itself was a social asset.
Unlike many of their white ancestors, these persons were born in
Dominica and considered it their home. Their attempts to make
sense of and control their world were not based upon the goal of
retiring home to Britain, but focused on bettering their lot in Dominica. Although they were dynamically related to both the powerless

black slaves and the powerful white administrators and planters, they eschewed recognition of their slave ancestry and imitated, where possible, their white ancestry, which often enabled them to obtain a better education, an inheritance of some capital, and a different life style.

Some free coloureds with property and slaves had come to Dominica from Martinique prior to the British arrival. The expansion of this relatively educated and wealthy social group of landed mulattos introduced the potential for greater social disequilibrium at the time of emancipation. Racism had grown considerably during the period of sugar plantations. In the period that followed, antipathies between whites and coloureds became linked to metropolitan versus local interests. During this same period, then, when ex-slaves were forming their peri-island village communities in Dominica, a struggle was being fought at the "élite" level between the representatives of metropolitan interests, who sought to maintain control of their world through preserving colonial relations, and the mulatto élite, who wanted to wrest away that control and centre their local world for themselves. The conflict took place in the local legislature, where representatives of metropolitan interests clashed with local influentials. In this contest, the principle of metropolitan appointments was pitted against the principle of democratic process. The battle was furious, and, at times, the political process became so unworkable that the island was subordinated to wider federal controls or to direct rule from Westminster as a Crown colony.

This period can seen as an attempt by the more affluent coloureds to decide matters for themselves and control their destiny in a context in which local decision making was continuously eroded by outside interests. They were as aware as the villagers of racial stereotypes and arbitrary decisions and the experience of metropolitan domination. Whereas the ex-slaves sought to handle these problems by removing themselves from metropolitan control as much as they could, the mulatto élite tried to work the metropolitan system in their own interests. They used the elective principle as a centring strategy to bring about change and gain greater control of the island's administration. However, their activities occurred within the context of the entropic, disordering effects of Westminster's decision to abolish slavery and emancipate the slaves. During this period of highly acrimonious debate, it became increasingly difficult for the metropole to pass the legislation it wanted to protect its interests. Thus, entropic effects were initially felt only locally, but eventually they fed back to the centre, which had to expend energy to maintain the order that served its interests.

THE AGE OF DEMOCRATIC REVOLUTIONS

The context in which the mulattos became a significant political force in Dominica was a period of Atlantic history that has been described as the "Age of Democratic Revolutions" (Knight 1978, 147). The French and American revolutions, the general maroon activity throughout the Caribbean, and the Haitian Revolution of 1804 were the most prominent events in a period in which newly emergent groups organized concerted attacks on the accepted structures of political power.

The Haitian Revolution, in particular, had a dramatic impact not only on neighbouring territories in the Caribbean, but on the entire Atlantic region. Among other things, it exacerbated the whites' and free coloureds' fear of their slaves. The greed of Haitian prosperous whites, the *grands blancs*, had fostered increasing ethno-caste divisions in the society. The pervasive hostilities in the society not only were racist, but included considerable social distancing of the *grands blancs* from poor whites (*petits blancs*). The metropolitan government strengthened these divisions, for it bolstered the interests of the *grands blancs* by trying to limit the activities of the free coloureds socially and politically, generating in the process considerable resentment. Wealthy coloureds responded by invoking the rallying cry of the French Revolution and demanding equal treatment, equal opportunity, and (most dangerous to the status group of the *grands blancs*) equal fraternity with those very *grand blancs* who were attempting to lord it over both them and the *petits blancs*. It is significant that the wealthy coloureds did not include black slaves in their demands for equality and fraternity, for the coloureds were as distant from black slaves as the *grands blancs* were from the *petits blancs*. Indeed, in the Haitian civil war, the blacks in the north, under Christophe, fought the mulattos of the south, under Petion (see Knight 1978, 157). Thus, the rise of the free-coloured group in Dominica occurred at a time when the intellectual climate provided those who wished to translate economic gains into political ones with an ideology to back up their demands. But the ideological mixture of democracy and racism made for a particularly volatile brew.

THE EMERGENCE OF THE FREE COLOUREDS AS A POLITICAL FORCE

The brief period of economic prosperity that followed British annexation was accompanied by important changes in the ethnic composition of the "influentials" (*gwos bougs*) in Dominican society.

Some free people of colour had already acquired coffee plantations from the French and supported them in their opposition to the British on the island. Free coloureds, however, were having an even more important impact in Roseau than in the rural areas, because they were taking over the skilled occupations of absent whites. By 1832, free coloureds represented 59.9 per cent of the town's population (Martin 1844, 284), and many of them were involved in its business. As they acquired land and businesses, they began to mount a political challenge to the established order.

Prior to emancipation, Britain had controlled most of its West Indian colonies through local legislatures that were subordinate to the British parliament. The metropole carefully guarded its direct control of external trade and defence and scrutinized the operations of the various West Indian legislatures. At the time of emancipation, these bodies were composed of a governor, a nominated Council, and an elected Assembly. This tripartite system did not run smoothly: the governor, as the representative of the Crown and also the head of the colonial government, had two roles, which were often in conflict. The Council consisted of members nominated by the governor on behalf of the Crown, from among the richest and most influential colonists, and acted as both an advisory body and an upper house of the legislature. The Assembly was composed of members elected on a very limited franchise, who "exercised considerable legislative power, including the sole right to introduce money bills into the legislature" (Dookhan 1975, 113). The result was continuous, often bitter, conflict between the governor, who was responsible for the administration, and the Assembly, which could oppose the governor at every turn, but could not actually control him save in financial matters. In Dominica, this conflict was compounded by disputes over eligibility for Assembly membership, which was initially restricted to the white and wealthy.

It was within a general political atmosphere of growing demands for freedom, accompanied by racist stereotypes and the authorities' desire to retain control, that, in 1823, the free coloureds of Dominica petitioned the Assembly for more participation in the island's affairs. The Assembly conceded that the coloureds were a majority in numbers, but refused their request on the grounds that they were lacking in education and wealth:

Well, we have not been able to discover out of the whole free coloured population more than 12 persons who are at all qualified by education to have the smallest pretense to such a right [the framing of laws and participation in administration] and even of that number part are Roman Catholic, which persuasion is followed by three quarters of the whole free coloured population of the island. In times of war, the coloured people have been loyal, but Court records are there to show that they are not a peaceful section of the community. To grant them the privilege to set as jurors is a mere waste of time, considering the small numbers of those who qualify. (Minutes of the House of Assembly 2 Feb. 1823)

The assembly added that, before considering coloureds' democratic rights, there were whites on the island to be considered first: "Need we go farther than the very island of Dominica in which we reside, to behold white proprietors, Frenchmen or their descendants, men of large landed property, wealth and talents, who have no right nor claim to political power, persons not belonging to His Majesty's Council or the House of Assembly nor created magistrates, not enjoying any office of trust or profit under the Crown" (Minutes of the House of Assembly 2 Feb. 1823).

The complex divisions in the community existed not simply along colour lines, but involved religion (Protestant versus Catholic) and language (French versus English) as well. Although not as extreme as those in Haiti, these factions in Dominica hindered the smooth operation of local government. In fact, one commentator, visiting the island in 1826, was forced to observe, "I am afraid the spirit ... is at present something drowsy in Dominica; there is no public voice to call forth or public encouragement to support the exertion of individual virtue and talent; the community is first divided by language, then by religion, and the not inconsiderable residue, which is supposed to represent the whole, is so torn to pieces by squabbles, as bitter as they are contemptible, that mere routine of Government was at a dead stand while I was on the island" (Coleridge 1826, 152–3).

The free coloureds were undaunted by such obstacles, and they continued to press for greater political participation. In 1831, their efforts were rewarded with the passage of the Brown Privilege Bill, which granted them full political and social rights. The following year, when the Emancipation Bill was passed, three coloured men and a Catholic were "welcomed" into the Assembly. Things developed quickly and, by 1838, coloureds formed a majority of members in the Assembly. This set the scene for a period of highly contentious politics,[2] for, although the elected representatives attempted to promote the interests of the local coloured élite, "the white attorneys, merchants and traders allied with the numerous absentee owners, constantly threw up legislative road blocks in the Assembly and the Council alike" (Boromé 1969b, 26–7).

The Dominican historian Lennox Honychurch (1984, 98) concludes of this political period, "In Dominica there had existed side-by-side two high societies: the mainly French mulatto families and the white attorneys and government officials." While the miscegenation of a growing number of the French-speaking Catholics contributed to the population of wealthy free coloureds, there were also impoverished French white planters on the island. Nor, as already noted, did all coloured persons belong to the mulatto élite.

Both Honychurch (1984) and Grell (1976) have argued that the mulattos in the legislature fought for "the welfare of the newly liberated citizens of the island" (Honychurch 1984, 98). Grell goes so far as to refer to a "black-mulatto coalition" (Grell 1976, 157). The House of Assembly did attempt to ameliorate the conditions of the poor and was concerned with certain welfare considerations. However, there is no evidence that it operated with the ex-slaves' interests high on its agenda, nor that mulattos, who had owned and abused slaves in the same way as the whites, were any more likely than the whites to turn around in a matter of months to champion the ex-slaves' cause. There was an enormous social gulf between the mulattos who found their way into the House and the ex-slaves who comprised the newly formed peasant communities. Proesmans, a local historian, is closer to the truth when he observes, "At this time, the coloured people and the Negroes were still two entirely separated classes of people. For instance, when Rev. Horsford, who arrived as a missionary in Dominica in 1837, speaks of the coloured class, he means mainly yet not exclusively, the free coloured class with little or no leaning towards the Negroes" (Proesmans n.d., 40). This difference was well recognized by the whites, who "took a socially stratified order for granted and viewed the separate identity and special privileges of the free coloured as a means of consolidating their own hegemony" (Lowenthal 1972, 47). Members of the mulatto élite, then, were not champions of the ex-slaves' interests in Dominica; they were champions of their own interests.

Notwithstanding the complexity of Dominican social structure, the major interest groups represented in the House of Assembly tended to polarize along colour lines, with the mulatto élite pitted against white planters, merchants, and attorneys, in an attempt to use the extant colonial political institutions to further their cause. They proposed bills, sought election, organized petitions, and tried to alter the composition of the House. They justified their actions by representing themselves as the defenders of local, Dominican interests, arguing that the white planters, administrators, and merchants were essentially transients in the island who variously represented the metropole. Thus the notion of "Dominican" came to be thought of in colour terms, fuelled by long-standing racial antipathies.

The mulatto élite was not using a new strategy. Slaves captured in Barbados in 1816 had "stoutly maintained ... that the island belonged to them" (Williams 1970, 321). Slaves and ex-slaves elsewhere identified with their territories. Moreover, the role of colour in social relations has been an acknowledged component of most analyses of the Caribbean. In some cases, it has been seen as the major criterion for ranking in the society (for example, Braithwaite 1953, 1954; Broom 1954; Greenfield 1966, 1961; Henriques 1968; Smith 1953). In other instances it has been considered as an important modifier of status (for example, Jackson 1972; Sherlock 1955; Simpson 1941; M.G. Smith 1956; R.T. Smith 1956). M.G. Smith (1965, 60–6) identifies five meanings of colour in the Caribbean: genealogical, phenotypical, associational, structural, and cultural/behavioural. Although Rodgers and Morris (1971, 241) comment that "the class/colour stratification common to other areas of the Caribbean is not well developed in Dominica," Spens (1969, 30) has argued that it plays an important role in status allocation, although it is modified by the possession of wealth. Lowenthal observed that "Dominican Creoles exaggerate Carib antecedents to emphasize that they are lighter than other islanders" and that "the closely interrelated, light-skinned upper class sharply distinguish themselves from all others of whatever shade" (Lowenthal 1972, 185, 85).

The social significance of colour in Dominica is complex, and its role as a centring strategy is somewhat unclear, but it was used as a major resource in the political battles under discussion here. Two newspapers emerged that openly identified themselves with a colour interest: *The Colonist* aligned itself with whites and *The Dominican* with coloureds.[3] This differentiation permeated deliberations in the House of Assembly, which were nearly always prolonged and acrimonious. Reforms such as poor laws and public education inevitably generated a crossfire between the two coloured-based groups, whose daily vituperation and vilification of each other was shrilly echoed in the two partisan papers. John Finlay, for instance, expressing the opinion of some leading whites, wrote that the coloured membership of the house was

mostly composed of men who are entirely ignorant of the first principles of government, and whose only reason for going there is to aggrandize themselves, and to bring ruin on the more respectable classes of society. They are uneducated, ignorant and revengeful; and most of them have neither status or property in the Island. The majority of these would-be-legislators is made up of Journey-men Printers and Tailors, Bankrupt shopkeepers, a Blacksmith and a few fourth rate planters. Very few of them articulate English decently, and a still small number are able to write it with any degree of accuracy or propriety. (*Dominica Colonist*, 1 July 1854, quoted in Boromé 1969, 27)

Condemnatory rhetoric was directed particularly at Charles Gordon Falconer, the clever – and coloured – vociferous editor of the *Dominican*, who led a group of influential politically active coloured persons that came to be called the Mulatto Ascendancy, six members of which were his relatives.[4] They were so successful in advancing their liberal views as a block that the whites suggested single-chamber government in 1853 and, four years later, in order to contain the "Falconer Crowd," formed the Dominican Association for the Reform of Abuses in the Administration of Public Affairs. The leadership of this association was assumed by Thomas Doyle, the white editor of the *Colonist*. Its purpose was to obtain a single-chamber government that, its members hoped, would reduce the influence of the coloured group and the wrangling that accompanied all decision making in the legislature.

In December of 1861, Lieutenant-Governor Price arrived in Dominica and tried to compile a voter registry.[5] His attempts caused such a furore in the Assembly that he was forced to dissolve the government in May of the following year and call for new elections. The situation proved interesting, for now the "Falconer crowd" found themselves temporarily out of favour. To Price's delight, the election created what he considered to be the "purest" assembly Dominica had seen "in years" (Price to Hamilton, 10 November 1862, CO 71/128), with Thomas Doyle, who had sought a unicameral government, as Speaker of the House. This enabled Price to push through the legislation requiring voter registration in 1863, and to create single-chamber government with a Legislative Assembly comprising nine Crown appointees and nineteen members elected by the people.[6] This unwieldy body did not have time to meet before Price died, on 25 October 1864, but when it did the new Legislative Assembly "failed utterly to satisfy Dominica's need, for as violent party feeling rose to unprecedented heights, no important business could be transacted" (Boromé 1972c, 28).

THE MOVE TO CROWN-COLONY STATUS

The colonial government was well aware of the impasse created by the opposing groups in the Assembly. It was particularly fearful that

James Garraway, a coloured merchant and senior Council member who had been opposed to Price but had temporarily taken over his responsibilities on his sudden death, would start to dismantle his revised constitution. In January 1865 it sent William Robinson, the coloured president of St Kitts, to replace Price and protect its interests. Robinson, aghast at the name calling and recriminations in the Assembly, was quickly convinced that single-chamber government would never work until the number of its members was considerably reduced. He decided to establish a smaller Legislative Council composed entirely of nominated members, a proposal earlier advocated locally by William Macintyre, a prominent white attorney, and other Englishmen with large properties (Robinson to Hill 7 April 1864, CO 71/130).

A bill to make Dominica a Crown colony, and thereby avoid the input of an elective principle in local political decision making, was introduced into the House of 8 March 1865, and was supported by a majority of members. A public outcry, led by the Falconer minority, ensued. Tempers rose and rumours of all kinds flew: slavery was to be restored, a curfew was to be imposed. People flocked to mass meetings. The political unrest proved effective. On 23 March, a deputation of coloured inhabitants was told that the Crown colony bill would be replaced by a modified bill in which the representative principle would be restored: seven nominees and seven elected representatives would make up the legislature. The bill was passed, amidst high security, on 12 April 1864.

But the unicameral system was still perceived negatively by a majority of coloured Dominicans. Some instigated rioting. The Goodwill estate, which was close to the capital and whose agent was Macintyre, was set afire. Police and marines had to be called to clear the court-house on 19 April 1865. Despite this unrest, the new act went into effect on 21 August. In the subsequent elections, to show their displeasure with the government, the electorate returned Falconer and his followers to the elected seats. To counter this, the governor carefully chose anti-Falconer men as the Crown's nominees. The scene was thus set for yet another round of contentious politics.

The local representatives of metropolitan interest were dissatisfied with the modified political system. They increasingly felt that there was no official member who could put forth metropolitan views. The nominees seemed a timorous, weak lot who were afraid to stand up to the elected members, although, at the time, Falconer appeared to be exercising a restraining influence on the coloured elected opposition: nominees either did not vote or they absented themselves. Quorums of five were hard to obtain. Members voted out of self-interest. For example, a bill to establish a telegraph system barely passed for fear that this would "open the island to capital and enterprise which would smash the 'power and patronage' of the local oligarchy, and even more important, make resistance to federation impossible" (Pine to Granville, 9 May 1870, CO 71/140). In all, the Assembly was, as Lieutenant-Governor Freeling described it in 1869, "a perfect farce" (Freeling to Pine, 12 August 1869, CO 71/139).

FEDERATION WITH THE LEEWARD ISLANDS

But things were changing. In 1868, the government side won over Falconer by appointing him to the position of colonial registrar. By 1870, four of the seven members of the Executive Council were coloured. This body voted unanimously in favour of federation with the Leeward Islands, and the Assembly passed federation by a vote of nine to five in September of that year. Falconer was one of the two elected members who voted in favour of the union. In 1871, Dominica and the Leeward Islands became a federal colony administered by a president but under a governor based in Antigua.

The incentive behind this move was the promise of an improved economy and efficient administration at a time when the economy was in very dire straits and the Assembly was a shambles. However, the policy did not work in Dominica's favour. Dominicans received third-rate appointments in the federal government, and not a single Dominican held an office in the government or on the bench. There was no sign of any economic improvements to the island. To make matters worse, the governor attempted to steamroller his plans through the Assembly. Matters came to a head in 1880, when Governor Berkeley personally chaired a meeting of a new Assembly, to which he had appointed three Antiguan federal-government officials as replacement nominees. At this meeting, he changed the rules, making a quorum any five members, resident or non-resident, and proceeded to rush through bill after bill, "some being introduced without so much as a printed or manuscript copy" (Hamilton 1894, 56).

A protest was delivered to Berkeley and a petition was sent to the Queen. The petition galvanized William Davies, the editor of a local newspaper who has been called "the Hampden of Dominica," into action. Boromé (1969b, 34) describes Davies as "the most skilful coloured political leader after Falconer." In 1885, the Assembly passed Davies's resolution requesting severance of Dominica from the Leeward Island Confederation. Only two official nominees voted. The colonial government advised that nominees should be either persuaded to vote for the government or be replaced by some who would do so. But, as Boromé (1969b, 35) observed, "potential nominees were not as plentiful as strawberries," which, in the Dominican context, made them a decided rarity. A plan was devised to extend the franchise in the hope that new and more tax-paying voters would seize the opportunity to promote their interests and oust the old, elected members. The intentions of the Franchise Act failed. In the subsequent election, all but one of the old Assembly members were returned, and the new members shared the view that decision making should be returned to Dominica.

This was the situation when a new governor, Gormanston, arrived from Britain, in 1886, with a brief from London to revise the tax laws. The members of the Assembly held significant mercantile and landed interests, and they were determined to thwart the governor's plans to broaden the tax base. They stalked Gormanston, stayed out of the Assembly in protest, and held public meetings. In the opinion of one local colonial administrator the clique in the Assembly were a bad lot, mainly coloured and led by an ambitious coloured man. Moreover, such "a Coloured Clique is the worst form of tyranny that could be endured: it is inimical alike to the Negro and the white and by the former race it is hated" (Harris CO 152/166). London pronounced the tax measures "wise and necessary for the Presidency" (Hamilton 1894, 53), and they were promulgated by the end of the year. In response, Davies, to further his interests and secure influence in the more representative government, created the Dominican Patriotic League.

Governor Gormanston was succeeded in 1888 by the apparently more conciliatory Haynes-Smith, and the elected members were quiet for a while. But by 1891, the seven representatives contemplated petitioning the Secretary for the Colonies for his removal and the *Dial*, another coloured Dominican newspaper edited by Davies, suggested that "he should be assassinated." This time, the trouble concerned the activities of Edward Robins, an English engineer, recently appointed to the Road Board. Robins ran into difficulties with the board and attributed the feelings against him to colour prejudice. A storm had greatly damaged his projects, sweeping away bridges and equipment and causing extensive flooding, and he was held to be partly responsible. Haynes-Smith was critical of Robins, but he ignored the coloured elected members' advice to castigate him and remove him from office.

These problems were aggravated when Haynes-Smith ordered the eviction of a man for tax evasion in La Plaine, an incident described in some detail in the last chapter. Haynes-Smith was himself in Antigua at the time, and he advised the Secretary for the Colonies from there that Crown-colony government should be imposed on the island. The Colonial Office responded with a commission of inquiry into conditions in Dominica, to be conducted by Sir Robert Hamilton, ex-governor of Tasmania, with a special directive to investigate relations between the government and the legislature, taxation, and revenue collection.

Hamilton arrived on 21 November 1893; after hearing the views of Haynes-Smith, spent the next five and a half weeks holding hearings in Roseau and in other communities around the island.[7] Sympathizing with the Dominicans, he recommended that the island be separated from the Leeward Island Confederation and placed under a lieutenant-governor. He proposed that the Legislative Assembly be composed of seven elected representatives and seven nominees, of whom only three were to be official, and that the Executive Council, which had been filled mainly by officials resident in Antigua, be made up of Dominican residents and local Department heads; suggested that taxation and methods of levying be altered and that a loan of £30,000 be raised to pay off the floating debt; and recommended that the upkeep of Roseau be removed from the insular revenue and become the responsibility of a town board that would tax the inhabitants for this purpose.

This report was not well received in London. Hamilton was rapped on the knuckles for harbouring ideas such as "Dominica for the Dominicans," which completely broke with Colonial Office policy of the previous sixty years. He was deemed to have fallen victim to "clever but slimy politicians who represent one of the least desirable results of the advance of civilization in our West Indian Colonies" (note on Hamilton CO 152/190). But Dominicans received the report joyously and, although relatively little came of it, it pacified the elected members who lived for a while in expectation of changes.

Hamilton's judgment that Dominica's lack of prosperity was more the product of economic and geographical factors than of political ones proved to be a most influential point with Dominicans. Chamberlain, the Secretary of State for the Colonies in London, who was determined to strengthen the West Indian colonies, concluded from the report that Dominica's major need was improved communication through road building. The island merited "exceptional treatment" because it had not benefited from the sale of Crown lands when it had been ceded to Britain in 1763. Hamilton asked the House of Commons for £15,000 to wipe out the floating debt and £100,000 for road building. He got the £15,000 to liquidate outstanding debts and £120,000 for colonial relief, of which he allocated £15,000 for roads in Dominica, on condition that the island agree that its finances be directly controlled by the Crown – in other words, that it acquiesce to Crown-colony status.

William Davies interpreted this economic argument for Crown-colony rule to be, in fact, a colour one, essentially a matter of white versus non-white interest. He declared a race war and swore that he would rather see Dominica burned to ashes than see it lose its Legislative Assembly. The proposal to make Dominica a Crown colony was defeated in the Dominica Assembly by a vote of eight to six, with seven coloured elected members and one coloured nominee voting down the resolution (see Boromé 1969a, 47); all six dissenters were white. Fleming's response to the government's defeat was to dissolve the Assembly and call elections.

All the elected members were returned to office except for D.C. Riviere, in the parish of St Andrews, who was defeated by the white owner of the Hampstead estate, James Colin Macintyre. Meanwhile, Fleming had replaced L.A. Giraud, the coloured nominee, with James Cox Fillan, another coloured person. On 11 July 1899, the House accepted Chamberlain's "friendly bargain" by a vote of eight to six, and the following day it determined the composition of the new Legislative Council to be six official and six nominated members, with an administrator having the deciding vote. All of the official members and four of the seven unofficial members were white.

These developments met with considerable opposition. Furious, the old elected members pilloried Fillan as "the most justly abused and despised coloured man throughout the length and breadth of Dominica" (Boromé 1969a, 49). The clergy had supported Crown-colony status because some of its denominational primary schools had been dissolved under the influence of the electors. It was savagely attacked for this in the *Guardian*, a coloured newspaper that had replaced the *Dial*, which had folded for lack of funds. A large crowd collected round the presbytery and the cathedral and cut the telegraph cable. But concerted protest quickly evaporated, and the coloured opposition retreated. Lockhart, a coloured representative of the House, resigned all of his honorary offices in protest against the lack of franchise. In 1919, he founded the Representative Government Association, which he presided over till his death, in 1924. Davies retreated to his fifteen-hundred-acre Melvill Hall estate on the northeast side of the island, later moving to Concord, where he and his wife were killed in the hurricane of 1916 and their house was blown into a ravine. The other old elected members passed from the scene.

Dominicans had fought hard to resist Crown-colony status, but when it came they allowed it to operate reasonably smoothly. This was largely on account of the governorship of Henry Hesketh Bell, whose arrival in September 1899 "signalled the beginning of the most brilliant administration the island ever experienced" (Boromé 1969a, 51). In six months, Bell visited almost every part of the island, and both local newspapers praised him for his vigour and diplomacy. This led Lockhart to found *The Leeward Islands Free Press*, another paper, to provide some sort of criticism. He accused Bell of vanity, of "fostering racial prejudice by setting up a social club at Queens Lodge for whites only, by excluding most coloured persons from government house receptions and by discriminating in appointments and salaries" (Boromé 1969a, 52). In spite of these recriminations, Bell completed a peaceful tour of duty of Dominica in 1905. For his part, Chamberlain came through with a road grant for Dominica in return for adoption by the Assembly of Crown-colony status. The Imperial Road was built through the centre of the island, linking Melville Hall, in the northeast, with Roseau, in the southwest. It was not until after the First World War that Dominicans again became restive with Crown-colony status.

A RETURN TO THE ELECTIVE PRINCIPLE

After the First World War, there was a general movement for a return to the elective principle in the West Indies. Lockhart led the way in Dominica, with his Representative Government Association. At a meeting in St Gerard's Hall in 1920, at which he presided, a petition was drawn up for withdrawal from the Leeward Island Confederation. Two years later, Major Wood, appointed by Great Britain to assess the condition of the West Indies, heard James Colin Macintyre, who had abrogated his former pro–Crown-colony position, plead for representative government. Wood also received a petition of twenty-three hundred signatures demanding withdrawal from the federation. He went along part of the way by recommending greater representation. In September of 1924, Dominica was granted a new constitution, with a Legislative Council consisting of six official and six unofficial members. Of the latter, four were to be elected.

The four coloured men elected in 1925 experienced increasing frustration as their votes were consistently swamped by the official members. Attempts were made to increase the representative component in government, but it was not until the 1936 constitution that a majority of unofficial members were to make up the Legislative Council. The next year, Dominica withdrew from the Leeward Island Confederation. The stage was thus set, after the Second World War, for the emergence of political parties and a new level for political life on the island.

AMONG THE METROPOLE'S centring strategies was the extension of administrative control over the periphery. This was achieved by appointing administrators from the centre, fashioning decision-making structures on the periphery, and, often, working through already existing indigenous political structures. The aim was to create a social order that operated in the interest of the metropolitan centre. As far as Dominicans were concerned, therefore, the governor and the appointees in the Assembly were persons selected by the metropole for their allegiance to the home government, and their job was to protect the interests of the metropole. This centring activity peripheralized those persons whose interests did not accord with those of the metropole – for example, local businessmen, planters, and the coloured élite of Dominica, who felt that decisions were being made with no concern for local priorities and found themselves relatively powerless to alter this. Yet the imported democratic principle, designed by the metropole to maintain political control of the colony, provided opportunities for local interests to express themselves and for decisions to be moulded in their favour, with the landslide of changes that followed emancipation. The result was a period of Dominican history during which there was a continual battle between the periphery's attempt to wrest control from the metropole and the metropole's attempt to keep control over local political decisions and aspirations.

The outcome of this was a period of local political activity in which efforts to create a political structure merely gave rise to an increasing inability to make decisions. The energy expended in local decision-making efforts only created more entropy – an inability to create order. The metropolitan government changed the administrative status and structure of Dominica every few years, from colony to Crown colony, to federated colony, and back, with the locus of official decision making moving from Dominica to Antigua to London and back. The changes were unsuccessful in decreasing the levels of unpredictability – the disorder being generated by the system.

It was in this turbulent context that a group of local dominicans put considerable effort into centring the peripheral situation. Initially, they were a divided community, with the traditional English and French division being complicated by the French practice of miscegenation, and the rise of the French free coloured. Increasingly, the cross-cutting language, religious, and colour factions polarized into a white/mulatto division, which reflected a conflict between metropolitan and local interests. Whites on the island sided with metropolitan interests, and the coloured élites with local interests.

Efforts emanated from the metropole to create and maintain order in an entropic periphery. The very process of trying to re-establish an orderly periphery and maintain the centre–periphery *holon* (whole) further destabilized the political organization of the peripheral society. Furthermore, the patterns of decision making that were imposed were conceived in a far more complex society. They were, in themselves, energy-expensive processes. The results were the entropic effects that one might expect on the periphery of a high-entropy society, including the failure of resources, the difficulty of making local decisions, and the chaotic, unpredictable consequences associated with truncated relationships.

In the final three chapters, we enter the present era, in which ethnographic data are presented and interpreted in terms of the processes that I have been discussing. As we follow the long-standing process of centring and peripheralizing into the present, events become telescoped and the pace slows down. How emancipation and the failure of sugar unfolded into the present economic structure of Dominica is the topic of the next chapter.

8 Capitalizing a Subsistence Economy

> While agricultural labour in all the British West Indies is the great *desideratum* and the cry for immigration is echoed and re-echoed, it is amazing to see how the labour which the planter has within his reach is wasted and frittered away; how the particular population upon which the prosperity of the colonies so utterly depends is neglected; how by mismanagement and unpardonable blunders of policy, the life of field labourer has been made so distasteful to the peasant that the possession of half an acre, or the most meager subsistence and independence, seem to him in comparison with estate service, the very acme of luxurious enjoyment.
>
> Sewell 1968 [1862], 154

THE CARIBBEAN CONTEXT

West Indian planters, at the time of emancipation, wished to remain within the metropolitan centred system, from which they derived their profits, and so they were preoccupied with the fear of labour shortages and their consequent effect on productivity. Besides feverishly generating strategies to keep the ex-slaves on the estates, planters sought new sources for their labour – in renewed migration and indentured labour. As a result, West Indian territories experienced a new wave of some half a million immigrant labourers, starting in 1838 and ending as late as 1924, which affected both the communities they left and the territories into which they came.

The majority of these people were East Indian. Some 238,000 went to Guyana, 145,000 to Trinidad, 21,500 to Jamaica, 39,000 to Guadeloupe, 34,000 to Surinam, 1,550 to St Lucia, 1,820 to St Vincent, 2,570 to Grenada, and 6,748 to Martinique (see Williams 1970, 348).[1] There were also a significant number of Chinese: approximately 34,834 were in Cuba in 1861 alone, and 14,002 were in Guyana. There were Madeirans and Javanese in Surinam.

Only four territories in the Caribbean in the nineteenth century did not participate in the vast demographic revolution which was in operation in the area as a whole: independent Haiti, Spanish Santo Domingo, which became independent in 1844, Spanish Puerto Rico, and British Barbados. Elsewhere the simple population pattern at the end of the eighteenth century – a few whites of the metropolitan country, some mulattos, and a majority of Negroes – became a heterogeneous mixture which included Indians, Chinese, Javanese and Portuguese, with the infinite gradations, shadings and mixtures produced by miscegenation. (Williams 1970, 350)

Dominica should be added to Williams's list, for it, too, did not participate in indentured labour. Although the planters in Dominica also faced major labour shortages, they were too poor to respond by creating an alternative labour source.

THE COLLAPSE OF SUGAR PRODUCTION IN DOMINICA

In Dominica, the legacy of slavery, with its ideology of racism, had been to blind both planter and ex-slave to the possibility of co-operative work relations. The general mistrust between planter and ex-slave had accompanied a mass exodus of ex-slaves from the estates and the development, as we have noted, of a peri-island peasantry. Because estates were poorly developed, they did not have the depth of resources available in other territories and were unable to purchase labour in the post-emancipation period. Instead, they either hung on through operation of the *metayage* system or they collapsed. It is indicative of the abysmal state of the Dominican economy around the time of emancipation that no indentured labour was introduced to work the island's estates.

In 1846, cane sugar from the West Indies, challenged by cane production in other territories and by the increasing efficiency of beet-sugar production in Europe, lost its monopolistic position in the British market. Nevertheless, indentured labour kept sugar alive, and even increased production in the sugar islands. For instance, sugar exports increased by some 21.9 per cent between 1882 and 1895 (Williams 1970, 351). In Dominica, however, productivity and sugar exports dropped significantly: between 1882 and 1894, production fell from 3,421 tons to 1,050 tons – a drop of almost 70 per cent (see Williams 1970, 366).

The long, slow erosion of the cane-sugar prices that began in 1846 led to the complete collapse of the Dominican sugar industry (Cracknell 1973, 79). "Between 1870 and 1878 ... cane-sugar prices fell by about 1/3 a cwt.; in 1884 alone prices fell from 20/- to 13/-a cwt.; and by 1897 prices were down to 10/- a cwt" (Dookhan 1975, 19). The drop in prices contributed to the abandonment of some estates, and to the severe curtailment of production on others. By 1897, there were only two sugar factories in Dominica, and only 975 acres were in cane. In 1894, sugar made up only 15 per cent of the value of Dominica's exports (Williams 1970, 372). Although several factors, including the abolition of bounties for beet production, the centralization of sugar production in some islands, and the decline in trade with Europe as a result of the First World War, fostered a temporary resurgence of the West Indian sugar industry elsewhere, it did not occur in Dominica at all.

THE RISE AND FALL OF THE LIME INDUSTRY

The changes in the sources and market value of sugar at the metropolitan centre affected the periphery, which had been developed explicitly to provide this monocrop. Planters, who had centred their world and organized their activities to supply the centre with sugar, now had to cope with a potentially chaotic, destructive situation. One strategy was to find an alternative crop which would enable them to remain within the ambit of the market. Some returned to the type of diversification that had existed prior to the sugar invasion, while others sought an equivalent to sugar. A number of unsuccessful attempts were made as early as the 1850s to find a substitute for sugar production in Dominica. A scheme to revive the cotton industry, for example, failed. Limes, however, proved to be different.

Dr John Imray, a Scotsman who had replaced his brother as a medical practitioner in Dominica in 1832 and quickly became the island's leading physician and an international authority on yellow fever and yaws, introduced Liberian coffee and resurrected lime cultivation in the island. Imray noticed that the lime trees that grew at the side of the road on the way to his estate produced excellent fruit that was left to rot. Aware of the nutritive qualities of limes, he learned how Sicilians extracted citric acid from lemons and set up his own small factory, which gradually led him to replace sugar with limes on his estates (see Cracknell 1973, 80). Other estate owners, particularly those in coffee, followed his example, and limes became an important element in the Dominican economy.

Limes did not require the same work-force as sugar, nor the same kind of investment from the planter. The fruit was far better suited to Dominica's terrain and did well in the cooler, rugged interior of the island. Furthermore, lime trees continue to bear fruit years after planting. Laughlin Rose & Company, of Leith, Scotland, became interested in the product. It entered the lime business first in order to supply ships with the fruit, but it went on to develop a lime soft drink. Laughlin Rose bought land in Dominica to grow limes, and the industry received a considerable boost when an American millionaire, Andrew Green, whose engineering company was making a fortune constructing the locks of the Panama Canal, arrived on the island. He bought the Canefield estate, then still in sugar, converted it to limes, and set up the most advanced citrus-processing machinery to date, powered by both steam and water wheel. The value of lime exports increased steadily, from £11,363 in 1892 (26 per cent of the value of exports) to £185,803 in 1914 (88 per cent of the value of exports) (Watts 1916, 200). Dominica became the largest lime producer in the world, and several planters substituted monocrop sugar production with monocrop lime production.

Planters also revived an interest in cacao, which had been an important crop during the French period. The British chocolate manufacturer Rowntree and Company owned three large estates in the northern part of the island, which were given over to cacao production (see Honychurch 1984, 119). The value of cacao exports rose from £9,748 (2.2 per cent of the value of total exports), in 1892, to £20,024 (9.5 per cent of the value of total exports), in 1914. Limes, however, remained dominant, and the economy essentially was based again on monocrop agriculture (Watts 1916, 201).

Limes brought prosperity and, under Henry Hesketh Bell's able administration in the first years of the twentieth century, Dominica underwent a period of rejuvenation. "In 1901 the Treasury statements actually showed a surplus of £5,000, something that had been unbelievable in Dominica" (Honychurch 1984, 115), and during the First World War trade soared. For the fiscal year 1914–15, the balance of payments was some £30,000 in Dominica's favour.

One of Bell's schemes was to open up the interior of the island to agriculture. To this end he used the financial aid Dominica received to build the Imperial Road, which snakes its way from Roseau up into the interior of the island to a point locally referred to as Bells, and then across to Melville Hall. He then encouraged whites to emigrate from Britain and settle along this road. As he put it, "I am already convinced that the right people to develop these new lands would be the same class of young men from home, who have been such a success in Ceylon, Burma and Malaya. This is the policy I am going to work on." He also developed a plan to settle three thousand Boer War prisoners from South Africa in the interior. Although this plan never materialized, some thirty or forty white families bought lots of considerable size and settled along the Imperial Road. However, this scheme turned out to be unsuccessful in the long run. Many of the white settlers who settled in the interior abandoned or sold off their estates before the outbreak of the First World War, finding the mountainous terrain and the inhospitable climate too difficult. Most of the remainder returned to Britain at the outbreak of war, never to return.

Dominica's reliance on a single crop proved disastrous. In May, 1922, the lime industry received a *coup de grâce* with the outbreak of withertip on an estate in the southern part of the island. The disease spread rapidly, and in three months it was to be found on every estate. Compounding the problem was red root disease, which affected the base of the trees. Exports the following year slumped to less than half, and continued to fall disastrously. The industry never recovered, though new experimental strains were later introduced. Acreage in limes dropped by two thirds between 1921 and 1937 (Cracknell 1973, 87). This had serious implications all round. In a memorandum to the Royal Commission in 1938, Pidduck observes, "In the years prior to 1921, when Dominica was the world's foremost exporter of limes ... (500,000 barrels per annum), outside capital was easily procured on loan. Today it is difficult if not impossible to incline anyone within or without the island to invest much in agriculture, and planters and peasants alike have to make their slender profits keep them and their families alive, pay interest on loans and develop their lands as best they can. The majority are unable to repay loan capital and many are in arrears for interest as well" (Pidduck 1938, 6).

The final blow for the economy as a whole came with the three hurricanes of 1926, 1938, and 1930 and the serious impact on world trade of the collapse of New York Stock Exchange in 1929.[2] Plantation after plantation went bankrupt. Peasants retreated further into subsistence farming. By 1937, the per-capita value of exports stood at 5s 9d, the lowest figure for the entire British West Indies, and the per-capita value of imports stood at £2 10s 7d, the second highest among the British West Indian territories (Cracknell 1973, 87). The result was a balance-of-payments deficit of some 800 per cent. A measure of the island's problems can be gauged from Harvey's memorandum to the Royal Commission in 1938: "The serious position economically into which the island has fallen can be seen at a glance on reference to the record of imports and exports from 1919 to 1937" (Harvey 1938, 4; see table 6).

The impact of this pattern of economic activity on the social structure of Dominica through the first half of the twentieth century was to polarize the urban political and economic centre and the isolated and dispersed rural peasantry, who were largely left to fend for themselves, locked into small, local networks in peri-island communities, some of which were accessible from Roseau only by

Table 6
Dominica: Exports and Imports, 1919 and 1937

Year	Exports ($EC)	Imports ($EC)
1919	256,789	203,330
1937	73,061	125,372

Source: Harvey 1938, 4.

boat. The lime boom exacerbated the marginalization of the peasantry because it required less labour than sugar. Peasants themselves
did not have the resources to develop limes as a cash crop because
there was a delay of several years between initial investment
(clearing and planting) and expected returns (harvesting of fruit),
which they could not afford. But, in the words of one informant,
"Things changed drastically after the war."

DEVELOPMENT OF A BANANA INDUSTRY

As we have seen, the peasantry accessed the market on an *ad hoc*
basis. Initially, the administration had seen the peasantry as an
unproductive nuisance, but the Royal Commission of 1897, reflecting
the stipendiary magistrates' reports that apprentices should grow
some export crops (CO 74/33), saw the peasantry as a potentially
productive local force.[3] Their development as such was slow to
materialize. Although bananas were easy to grow, the plants were
very susceptible to wind damage and were often ravaged by Panama disease. Thus, they were grown on a relatively small scale in
Dominica prior to 1948, and the importance of the crop fluctuated
(see table 7). In 1948, however, a new strain of banana was introduced, and in 1949, Antilles Products Ltd agreed to sell all export-
able bananas in Britain for the next fifteen years. Two founders of
this company, P.J. Foley and G.B. Brand, set up their own estate at
Woodford Hill, in northeast Dominica. In 1952, Geest Industries
picked up the banana contract from Antilles Products and went on
to become highly successful:[4] "[At its inception, Geest's] nominal
capital was only £75,000. By 1981, profits alone exceeded £1 million.
Moreover, since 1972, Geest Industries itself has become part of a
much larger conglomerate, Geest Holdings Ltd., whose subsidiaries
are involved in various types of activities from foodstuffs distribution and agricultural engineering to computer services and leisure
travel" (Trouillot 1988, 164).

The sturdier plant introduced in 1948 made market production
more attractive to the peasantry, and this was reflected in the value
of banana exports as a percentage of total export values: banana

Table 7
Agricultural Land Use in Dominica, 1938–61

Year	Acres in Cane	Cacao	Coconuts	Bananas	Citrus	Vanilla	Pasture	Provisions
1938	200	1,000	1,500	1,000	–	–	–	100
1944	300	1,000	2,000	700	150	150	–	1,000
1946	1,305	1,523	4,083	6,281	2,500	–	4,914	6,640
1952	–	1,100	3,000	4,000	4,925	–	–	–
1961	424	1,740	7,052	8,389	4,745	–	4,336	1,666

Sources: West Indies Census of Agriculture, 1946; West Indies Census of Agriculture 1961.

exports rose from about 25 per cent, in 1953, to almost 77 per cent in 1966. The absolute value of banana exports rose by some 148 per cent in the nine-year period 1960 to 1969 (see table 8). An increasingly significant proportion of this production came from peasants.[5]

The major players in this new monocrop development were, of course, to be found in the metropole: Geest Industries and the British government. Geest had considerable marketing facilities in Britain, to which it linked a series of "banana boats" that transported the fruit from the Windward Islands for sale in Britain. The firm cooperated with the British government in developing bananas as an important cash crop in these islands. While the profits accrued to Geest, the peasant growers had access to a ready source of cash on an individual basis and experienced an increase in their standard of living. But along with access to cash and its purchasing power, they encountered a new market dependency. They were once again pulled into the periphery of the metropolitan centre.

The British government, with its primary interest being to support domestic industry, protected Windward Islands bananas imported by Geest on the home market. It provided monies to the island in the form of grants for banana husbandry and for developing new roads to provide access to banana-growing areas. This greatly facilitated banana production: peasant growers could "head out" their bananas from their inaccessible gardens to the nearest road, whence they could be transported to the ports (or, more recently, to boxing plants). In 1950, to further entrench bananas in Dominica's economy, the Commonwealth Development Corporation (CDC) bought two estates on the windward side of the island: Castle Bruce, which had been abandoned for many years, and Melville Hall, which had been bought by the Government of Dominica as a site on which to build an airport. The CDC planted fourteen hundred acres of Castle Bruce, mainly in bananas, and nine hundred acres of Melville Hall in cacao, coconuts, and bananas. Geest, meanwhile, purchased estates at Woodford Hill, Portsmouth, and Brantridge, in the north and central part of the island.

Table 8
Value of Banana Exports, 1960–70

Year	Value in $EC(000s)
1960	4,125.5
1961	4,783.9
1962	4,875.1
1963	5,417.1
1964	6,717.7
1965	7,475.0
1966	7,421.1
1967	8,225.6
1968	9,387.6
1969	10,225.0
1970	7,758.3

Source: Annual Statistical Digest No. 4,
1970–1972, table 71.

These signs of metropolitan interest and commitment to bananas were not lost on the urban élite in Dominica. Wealthier residents of Roseau saw a new resource for their centring strategies and started to buy land in the interior, where they retired on weekends to enjoy the cooler mountain air and tend their bananas. Indeed, there emerged a new type of "middle-class part-time farmer who understands little else about agriculture but the production of bananas" (White 1967, 66).

While the initial thrust of bananas production occurred on estates, its success lay in its adoption by small peasant farmers, who found the fruit an ideal cash crop and incorporated it into a new, more market-oriented centring strategy. Bananas provided them with a small but steady source of cash, for the fruit is non-seasonal and can be harvested and marketed weekly. Furthermore, bananas do not require a large initial capital outlay and bear fruit within a short period after being planted. The result was the biggest change in the Dominican land-use pattern since emancipation (Momsen 1970, 264) and a dramatic impact on the merchant community in Roseau. In 1961, 73 per cent of the farms and 94 per cent of the acreage was in freehold ownership (West Indies Census of Agriculture 1961, 891). There followed a steady increase in the number of small farms of between five and ten acres and a decrease in those of over one hundred acres: between 1946 and 1970, there was a 32 per cent increase in the number of small holdings, and a 77 per cent increase in the number of acres in small holdings. There was also a 32.6 per cent decrease in total farmland acreage. By 1970, 90 per cent of the banana growers had farms of fewer than five acres, and the majority of these were fewer than three acres (see table 9).

By 1960, there were few large estates in Dominica: "Only twelve estates exceed 1000 acres in size and only three exceed 2000 acres,

Table 9
Changes in Small Holdings and Total Farm Land, 1946–61

Size of Holdings	1946	1961	1970
Under 5 Acres			
Holdings	5,354	6,847	7,105
Acreage	8,120	10,051	18,592
5–9 Acres			
Holdings	379	1,160	1,336
Acreage	3,646	7,047	
10–49 Acres			
Holdings	955	667	580
Acreage	17,509	11,916	
50–99 Acres			
Holdings	89	78	60
Acreage	5,753	5,050	
100 Acres and Over			
Holdings	110	97	50
Acreage	42,363	40,767	
Total Farm Land Acres	80,800	76,163	54,419

Sources: West Indian Census of Agriculture 1946, 74; West Indian Census of Agriculture 1961; Agriculture Statistics, Dept. Agriculture, Dominica.

one of which is the 3,700 acre Carib Reserve" (Clarke 1962, 15). Foreigners held approximately 12 per cent of the farms larger than fifty acres in 1970 (Watty 1970).[6] Plantations tended to go out of bananas because of labour shortages, inadequate feeder roads, and increasing costs of "heading out" bananas. Peasants, on the other hand, were quite able to tend their small plots, perhaps with some co-operative help, and to carry bunches of bananas down from their gardens to the roadside on their heads. Despite the trend for estates to go out of banana production, Geest expanded its holdings from one thousand acres, in 1956, to four thousand acres, in 1969.

The pattern of land tenure that had emerged with emancipation had repercussions on the efficiency of banana production (see Weber 1973, 192). In many cases, the gardens were in isolated areas, up in the "heights," and banana stems had to be headed out considerable distances to pick-up points, where they were loaded onto trucks. Heading out bruised and damaged the fruit, which was then rejected by the buyers, so feeder roads were built to minimize this form of transport as much as possible. But, as noted earlier, road building in Dominica is particularly difficult and expensive, and the results are often relatively short-lived, as roads get washed out and bridges washed away in the torrential rains. Thus, the local costs of developing the banana industry were high. As one economic expert observed, "Owing to the nature of the land in Dominica it costs about $100,000.00 to build a mile of main road ... A programme is envisaged in which 16 miles of main road per annum would be constructed ... A programme covering 16 miles a year of surfaced feeder roads at $50,000.00 per mile would cost $8,000,000.00 over ten years" (O'Loughlin 1963, 84–5). This was a considerable figure for the island at that time. The number of miles of road rose from 203.8, at a maintenance cost of $65,425, in 1949, to 447.0 at a cost of $927,206, in 1970. In other words, while the number of miles of road little more than doubled, the cost of building and maintenance rose some thirteen times. In 1972, the estimated total cost of feeder-road construction was $550,000 (*Estimates* 1972, 231).

According to data from the Agricultural Department, there were 8,085 land holdings in 1972. Of these, 0.2 per cent (16) were over five hundred acres, and 88 per cent (7,105) were under ten acres. Sixteen per cent (1,297) of the holdings were reported as family land. In this last case, as already noted, land is held by an extended family, all of whom have equal right to usufruct on the entire holding. The co-owners have to agree if they, or an individual among them, want to partition the land; when there is a move to do this, heirs to the property are often very hard to trace. Often, in cases where all the owners can be identified and would agree to partition the land, the resulting plots would be so small that the exercise becomes worthless. Dominicans therefore tend not to cultivate family land.[7] As a result, there is "a substantial amount of unused land in areas already served with roads" (Campbell 1965, 3), as peasants prefer to resort to marginal lands of lesser potential in "the heights."

ORGANIZATION OF THE BANANA INDUSTRY

The major forces involved in the organization of the Dominica banana industry in the metropole were Geest Industries and the British government; in Dominica, they were the Dominica Banana Growers Association (DBGA) and the growers themselves. Clearly, the locus of power and decision making and the centre of the industry were in the metropole: Geest controlled the marketing, transportation, and production of bananas by creating certain structures, from estates, to shipping lines, to a network of marketing outlets in Britain, and also by setting the price paid to peasant growers and the standards they had to meet. It also networked with the British government in the pursuit of its interests. This last strategy is all-important, for Geest has held the exclusive shipping and marketing contracts for Dominica's bananas for over thirty years, since it bought out the interest of Lesser Antilles Products.

Why did the British government commit itself to supporting Dominican bananas, and thus Geest, on the domestic market? For the second time in its history, Dominica's strategic location made it an area of some interest to metropolitan powers because it appeared to be vulnerable to a communist takeover. Castro's successful revolution in Cuba raised the region's importance, and a stable, prosperous peasantry in Dominica came to be seen by the metropole as a distinct advantage. Just as the island's value had once lain in its strategic position between Guadeloupe and Martinique and therefore in its potential for breaking up French hegemony in the region, now it was important because it had the potential to inhibit a communist hegemony in the region. The British government made bananas a risk-free business for Geest by guaranteeing access to the British market. This would facilitate peasants' production, and their resulting "affluence," it was argued, would ensure their allegiance to the "Free World."

The British market for Windward Islands bananas existed because imports from Latin American countries could be restricted by the anachronistic use of the 1939 War Emergency Powers Regulation, issued and still in force, under the 1935 Defence of the Realm Act. Geest therefore had to pay the islands only the residual value of the bananas after all its costs plus margins had been deducted, was thereby assured of profits, and had to pay the island growers just enough to make sure that the banana production continued. This economically advantageous state of affairs was made even more attractive to Geest by the British government's readiness to provide aid tied to the island's banana industry. With these measures, potential competition from large-scale operations in Latin America, which produced a more attractive but less flavourful fruit than Dominica, was easily contained. There were other advantages too: Dominican bananas were some fifteen hundred miles closer to the British market than those in Latin America, which reduced their transport costs, and they did not suffer from Black Sigatoka, a banana blight that invaded many Latin American plantations. As well, because they were produced by small holders and family-based operations, rather than by large plantation-type organizations using wage labour, the enterprise was far less prone to problems associated with labour productivity.

In Dominica, the industry's interests are handled by a statutory body, the DBGA, which is responsible for disease control, the banana extension service, payments to farmers, and the delivery of output to the wharf for shipping (Prins 1984). The DBGA receives the residual value of the bananas (usually between 20 and 25 per cent of the retail price in Britain) after Geest has deducted all the costs and profits associated with its shipping, ripening, and marketing operations. It attempts to improve and maintain industry standards and productivity on the island and, through WINBAN (Windward Islands Banana Growers Association – the regional umbrella), negotiates banana-contract prices with Geest. Although the DBGA appears powerful on the local scene, Geest continues to exert enormous influence over its decisions. Thus, the association's local centring ability is eroded by its dependence on metropolitan players.

In 1971, for example, Geest ordered that bananas be bought "by the hand," as they are found in shops, rather than "by the stem," as they are cut from the plant. This decision benefited Geest, for it meant less processing for the firm and an ability to reject more poor-quality fruit at source. The DBGA hired a Canadian consulting team, which recommended that the purchase of bananas on the island be centralized by creating twelve "boxing plants," strategically placed throughout the island, to which bananas would be brought to be "dehanded," selected, and boxed. The boxes of better-quality bananas would then be trucked to export centres at Roseau and Portsmouth. Twelve boxing plants were built; then, in response to grower pressure for better access, the number was expanded to seventeen. This scheme clearly benefits Geest, though it costs the firm nothing, whereas some of the costs for running the plants are borne by the DBGA, which is responsible for the managing the operation and for providing cartons.

In order to control its costs, the DBGA has had to pass them on to the peasant growers and the organization itself has had to expand. In 1972, there were 133 staff in the association (see *Dominica Banana Growers' Association Annual Report*, 1972, 11–12), with salaries totalling $116,865.66 (*Dominica Banana Growers' Association Annual Report*, 1972, schedule 3). Six of them were in administration, nineteen in finance, and the remainder in operations. Seventy-two positions were created by the boxing-plant reorganization of the early seventies, and these salaries have to be paid out of the monies generated by banana production. The economic position of the peasant grower in this whole scheme is starkly captured in a statement by Bunge (1983, 61): "The poor farmer is paid 14 cents, British West Indian (BWI) currency, for a pound of his bananas, delivered on demand and in good condition to the British firm Geest Industries Limited, at Geest's warehouse at the deep-sea port just north of Roseau. My wife has paid as much as three dollars BWI in the Dominion Food Store at the Jane-Finch Mall in Toronto, Canada for a similar pound of bananas. The Coulibistrie farmer is paid only 5 *per cent* of the final retail price for his labour."

THE IMPACT OF BANANA PRODUCTION

Although the producers receive a very small proportion of the profit from the banana industry, a major impact has been the cash it puts into the hands of the peasants. In 1962, bananas netted $EC 2,982,544; in 1969, they netted $EC 6,033,269 (see table 10). Previously, Dominicans had experienced a most restricted cash flow. For instance, in 1929, only 0.2 per cent (ninety-six people out of a population of forty-three thousand) had an income sufficiently high to pay tax, and only six people had an income over £1,000 per annum. Wages were 1s 3d per day for men and 10d per day for women. In 1939, 2.12 per cent (1,050 out of a population of 49,483) were wage earners (Cracknell 1973, 87–8). In 1963, 8 per cent (4,771 persons out of a population of 59,496) were assessed for taxes and, thirty-three people had an income over $10,000 (*Annual Statistical Digest* no. 4, Table 23). Thus, revenue from bananas increased the cash flow on the island considerably and integrated the peasants into the cash economy for the first time in Dominican history.[8] This had a marked effect on the living standards of the peasants in rural areas and on the mercantile sector in Roseau.

In 1935, Harrison (1935, 76) described the Dominican rural scene in this way: "Native homes are of local woods, covered with shingles of local manufacture. A few shingles are imported from British Guiana for use in better homes ... The foods in most common use are native vegetables, native fish and salted fish from Canada ... Most of the labourers on the estates live in villages adjacent to or within easy walking distance of the estate upon which they work." The traditional way of life in the island villages had changed little from the previous century. Although there was some labour on the estates for cash and some sale of domestic produce in the market, the majority of the population were caught up in subsistence farming and a cycle of non-monetary exchanges. Cash was used for "luxuries." For example, "The native ... augments his income and obtains the wherewithal to buy for himself, his wife and children, clothes and articles of dress, of which he is very fond. Garments with outstanding colours are generally what are worn ... the head dresses of many of the women are gorgeous in colour, very effective, but too striking in appearance and arrangement to suit the European female mind" (Grieve 1906, 24–5). On the whole, economic activity was not geared to producing a surplus.

Village life began to change as cash started to penetrate the local economy. The size and type of holding, its accessibility, and its fertility became important factors in generating a surplus and thus

Table 10
Banana Production, 1962–71

Year	Total Stems	Boxes	Tons [000s]	Cwt/ Stem	Growers Paid ($)	Price Per Lb [Cents]
1962	2,393,928		28.2	26.4	2,982,544	4.2
1963	2,446,970		30.7	28.1	3,328,293	4.8
1964	3,474,056		42.2	27.2	4,956,875	5.2
1965	4,006,089		49.8	27.4	4,906,095	4.4
1966	3,495,017		42.9	27.5	4,132,922	4.2
1967	3,551,105		46.8	27.5	4,518,678	4.3
1968	4,099,128		54.9	30.0	6,184,369	5.0
1969	3,819,519		57.7	33.8	6,033,269	4.6
1970	2,776,901	322,672	44.4	32.6	4,182,270	4.2
1971	1,418,261	1,192,369	38.2	34.0	3,446,620	5.2

Source: Dominica Banana Growers Association Annual Report 1971, 2.

making a profit from one's banana enterprise. Those who could afford fertilizer and who managed their land better could generate more cash. Entrepreneurial ability led to greater occupational differentiation in villages as individuals became involved in truck-driving and store operations. Evidence of greater social inequalities emerged. Some houses were still built of shingles, but others took on tin roofs and some were constructed of concrete block. Whereas, previously, most houses were lit at night by kerosene lamps and meals were cooked on kerosene stoves, many houses were now serviced by electricity and boasted such appliances as refrigerators, stoves, and radios. Some houses had telephones. Plantain, dasheen, okra, fish, and salt fish remained the staples of the daily diet, but tinned milk, tinned meat, and other imported foods were increasingly adopted. The cash for these purchases came from bananas or banana-related activities.

Access to cash led to increased local entrepreneurship. For example, during my fieldwork in the island in 1972–3, I found one young man who had access to five plots of land, varying in accessibility and in size from three acres to twelve acres, on which he had planted bananas in 1958. Two of the plots were family land. Augustine (a pseudonym) worked hard. He had made some money from bananas and bought a truck on credit. Subsequently, he bought a second truck, which he used to transport bananas on "banana days" (when the fruit was collected and taken to the boxing plants) and converted into a "bus" with benches on the remaining days. He then built a concrete-block house on land directly in front of his home, which he rented out, preferably to "white people." His son helped him with his bananas while he drove the truck; one of them was training to be a carpenter and hoped to find work in Roseau. Augustine was negotiating to buy some land on which he wanted to build some "tourist homes." In another village, a retired police inspector and his wife ran the main shop, which was the hub of local social and political activity. His trucks took people to Roseau to shop. He owned two fishing boats and received a share of the catch from each. A third individual had concentrated on improving his banana yield, and he had been so successful that he was held up as a model to all peasant growers in the Windward Islands. He was well known for his excellent banana husbandry and the good quality of his fruit. He owned his own transport and had improved the roads to his land.

Rodgers and Morris (1971, 245) carried out a study of vocational specialization in sixty-five communities in Dominica in 1969. While all of the communities contained peasants and almost three quarters of them contained teachers, a sizeable number also had shopkeepers, agricultural labourers, drivers, nurses, and fishermen. Although teachers and nurses are government-salaried occupations and thus are not directly products of banana production, the large number of shopkeepers and drivers is a more direct result of the impact of cash from bananas. Rodgers and Morris do not distinguish between part-time and full-time occupations and the fact that the majority of Dominicans attempt to diversify their economic resources as much as possible by juggling a number of different occupations. Nevertheless, the number of people identifying themselves as drivers in this survey attests to the impact of bananas on the occupational structure of the local community.

These changes also affected large landowners. The nature of banana horticulture was such that most Dominicans preferred working for themselves to working for someone else, and they did so.[9] This exacerbated the labour shortages that have existed since emancipation.[10] As a result, large landowners tended to underutilize their land, sometimes considerably so. Large acreage was therefore not consonant with land-based prosperity. For example, in 1972, one owner of a 300-acre estate, inherited from his father, worked only ten acres, employing three men and three women, whom he found "lazy." He "went out of bananas," finding them unprofitably because of the cost of labour. Another individual managed a 1,000-acre company estate, of which only 650 acres were cultivated "because we can't get enough labour." A third inherited 150 acres from his father in 1947. He worked 95 acres of it, of which only 8 were in bananas; he concentrated on citrus because it required less labour and was less prone to wind damage.

Besides affecting the village dwellers and the larger landholders, banana production also affected Roseau. In 1920, Franck (348–9) described the town as "scarcely more than a village ... It is so small that all its business is carried on within plain sight from the steamer deck, though it strives to look important with its few two story stone buildings ... The highway up the valley lasts a bare three miles before it dwindles to a mountainous trail that struggles constantly upward." Some thirty years later, Pope-Hennessy (1954, 12–13) had little to add: "Roseau is a shack town of unpainted hen-coop houses made of shingles and roofed with patched and rusted corrugated tin ... The Town limits of Roseau stop in a simple and endearing suddenness. There are no suburbs and virtually no slums." In the aftermath of the banana boom, a middle-class suburb, Goodwill, sprang up; in 1972, it had a population of 4,940. A large number of the houses in Roseau are of concrete. The government has been involved in "slum clearance" programmes in the Elmshall and Newtown areas. The population has increased, and now Greater Roseau accounts for approximately 25 per cent of the island's population.

There was one hotel on Dominica in 1920, but by 1970 there were five in or close to Roseau and another two at a distance from it. There were also five guest houses in the town. In the early 1900s, the major merchant enterprises were chemists, general dry-goods stores, and hardware stores (see MacMillan 1912, 401). In 1973, there were two large supermarkets, one of them air-conditioned, and shops specializing in clothes, electrical appliances, shoes, travel, insurance, printing, cameras, cars, ice cream and drinks, books, and records. There were also a few small production enterprises – grass-mat and basket making, soft-drink manufacture, baking, ice-cream production, fruit canning, a poultry business, two laundries, and so on.

The group to benefit most conspicuously from the expansion of the retail sector generated from increased cash flow was the Syrians. "Syrian" is an emic generic term used in the Caribbean to describe individuals whose families originated in the Middle East, either in Lebanon or Syria. The majority of Syrian families in Dominica came from around Tripoli, Lebanon, but had been in Surinam before coming to Dominica. In all cases, Syrian families were originally from villages rather than towns, and Dominica was seen as the terminal point of their migration. Two Syrians said that they would eventually like to return "home," and in several cases money was sent to the old country and communal family land was still reckoned as available to them there. But the general impression was that, in fact, these individuals discounted any real possibility of returning to

Lebanon and considered Dominica their home. Economic problems and land pressure in Lebanon had induced the migration initially, and there was no improvement in these conditions to warrant their return.

The Syrians arrived in Dominica over about a seventy-year period, with the earliest settling in Dominica around the turn of the century and the latest in the mid-sixties. Although they exhibited a certain mutual support and shared ethnic identity, each family was expected to make its own way. This resulted in a relatively wide range of economic "successes," both within and between Syrian families. Their success lay in their hard work, their business acumen, and their readiness to branch into different fields. All three of the most successful Syrians expanded their businesses in the sixties. One built a large supermarket, a hotel, and a new garage, where he operated the island's Volkswagen and Peugeot dealerships. He laid his success clearly at the door of the banana industry. As he put it, "What bananas meant for me was that suddenly trucks were coming to town and leaving town loaded with beds and chairs, with tables and propane cylinders. The store was crowded with people." Another Syrian's sons had each pursued a different career: one started a soap and copra factory, another an electrical supply store, and a third a supermarket. A third Syrian family ran a Ford car dealership and a grocery store. All of them profited from the cash flow that bananas generated.

The banana boom also positively affected the traditional mulatto merchant enterprises, but to a lesser extent than their Syrian competitors. Their pattern of responses was different from the Syrian and Dominican entrepreneurs. In the case of old-family mulatto enterprises, the banana boom led to the consolidation of the various family firms, but not to their diversification. The profits they gained from peasant purchases in the capital were used much more conservatively to bolster the existing line of business.

Finally, the banana industry drew the Amerindians back into a peripheral relationship with the market. In fact, some of the most productive banana lands were on the Carib reserve. The Carib took up this cash crop and became recognized as efficient banana producers.

THERE MAY BE some debate over economic explanations for the abolition of slavery, but the social and economic impact of the decline in the value of sugar on Dominica cannot be denied. Profits from sugar had been the major component for metropolitan centring in the Caribbean, and a drop in the value of this commodity at the centre inevitably altered relationships both between the centre and the periphery and within the periphery. This increased the level of unpredictability in Dominica. Planters had to recentre their world, and they did this by selling out, declaring bankruptcy, or seeking an alternative commercial crop. Some found the last in limes, a product that was not as labour-intensive as sugar, but was of interest to a metropolitan-based company. Order was restored by the remaining planters, based upon the traditional role of monocrop exploitation and export to the metropole, where, again, the major profits were realized. However, such an economy is very vulnerable to both disease and metropolitan market fluctuations and when the lime industry collapsed, so did the Dominican economy. The entropic effect of this kind of centring exercise is that it denudes the economy of other viable resources and reduces alternatives. Meanwhile, during this period, the Dominican peasantry were largely immune from the disordering effects of this situation, being largely removed from the metropolitan periphery in their diversified subsistence, peri-island villages.

A major social and economic change occurred in Dominica when bananas were reintroduced in the early fifties and Geest Industries took over marketing them. The metropole targeted the Dominican peasantry, and banana production was quickly adopted by small-scale peasant operators through most of the island. It drew both the peasants and the Amerindians back into contact with the centre, and with a cash, capitalist economy. This diversion of the flow of peasant resources toward the metropole had an important reordering effect on the island. The social structure of Dominican villages changed with the introduction of a more complex intermesh of local relationships and new dimensions of social inequality into the villages. It brought about divisions in the island, between banana producing and non-producing areas (the north is more suitable than the south), and it increased competition for resources. It permitted the merchants in Roseau to expand their businesses considerably and increased their profits. But it also peripheralized both the merchants and the banana producers as it brought them into a system that was organized and controlled from abroad.

One forum where Dominicans attempted to resist this peripheralization was the DBGA, which was created to represent the interest of local growers and became an important locus of Dominican attempts to influence the banana-growing enterprise on the island. The DBGA used various strategies to "rationalize" banana production, such as creating centralized boxing plants, increasing its own complexity

and size, and the like. Although these changes were designed to
further the interests of the local growers and create a more predictable environment within which to operate, they most benefited the
players at the metropolitan centre, specifically Geest Industries and
the British consumer. Moreover, these schemes further peripheralized the peasant growers by reducing their profits because they had
to bear the costs of these strategies.

The metropolitan political context within which these events took
place is important. After the Second World War, power relations in
the world system shifted. Competition between East and West
became embedded in the ideological oppositions of (autocratic)
socialism and (democratic) capitalism, and Caribbean territories took
on a new strategic importance in this confrontation. There was a
metropolitan need to guarantee political stability in the region, and
the creation of a peasant-based banana industry in Dominica was
part of a larger strategy to counter the infiltration of communist
sympathies. This pattern of creating an order in Dominica to arrest
the centring strategies of another metropole was not new, but the
continuation of a component of Dominican history that had existed
for almost two centuries.

In sum, banana production was a centring strategy orchestrated
from the metropole. Its aim was to co-opt the peasantry and generate a more complex social order in the island. This produced a
wider base for local efforts to centre the periphery and to create a
new order in their interests. Such efforts have proved ineffective: the
Dominican order has remained dependent on the metropole. However, although economic independence has not been achieved, the
development of political autonomy has made some progress. This
will be discussed in the next chapter.

9 Democracy: Bringing Decision Making Home

> What is significant about these elections is that for the first time members of the labouring classes made their presence known directly in the political system.   Singham 1967, 135

> But the various colonial areas were not dominoes responding to some inevitable "historical tidal wave of nationalism" any more than the European governments had a set response to every colonial challenge whatever its nature. Nationalism in each case had its local pedigree and its own internal tensions composed of unique constellations of class, ethnic and regional alignments. So, too, different governments in Paris and London acted in noticeably different fashions. In this sense, there were multiple decolonizations, whose discontinuities, ambiguities, and uniqueness must be respected, however much they interfere with the desire to reduce history to a crystalline pattern, to discover a single formula which makes sense of its complexity. Smith 1978, 101–2

THE CARIBBEAN CONTEXT

As the world system developed, metropolitan centres found that they could obtain Third World resources through the economic structures that had emerged, and that the need for costly administration of their colonies was no longer necessary, efficient, or desirable. Thus, the metropolitan powers were ready to divest themselves of their colonies, and they took advantage of local efforts to centre peripheries to rid themselves of the administrative responsibility for them. Sometimes, as was the case of Dominica, this involved a staged withdrawal process in which internal government was relinquished but external and defence portfolios remained with the metropole.

The first half of the twentieth century found the British Caribbean territories as a whole still tied economically to the production and export of sugar, despite the previous half-century's tremendous reduction in sugar-producing estates, from about twenty-two hundred, in 1838, to about eight hundred, at the dawn of the twentieth century, despite the attempts of some territories to diversify – Guyana into rice, Jamaica into bananas and, later, bauxite, Trinidad into petroleum. "Until the Second World War the fluctuating fortunes of the sugar industry remained the chief barometer of the general economic condition of the English Caribbean" (F. Knight 1978, 175).

This situation worsened with the Great Depression: sugar prices plummeted further; foreign labour markets in the United States, Cuba, and Panama closed; wages all but disappeared; and there was large-scale unemployment, and increasing poverty and malnutrition. In 1935, "nearly half the wage-earning population of Jamaica obtained only intermittent employment and both government and private employers adopted the policy of 'rotational employment' – a worker worked for a fortnight and then was discharged to make way for another ... The Barbadian labourer was fed worse than a gaolbird; he could not afford milk in his tea ... The daily consumption of fresh milk in Kingston, Jamaica ... was one fifteenth of a quart per head" (Williams 1970, 446, 450, 451). Local attitudes, in this period, moved slowly from a disgruntled colonialism to a vibrant nationalism. There were bursts of protest, expressed in riots and labour unrest, throughout the Caribbean from 1919 to 1929 and from 1935 to 1938. There was support for radicals such as Marcus Garvey and Sandy Cox, in Jamaica, and A.A. Cipriani, in Trinidad. Labour unions sprang up, spread rapidly, and became the bedrock for the formation of political parties. After Bustamente's Labour Party won the elections in Jamaica in 1944, able labour leaders followed him elsewhere – Bradshaw in St Kitts, Adams in Barbados, Gairy in Grenada, Williams in Trinidad, and Jagan and Burnham in Guyana.

THE INTRODUCTION OF TRADE UNIONISM
IN DOMINICA

Although Dominica hosted the Roseau Conference in 1938, at which Caribbean leaders, concerned with socialist and labour issues, discussed regional nationalism, Dominica itself was not going through the same political questioning that was occurring elsewhere in the Caribbean. This was not because economic conditions were better. When the Moyne Commission visited Dominica, in 1938, it was particularly struck by the wretched conditions it found there: "Of all the British West Indian Islands, Dominica presented the most striking contrast between poverty of a large proportion of the population, particularly in Roseau, the capital, and the beauty and fertility of the island" (Moyne Commission 1945, quoted in Cracknell 1973, 91).

While the situation in Dominica did not give rise to a militant nationalism, trade unionism did emerge. The Moyne Commission, which had been given the mandate to investigate the social and economic conditions of the British Caribbean territories, suggested, in its report, that the Dominican middle class should see no further constitutional changes until conditions were improved on the island. At the same time, it recommended that legal obstacles to the formation of unions be removed.

One Dominican, who spoke before the Moyne Commission, took advantage of the new possibility to create trade unions. This was Christopher Loblack, a stonemason for the Public Works Department. Grell goes so far as to suggest that Loblack "was responsible to a large extent for the Commission's decision to remove legal and legislative barriers to worker organization and demonstrable protest" (Grell 1976, 191). On 11 January 1945, Loblack, with R.E.A. Nicholls and Austin Winston, formed the Dominica Trade Union, the first on the island.[1] Within six months, it had twenty-six branches spread around the island (see Honychurch 1984, 173). At about this time, the Dominica Workers Association was founded in the north of the island, and within four years the Union of Teachers was registered. Although the trade-union movement in Dominica did not spearhead a move toward democracy and autonomy, it was to play an important role in shaping the political evolution of Dominica, once democratization was introduced by the metropole, becoming a mechanism for local Dominicans to attempt to centre their world through control of the local political process.

UNIVERSAL ADULT SUFFRAGE

Universal adult suffrage, representing the first step by Britain in divesting itself of colonial responsibilities, was introduced in Dominica in 1951, at about the time that bananas were beginning to integrate peasants economically into the wider society and ensure the continuation of a centre-periphery relationship between Britain and Dominica. Universal adult suffrage incorporated the peasants into the wider local political process just as they were about to be embedded in the wider metropolitan market. The impetus for both banana production and democratization came from the metropole's centring interests.

It is, perhaps, not surprising that the possibility of adult suffrage was viewed by influential Dominicans with apprehension. They were unenthusiastic at the prospect of the mass of the people being able to exercise political power. A newspaper headline of the time read "Dominicans do not need adult suffrage" (*The Chronicle* 5 April 1950, 5). The editorial criticized Britain for thrusting adult suffrage on an unready people rather than paying attention to the nascent banana industry. The local social élite expressed concern at the thought that the mass of the people would be able to select their leaders. The peasants, who were just entering the cash economy, were indifferent to the issue. Thus, the political changes being introduced emanated from abroad and were not a response to local pressure.

Democracy dawned in Dominica as the island's economy began to depend on peasant banana exports. As noted in the previous chapter, this was a period when new social groups were emerging with local interests to defend. The Dominica Banana Growers Association was created to manage the industry in the interests of Dominicans. Local merchants, who were profiting from the cash brought in by bananas, sought to defend their business interests. Syrians and new Dominican entrepreneurs began to compete very successfully with the traditional mulatto élite in the mercantile sector. As for the latter, many of their estates had fallen into decline and their economic base had eroded, although their better education and traditional status continued to provide them with influence in the society. There had been a white exodus from Dominica, beginning with the collapse of the lime industry, which continued until few whites remained on the island, principally transient "experts" belonging to some form of aid programme or other. The Carib reserve turned out to be on prime banana lands, and Amerindians, like their fellow peasants, were drawn into the metropolitan periphery as they turned wholeheartedly to banana production. These were the social groups that were to participate in the new democracy.

Britain envisaged the Westminster political model for its colonies in the West Indies. Within a short time after the end of the war, "each territory had a more or less established two-party system, and a number of able, popular eminent politicians" (Knight 1978, 179). In Dominica, however, the introduction of the franchise led initially to a period of "no-party" politics (Thomas 1973, 164 ff). Thus, from 1951 to 1957 a series of *ad hoc* candidates, rather than political parties, contested the elections. Individuals who were considered wealthy or who were influential in their localities held office, but often only for a single term (see table 11). The electorate quickly demonstrated its democratic expertise: it dismissed those whom it regarded as working in their own interest rather than on its behalf, and rewarded those it considered its champions with re-election.

This pattern is evident in the election returns. *Bourgeois* (mulatto élite) and *gwoh bougs* from Roseau were elected once and then defeated, whereas people from the community, who were perceived

Table 11
Number of Votes for Selected District Candidates in Elections, 1951–57

District	Candidates	1951 Votes	1951 %	1954 Votes	1954 %	1957 Votes	1957 %
Roseau N.	Jules	358	32.0				
	Winston	717	64.0			109	11.0
	Boyd			145	15.5	217	21.8
	Ducreay			751	80.6	651	65.3
Roseau S.	Baron	553	48.3	697	60.0		
	Charles, L.					271	23.3
	Dupiguy	287	19.3			154	13.2
	James	226	15.1				
	Royer	125	8.4	125	11.3		
	Harris	688	46.2	395	35.8		
Eastern	Alfred	596	28.0	159	7.1		
	Didier	542	25.5	919	41.2	1,165	52.2
	Laville			852	38.2	985	44.2
Western	Henry					912	31.4
	Charles, J.	847	29.2	1,352	48.0	605	20.8
	Allfrey					562	19.4
	Jeffers	1,242	42.8	197	7.0		
Southern	Fontaine	602	22.1				
	St Luce	959	35.3	1,618	62.4	1,139	43.2
	Pemberton			912	35.2	645	24.5
Northern	Laville	778	39.8	1,470	85.4	1,628	58.5
	Telemaque	591	30.3			469	26.6
Portsmouth	Douglas	1,607	55.0	1,917	67.4	1,250	43.6
	Bertrand	321	11.0	753	26.5		
	Leblanc					1,347	46.9
Northwestern	Prosper	967	35.4	638	25.5	766	31.6
	Shillingford	1,512	61.7	1,383	55.3	1,053	43.4
Total Eligible Voters		23,288		23,835		23,343	
Number of Votes Cast		17,680		16,746		17,634	

Source: Dominica, Report on the Legislative Council General Elections, 1951, 1954, 1957.

either as empathetic or as locally important, were re-elected. Pemberton, Winston, Boyd, Harris, Charles, Baron, and Douglas, considered part of the first group, had single terms as elected representatives. For instance, Pemberton, an estate owner, was seen as wealthy, and this initially favoured his election. His dislike and handling of squatters on his land, however, led to his defeat in the next election. R.B. Douglas was the natural choice for election in his area the first time around – he owned the boats that provided the only contact between Portsmouth and Roseau, as well as the largest store in Portsmouth and the largest local banana plantation. But the second time around, he was unseated by a charismatic agricultural extension officer who spoke patois when he campaigned – Edward Leblanc. The next stage of political development was to occur when political parties were introduced.

PARTY POLITICS IN DOMINICA

Party politics was born in 1955, when Phyllis Shand Allfrey, then residing in Britain and strongly influenced by Fabian socialism, formed the Dominica Labour Party with her British husband, Robert. In 1956, the Allfreys returned to Dominica after a twenty-year absence and, together with Christopher Loblack, the trade-union organizer, worked hard to convince the electorate that their party had the peasants' and workers' interests at heart, despite Allfrey's colour and background. In her words, they keyed the masses to the term "labour." Theirs was an unlikely alliance. Allfrey was a planter-writer from an upper-middle-class white Creole background, and Loblack was a coloured ex-mason in the Public Works Department, from working-class origins. The political ideology of their party was socialist-humanist, with no pretension to radical revolutionary change.

In response to the challenge from the newly formed Labour Party, a group of middle-class political independents, already holding political office, banded together to form the Dominica United People's Party (DUPP) under the leadership of Frank Baron, who had been an elected representative in 1951. The 1957 general election saw the two parties face off and heralded the fractious and volatile factionalism that marked subsequent Dominican politics. The Labour Party was soundly defeated in the 1957 general election, with Allfrey herself suffering personal defeat in the Western District at the hands of the local favourite, Elkin Henry. Though a competent leader, Allfrey could not match Baron's charisma and the energy he put into organizing his party prior to the election. In addition, many labourers who worked for middle-class employers were threatened with economic reprisals by their employers if they voted for the Labour Party.

In 1956, the British parliament passed the Act Constituting a Federation of the West Indies, and elections were held for the House of Representatives in March, 1958, along party lines. Matters were very different in this election: Labour enjoyed a landslide victory in the federal elections in Dominica. Allfrey won her seat and Leblanc was runner-up (see table 12). Several factors may explain the Labour Party's success. First, many notables and elected members did not run because they believed that the confederation would fail. Secondly, some non-labour supporters encouraged Allfrey's victory because they believed that, should she be elected, she would have to leave the island, which would weaken the Labour Party's organization and they would be better off in the next national elections.

Table 12
Electoral Returns in the Federal Elections of 1958

Representative	Party	Votes Cast
Allfrey	Labour	9,345
Bellot	Labour	1,836
Leblanc	Labour	8,968
Lestrade	Independent	1,101
Lockhart	DUPP[a]	1,492
Royer	DUPP	975

Source: Dominica, Report of Federal Elections, 1958.
[a] Dominica United Peoples Party.

Under Baron, a major change in the island's constitution was negotiated which broadened the scope for local decision making and paved the way to internal self-government. As Chief Minister, Baron replaced the administrator as head of the Legislative Council. New ministries and a number of constituencies were created. When the confederation failed in 1962, Allfrey returned to Dominica. She found that Leblanc, who had resigned his federal post to contest the local elections, had become powerful. There was a serious difference of opinion between the two: Allfrey advocated changes within the colonial structure, while Leblanc advocated a more radical break with the metropole and greater independence from the Dominica Trade Union. In the 1961 elections, Allfrey misjudged her support, challenged his leadership, and lost. She and the faithful Loblack were dismissed from the party. The Labour Party won the next election by a ten-to-one margin. The composition of the party started to change as certain professionals aligned themselves with Leblanc. The most significant new members of the party were the Armour brothers – Jenner and Ronald – lawyers from an important landed professional family in the north of the island.

No cohesive ideology underlay the genesis of the DUPP, which had been organized merely to preserve the interests of those already in political office. When four members of the government resigned in 1961, the DUPP was soundly beaten by the Labour Party, led by Leblanc. After a weak attempt to contest the 1966 elections, Baron resigned and the DUPP evaporated; some members formed the short-lived National Democratic Movement, while others aligned themselves with an emerging new party, the Freedom Fighters, discussed below. In effect, no opposition party existed between 1961 and 1968 (see table 13).

In 1968, an address to the Roseau business community on the underlying problems in Dominica at the time hinted at communist infiltration of the island. This speech was reported in the "As It Is" column of the Dominica Herald as serious criticisms of the govern-

Table 13
Election Returns for the Labour and Opposition Parties, 1961–70

Party	1961		1966		1970	
	Votes	%	Votes	%	Votes	%
Labour	807	60.5	1,067	60.0	1,256	57.8
Opponent	321	24.0	461	26.0	755	34.7
Labour	912	39.0	1,374	53.3	1,417	48.5
Opponent	843	36.1	1,075	41.7	1,254	43.0
Labour	743	34.5	1,199	49.5	924	35.0
Opponent	872	40.4	1,036	42.8	923	35.0
Labour	179	13.3	969	66.8	977	63.6
Opponent	564	42.7	418	28.8	353	23.0
Labour	492	30.9	728	44.3	528	29.0
Opponent	512	32.1	918	55.9	1,144	62.8
Labour	329	24.9	705	55.0	729	52.7
Opponent	485	36.6	542	42.3	539	39.1
Labour	1,149	64.2	1,397	72.3	616	28.2
Opponent	453	25.3	425	22.3	758	34.8
Labour	941	77.8	976	75.8	851	62.4
Opponent	214	17.1	248	19.9	472	34.6
Labour	707	56.9	1,193	84.5	942	65.0
Opponent	422	34.0	153	10.8	267	18.4
Labour	759	51.0	1,190	76.5	1,030	65.8
Opponent	588	39.1	86	5.5	423	27.2
Labour	830	47.0	937	45.8	607	29.1
Opponent	636	36.0	693	33.9	1,214	58.1

Source: Dominica, *Report on the General Elections*, 1961, 1966, 1979.
Note: In 1961 and 1966, the opposition party was the DUPP; in 1970, it was the Freedom Party.

ment. The government reacted by deporting the person who had made the speech and passing the Seditious and Undesirable Publications Act in an attempt to muzzle media criticism. A group calling itself the Freedom Fighters sprang up in Roseau in reaction to what it perceived as the imposition of unwarranted Draconian measures. The group, consisting mainly of urban upper-class merchants and professionals and supported by religious leaders, succeeded in getting the government to rescind the act.

Shortly after this, five members of the Freedom Fighters won seats on the Roseau Town Council. The government feared that it would lose control of the capital and proposed to dissolve the Council. The Freedom Fighters organized a rally, prevented some ministers from entering the House of Assembly, illegally entered the House themselves, and disrupted the proceedings. Eugenia Charles, a Roseau barrister and the daughter of renowned local entrepreneur "millionaire" J.B. Charles, organized a fund in defence of those who were indicted in this incident. A solid opposition, representing largely the interests of Roseau and the business community, crystallized. After the incident, the Freedom Fighters disbanded, but some core members, led by Eugenia Charles, formed the Freedom Party to contest the 1970 elections. The party included Phyllis Allfrey and Christopher Loblack, who joined it to oppose the very party they had created, now led by Leblanc.

The context of these developments was the decolonizing strategy of Britain, whose declaration of universal adult suffrage provided a new resource for which local forces competed. This created a new form of unpredictability, as individuals and groups profited from local outcomes, but the overall political relation of Dominica to the metropolitan centre changed little. In 1967, however, Dominica was declared an associate state. Britain formally retained control over only defence and foreign policy – the portfolios, incidentally, that most reflected the traditional metropolitan-periphery relationships.

The 1970 election, the first to be held under Dominica's new status, was accompanied by a crisis. Shortly before it was held, three ministers in the Labour Party were dismissed, ostensibly for conspiring to overthrow the leader, Leblanc. The more likely reason is that they were concerned at the growing importance of Ronald Armour in the Party and his influence over Leblanc. The dismissal caused a party split. Leblanc retained his supporters, formed the Leblanc Labour Party, and won easily over the faction led by Ducreay, who then formed the Dominica Labour Party, and over the newly formed Freedom Party.

The political parties in Dominica were beginning to reflect different interest groups in the society, and the elections were becoming a major contest between these interests. Half of those who won seats for the Leblanc Labour Party, for example, identified themselves with agriculture or labour backgrounds and with the rural areas in which they ran (see table 14). There were now clear working-class and locality links to the political leadership of the government: the Minister of Agriculture was a farmer from Delices; the Minister of Home Affairs was a farmer and union organizer from Portsmouth; the Minister of Communications and Works was a trade-union organizer from Roseau; the Prime Minister was an ex-agricultural inspector from Vieille Case. These people were all of reasonably humble backgrounds and had received little formal education. The clear exception was the barrister, Ronald Armour, who was the youngest of five brothers, all professionals, whose father had been a medical doctor from Trinidad residing in the north of Dominica. There were also H.L. Christian, an ex-teacher and social

Table 14
Winners of the 1970 Elections by Constituency, Occupation, Origin, Party, and
Percentage of Votes

Winner	Constituency	Occupation	Origin	Party	Vote (%)
P.R. John	Roseau N.	Trade Unionist	Roseau	LLP[a]	57.8
R.O.P. Armour	Roseau S.	Barrister	Both	LLP	48.5
E.T. Shillingford	Western	Tailor	Country	LLP	35.0
E.O. Leblanc	N. Western	Planter	Country	LLP	63.6
A. Moise	S. Western	Planter	Country	DFP[b]	62.8
H.L. Christian	Eastern	Pensioner	Country	LLP	52.7
W.S. Stevens	N. Eastern	Pensioner	Country	DLP[c]	34.8
T. Ettienne	S. Eastern	Farmer	Country	LLP	62.4
J.L. Royer	Northern	Peasant	Country	LLP	65.0
E.A. Leslie	Portsmouth	Planter	Country	LLP	65.8
R.S. Fadelle	Southern	Planter	Country	DFP	58.1

Source: Dominica, Report on the House of Assembly General Elections, 1970.
[a] LLP=Leblanc Labour Party
[b] DFP=Dominica Freedom Party
[c] DLP=Dominica Labour Party

worker; Eustace Francis, a coloured lawyer of humble origins in
Grand Bay, who was speaker of the House of Assembly and the
editor of the government paper, The Educator; Victor White, chair-
man of the DBGA; Waddi Astaphan and George Karam, prominent
Syrian merchants; and Charles Maynard, a lawyer, ex-civil servant,
and co-director of Astaphans Stores, also of humble origins. This
party received scant support from gwoh bougs and Roseau merchants.

The Freedom Party represented a different set of interests and
came from different roots. The leader, Eugenia Charles, was a
successful businesswoman, with a law practice and shares in the
Fort Young Hotel, in Dominica Construction, and in estates. This
enabled her to be accepted by and to represent the interests of the
local mulatto élite. Prominent members, along with Phyllis Allfrey,
were Rupert Sorhaindo, the youngest of four brothers with professional occupations (the eldest brother was the island's gynaecologist;
the second eldest was Financial Secretary in the civil service; the
third eldest brother was an optician in Roseau); and Stanley Fadelle,
an "old family" merchant. Thus, the opposition reflected the traditional merchant and professional class in Roseau and the non-
banana-growing areas of the south of the island.

EXPANSION OF THE CIVIL SERVICE

These political changes were accompanied by the expansion of the
administrative arm of government – the civil service. The number of
civil servants in Dominica rose from 929, in 1950, to 1,832, in 1970 (a

97 per cent increase), while the population increased from approximately 50,000 to 70,000 (a 40 per cent increase) (see Dominica Estimates, 1950, 1970). Sixteen of the new positions were at the upper levels of the bureaucracy (permanent secretaries, chief technical officers, heads of departments), and their substantial salaries had to be met from taxes wrung from a mass of subsistence cultivators and a small urban merchant middle class.

Besides being expensive, this development often led to hostility between a better-educated bureaucracy and the ministers to whom they reported. As Singham (1968, 13) observed, "One of the consequences of this type of constitutional order, particularly in the stage of partial self-government, is that it has intensified the tensions between the bureaucracy and the legislature ... in small, agrarian colonial societies these tensions become especially acute." There were also strains between the old top civil servants, who had arrived at their positions largely through experience and "good family" background, and the new top civil servants, who were often from more humble backgrounds but had university degrees. Finally, there was the difficulty of professionalizing a civil service in a small-scale society where the notion of bureaucracy is not well developed and the bonds of kinship, school friendships, and locality intrude on the impersonal role of a bureaucrat.

Despite these problems, the civil service provided needed white-collar jobs in a society some of whose young persons were earning university degrees. The role of youth in the politics of this period is important and will be discussed shortly. It is ironic, however, that government became the major avenue for employment for a radical group of educated youths who inveighed against it but had obtained their position through the administration's education policies, which promoted university education.

DEMOGRAPHY

Dominica had maintained a relatively stable population in the past because of considerable amounts of emigration.[2] Retrenchment on immigration worldwide changed this, and the brutal restriction of this avenue has created a new demographic situation in Dominica (Chardon 1971, 1), following the classic form for developing countries. The World Health Organization and similar bodies have very effectively lowered the death rate through improved health care, training, and medical facilities, but have done little to slow the birth rate. The result has been an extremely youthful population, a factor which itself tends to compound the birth rate.

A comparison of Dominican age structure from 1946 to 1980 (see table 15) shows that the number of people under fifteen years of age has almost doubled, creating an age structure in which 50 per cent of the population is under fifteen. Given a birth rate of 38.5 per thousand in 1968 and the number of live births by age of mother in 1969 (see table 16), then it appears that 43.2 per cent of births for 1969 were to women below the age of twenty-five. This provided a firm base for rapid population expansion, pointing to a doubling in twenty-five years. However, table 16 also reveals a substantial decline in the birth rate in the 1970s, which qualifies the above conclusion. The general fertility ratio for Dominica in 1960 was 214.4; in 1981, it was 161.2 (*Population Census* 1980–1981, vol. 3, 44).

These figures indicate a 17.5 to 18 per cent population increase in the seventies and eighties, compared with a 5 to 10 per cent increase in the nineteenth and early twentieth centuries (see Smith 1972, 128). Such figures have important implications for education, social services, and the overall economic and political prospects of the country. In 1970, 5.9 per cent of those over fifteen years of age had received no education, 83.6 per cent had attended primary school, 9.2 per cent had attended secondary school, and 0.8 per cent had attended university (see table 17). This youthful population also had altered the proportion of dependent young people in the population, producing a higher dependency ratio (see table 18).

These trends affected employment opportunities. A comparison of statistics for 1960 and 1970 indicates a drop in employment from 37.5 per cent of the population to 26.8 per cent. (These figures, however, do not include self-employed banana growers, whose numbers had increased significantly since 1960.) This population distribution put stress on housing: in 1960, for instance, there were 337 cases of thirteen or more people living in one room and 1,908 cases of ten or more living in one room.

While these demographic trends had important implications for the social and economic outlook of the country, they also had important political implications. A very large percentage of the electorate of the new associate state were young, and they were open to new ideas.

THE RADICAL YOUTH MOVEMENT

Although the labour Party relied on the votes of a successful peasantry, the demographic profile of the island clearly indicated that youth formed a sizeable cohort of potential voters. Government emphasized an education policy that focused on the extension of

Table 15
Age Structure of Dominica, 1946–81

Year	Under 15	15–44	45–64	65+	% Population under 15
		Age			
1946	18,437	20,305	6,618	2,252	38.7
1960	26,800	21,611	8,207	4,511	43.8
1970	34,118	22,543	8,687	4,101	49.1
1981	29,406	29,701	8,908	3,661	39.8

Sources: 1946 West Indian Census; 1960 Eastern Caribbean Population Census; 1970 Population Census of the Commonwealth Caribbean, vol. 6; 1980–1981 Population Census of the Commonwealth Caribbean, vol. 3.

Table 16
Live Births by Age of Mother, 1969

	Under 15	15–19	20–24	25–29	30–34	35–39	40+	Unknown	Total Births
Live Births	10	467	682	494	312	236	112	381	2,694

Source: Demographic Yearbook, Special Issue (1979), 40.

Table 17
Population Fifteen Years and Over by Highest Level of Education, 1970 and 1981

Year	Total	Pre-School	Primary	Secondary	University	Other
1970	35,430	19	29,616	3,261	278	163
1981	24,471	1,494	18,889	3,847	95	131

Sources: 1970 Population Census of Commonwealth Caribbean, vol. 6, 16–19; 1980–1981 Population Census of Commonwealth Caribbean, vol. 3, 27.

Table 18
Percentage of Population under Twenty Years of Age
and Dependency Ratio, 1946–81

Year	Under 20 Years (%)	Dependency Ratio
1946	48.5	768.5
1960	53.6	1,050.1
1970	60.6	1,223.8
1981	52.5	1,028.5

Sources: 1946 West Indian Census, Windward Islands; 1960 Eastern Caribbean Population Census; 1970 Population Census of the Commonwealth Caribbean, vol. 6; 1980–1981 Population Census of the Commonwealth Caribbean, vol. 3, p. 8.

educational opportunities. Most of the policy was directed at primary-school expansion, but of considerable political significance were the monies devoted to post-secondary education. Financial awards were made available for Dominicans to go to university or pursue other programs abroad. Thus, significant numbers of young Dominicans pursued post-secondary education abroad, where they were exposed to radical political ideologies, especially on the University of the West Indies campuses. These individuals raised their aspirations but saw little chance of fulfilling them in Dominica, whose social structure could not accommodate many specialists – by 1972 all the medical specialties on the island, for instance, were filled by Dominicans. There were virtually no openings for university graduates outside of teaching and the civil service, and when university graduates took these jobs, their potential was usually underutilized. These persons formed a young educated category critical of both government and opposition, and of neo-colonialism in general. They had been exposed to, and some adopted, the more radical centring ideas of black power. The Movement for a New Dominica was formed to give voice to this youthful sector of Dominican society. It constituted a radical opposition to both parties, which, in turn, viewed it with concern.

Black power became an ideological force in Dominica in 1970, under the leadership of Hilroy Thomas, a teacher at St Mary's Academy, one of the denominationally run secondary schools in Roseau. Thomas had successfully petitioned government for more support for schools. The heads of the schools were perturbed, fearing that the government was manoeuvring to take them over. Thomas tried to create a secondary-school teachers' association to further press government, but he was dismissed from his post, ostensibly for not wearing a tie. He left the island for "further studies." In 1972, the movement regrouped under Julian Johnson and Gordon Moreau, both of whom had been to university. It adopted a name – the Movement for a New Dominica (MND) – and organized a series of summer seminars on such topics as decolonization, black power, the church, the press, economic dependence, slavery and social stratification, the disturbances at the House of Assembly, and the like. The thrust of the talks was to generate public interest in restructuring the society, and this was presented as the MND's required goal.

The leaders of the MND were, as indicated, university students or graduates, many from humble backgrounds. Most, though not all, were male. They represented the interests of educated youth in a context of heightened expectations but limited occupational opportunity. Their social goal was the overthrow of the élite and "the collective ownership, control and development of Dominican land and financial resources for the collective development of all Black People of Dominica" (Douglas 1974, 35–6).

The movement involved more than mere rhetoric. In August, 1972, Atherton Martin, a young Dominican recently returned from

Cornell University with a master's degree in agriculture, was employed as a manager on the CDC plantation at Castle Bruce.[3] He refused to carry out the request of the general manager to lay off fifty-three workers on the estate, ostensibly on grounds of financial exigency. He was fired. The village of Castle Bruce immediately rallied to his support. Martin organized several village meetings and proposed that the village approach government for a loan to purchase the estate. After many meetings, the proposal was accepted, and Martin became something of a hero. The estate was divided up on "collective" lines, and local Dominicans took over its ownership and operation.

THE POLITICAL SCENE

By 1972, three interest groups had crystallized on the political scene, reflecting different strategies and resources to centre their world and create the order they considered requisite. First, there were political-interest groups that represented the rural banana-based peasantry located largely north of Roseau, where the better banana lands were to be found. They were supported by a new group of merchants in Roseau whose financial success was the result of the banana industry and had occurred within a single generation. Second, there was a largely non-banana-based peasantry in the south, which felt that its interests were insufficiently regarded by the Leblanc government (which represented banana interests), and the traditional mulatto merchant class in Roseau, which felt that the new political leaders were upstarts and lacked the leadership characteristics to govern adequately. Finally, there were unsettled young people who saw limited local opportunities for their growing aspirations and blamed the neo-colonial situation for the ills of the country. Each group showed a healthy suspicion of the other. There was also evidence of brewing conflict between the legislative and administrative arms of government, the latter represented by the powerful Dominica Civil Service Association.

What is evident in these developments is that the old guard of anti-colonial, anti-metropolitan protest was bypassed by the political developments of the mid-twentieth century. As one *mulatre* informant commented, "All our work was for nothing. Look who we have in power today. People with no education and no manners!" Bananas and the vote provided new resources for the mass of Dominicans to try to centre their world. In the process, old suspicions and animosities, between classes and colours, between rural and urban dwellers, carried new significance in determining the outcome of political decision making. At this time, in the 1970s, the traditional "good families" of the mulatto élite felt that they were a beleaguered remnant of a more influential past. Not only did the economy no longer need their estate, but they no longer had the ear of administrators, and their access to important civil-service positions was being short-circuited by the appointment of younger university graduates. From being the leading edge of Dominican protest against the metropole as they had been in the late nineteenth century, they now found themselves resented, ignored, and relatively powerless as political decision making was brought back home. If there was a group that felt even more alienated from current developments, it was the very small handful of long-term resident whites. The closure, in 1973, of the Union Club, which had been created as a coloured alternative to the "white" Dominica Club, and the opening of the latter's doors to ex-Union Club members symbolized the end of an era, the demise of what they had stood for. The typical centring strategy of these groups was to look backward to a better past, and to hunker down to pursue business as usual, as if nothing had changed. This strategy created intergenerational tensions with their children, however, who feared that the marginality of their parents would translate into a sparse-looking future for themselves.

Finally, paradoxically, while the mass of Dominicans were exercising their freedom by choosing to embed themselves in market-orchestrated relations, there was a political movement, on the part of young people hostile to all forms of political and cultural dependence, to sever completely the ties of metropolitan domination. They considered the extant political leaders to be merely neo-colonial puppets in the theatre of metropolitan interests. The Movement for a New Dominica was an affiliate of the Rastafari movement, which "carried with it a certain continuity from the days of slavery, a continuity of resistance and confrontation with white racism. The Rastafari movement, in all its contemporary manifestations, challenges not only the Caribbean but the entire Western World to come to terms with the history of slavery, the reality of white racism and the permanent thrust for dignity and self-respect by black people" (Campbell 1987, 1). Unlike the peasantry, however, Rastas rejected the two-party system and, instead of participating in the political game, they sought to create their own culture, a new Caribbean identity, in political independence that mirrors the ex-slaves' quest for economic independence at emancipation. They were the ultimate political expression of bringing decision making back home "a desperate call for an alternative counterculture more suitable to the needs of black people in these times" (Forsythe 1985,

62). The Rastafari ideology built on the racism that had permeated the slave experience. As Walter Rodney (1969, 39) articulated their ideas, "Colour had become important because the white man found it convenient to use racialism to exploit the black peoples of the world. As Africans, we will use the question of race to unify ourselves, and to escape from the oppression of white men and their black lackeys."

IN THE WORLD system that emerged with Western industrial society, the entropic effects created by the centre on its extensive periphery fed back to the centre. The metropole experienced increasing costs in trying to administer its colonies. Eventually, the growing costs of holding an empire together began to be felt. To alleviate this situation, Britain began to divest itself of its colonial administrations, and Dominica was one of many territories where it dismantled the political order it had put in place. The decolonization of Dominica, like emancipation, can be seen as a decision by the centre that was thrust on the periphery. For many on the periphery, this appeared to mark a new era of self-determination and local decision-making potential. The problem was that the aspirations and expectations among Dominicans were hard to fulfil from their marginal, peripheral position in the world system.

The processes of democratization and decolonization in Dominica produced new sources of unpredictability as the old order for political decision making was removed. In this political void, various individuals, then interest groups, and, later, formal political parties tried to centre their world by seeking political office and attempting to create order in the face of receding metropolitan administration. The result was a volatile period. Factions emerged within parties, parties expelled individuals, new parties were formed on the eve of elections to accommodate differences of opinion within the party, with some parties surviving and others not. Political activity reflected a kaleidoscope of territorial, colour, class, and generational interests.

The changes permitting Dominicans to use the political process occurred at a time when, economically, the mass of the people were being pulled more fully into a capitalist system centred in Britain. The cost of their newfound affluence was loss of the control over their own economic destiny, something they had had as subsistence growers. The political changes leading to greater independence from Britain had virtually no effect on the continued economic peripheralization of Dominica. While Dominicans appeared to have achieved much greater freedom to choose leaders and make decisions, they remained as embedded as ever in metropolitan-centred networks to satisfy their growing needs. Thus efforts to centre the periphery continue, but are never realized, as the ability to make decisions and control the flow of information and resources is constantly thwarted. The control and flow of resources is essentially out of the island to centres in the world system outside – where the decisions are made that determine the nature of the Dominican order. As we have seen, such an order is fragile and continuously generates high levels of uncertainty and unpredictability. What has happened in Dominica since 1972 is the subject of the final chapter.

10 Four Hundred and Eighty-Five Years Later: Independence?

Each great period of science has led to some model of nature. For classical science it was the clock; for nineteenth-century science, the period of the Industrial Revolution, it was an engine running down. What will be the symbol for us? What we have in mind may perhaps be expressed best by a reference to sculpture, from Indian or pre-Columbian art to our time. In some of the most beautiful manifestations of sculpture, be it in the dancing Shiva or in the miniature temples of Guerrero, there appears very clearly the search for a junction between stillness and motion, time arrested and time passing.
Prigogine and Stengers 1984, 22–3

Physical changes were quickly evident on my return visit to Dominica in 1984. There was a new airport at Canefield, just north of Roseau, that made access to the capital from outside the island far easier. Major road projects were being financed and operated by the three major aid donors to Dominica, USAID (United States), CIDA (Canada), and ODA (Britain), and there were considerably more cars and many mini-vans being used to transport people to and from the villages around the island. An offshore medical school was located near Portsmouth, and a prosperous suburb was emerging near Mahaut, north of Roseau. Patois, which seemed so widespread during my fieldwork in 1972–3, having been legitimized by Premier Leblanc, was now often talked of as a threatened language. Children were not learning it and were speaking English (Creole) in the schools.[1] Many shells of buildings for industrial or office use had been built on the outskirts of the capital, but were vacant. In general, there seemed to be more activity and, indeed, more people. But the Geest boats and the banana trucks plied their trade as usual. What had really changed in Dominica?

POPULATION

The total population of Dominica according to the 1981 census was 73,795, and the population density was 108.3 per square kilometre. If one compares a breakdown of the populations of 1970 and 1981, there are some interesting developments. There appeared to be greater unemployment in 1981: 66.1 per cent of males and 31 per cent of females worked in the week before the 1981 census, down from 76 per cent and 34 per cent, respectively, for 1970. However, if the overall population increase is taken into account, the figures reflect a fairly stable employment picture (see *1980–1981 Population Census of the Commonwealth Caribbean*, 3: 13–15). A breakdown of the occupational grouping of the economically active population reveals two significant sets of figures: a near-doubling of clerical occupations, from 8.9 per cent to 15.5 per cent, and a drop in agriculture and related occupations of almost 10 per cent, from 29.7 per cent to 20.4 per cent (*1980–1981 Population Census of the Commonwealth Caribbean*, 3: 23), although agriculture remains the major source of employment, involving approximately 44 per cent of the male work-force and 20 per cent of the female work-force.

The population per square kilometre of cropped arable land was 488, and the GNP was $60 million US (Basic Statistical Data on Selected Countries – with populations of less than 5 million – 1984). According to the Chief Establishment Officer, who very kindly compiled these statistics for me in 1984, there were twenty-three senior civil servants, excluding five specialist medical officers, and seventeen medical officers. Besides an increase in the number of top civil servants, there was an overall increase in those working for government, from 17.45 per cent, in 1970, to 18.55 per cent in 1981 (*1980–1981 Population Census of the Commonwealth Caribbean*, 3: 22).

If one compares the 1970 and 1981 figures regarding households, one finds an increase in the households of under five persons and a decrease in those of over five persons. But the greatest increase in households, some 20 per cent, is of single persons, who account for only 5 per cent of the total population, while households comprising seven or more persons account for 21 per cent of total households and 43 per cent of the population. In the latter year, housing also tends to have more rooms and more amenities.

The 1981 figures reveal a marked decline in marriages, especially among males: 27 per cent of males never marry (up 5 per cent) and 33 per cent of females never marry (up 3 per cent). In contrast, common-law and visiting unions have increased. As might be expected, this has important implications for the formal legitimacy rate. According to the *1980–1981 Population Census of the Commonwealth Caribbean*, 19.9 per cent of the births in the year before the census were in married unions, 23.8 per cent in common-law unions, and 37.5 per cent were in visiting unions. Just over 10 per cent of respondents recorded that they had never had husband nor a common-law partner.

In sum, not only had the population of Dominica grown, but people were choosing to do things somewhat differently. Most significantly, the work force had changed, with a decline in agriculture and an increase in clerical work.

ECONOMY

It was obvious when I visited Dominica in 1984, that hurricanes David (1979) and Frederick and Allen (1980) had wrought severe damage on materials and crops. The wreckage of buildings was still very evident, and forest cover was clearly struggling to recover. Through massive reconstruction efforts and improved fiscal control, the country was recovering economically, and the World Bank predicted a favourable economic-growth potential over the medium term (see World Bank, 1983, 1. This report is cited with the permission of the Minister of Finance, Dominica Government). But while the disasters had stimulated some local construction development and trades, these opportunities appeared to be declining.

The Dominican economy had contracted sharply between 1972 and 1975, and only partly recovered in 1976 and 1977. GDP rose from EC$ 21.1 million, in 1961, to EC$ 37.1 million, in 1970 (Annual Statistical Digest No. 4, table 62). However, the growth rate declined from 6 per cent to 4.8 per cent. The labour-participation rate declined from 77 per cent in the sixties, to 69 per cent (an estimate), for 1980, and the number of young men entering agriculture fell by half between 1946 and 1970 (UNESCO 1981, 4). It should be noted, however, that a great deal of the work that Dominicans do is not of the kind that makes its way into official statistics, since there is still a tendency toward jobbing.

Agriculture remained the basis of the economy, accounting for 31 per cent of the GDP in 1981 (Europa 1990, 882), though there had been efforts to diversify economic activity. Banana output peaked in 1969 and started to decline in 1972 and 1973, fluctuating until 1979 and 1980, when production dropped dramatically because of the hurricanes. It was estimated, based on the two previous years' production, that the island lost approximately 70 per cent of its normal annual crop to hurricane damage, at a revenue loss of EC$ 453.8 million (Prins 1984, xxxix). However, banana production has remained the backbone of the Dominican economy (see table 19).

The banana industry has faced some serious difficulties. By 1984, the number of banana-producing estates had dropped from nineteen to two. Geest completely abandoned banana production and remained involved solely in the marketing and shipping of the fruit,

Table 19
Dominica Banana Growers Association
Export Sales of Bananas

Year	Tons
1961	28,756
1962	28,239
1963	30,738
1964	42,232
1965	49,756
1966	42,919
1967	46,796
1968	54,909
1969	57,677
1970	44,420
1971	38,235
1972	35,610
1973	27,928
1974	30,939
1975	27,117
1976	32,807
1977	30,659
1978	37,866
1979	15,706[a]
1980	7,498[b]
1981	26,943
1982	26,807
1983	28,700

Source: Prins, 1984.
[a] Hurricane David and leafspot epidemic.
[b] Hurricane Allen.

and the government acquired nearly all of the large estates, many as an attempt to forestall violence on them. Successful land reform has been implemented where former estate workers have acquired lands. The industry has become even more peasant-based, which has increased the proportion of fruit produced on fragmented holdings, and thus exacerbated problems of transportation and quality control. In 1983, 90 per cent of the growers sold less than fifteen tons per annum (Prins 1984, i), and bananas were still "the only source of regular cash income in most rural areas" (Prins 1984, 3). Various "rationalizations" were implemented in the banana operation, and these generated unintended negative consequences. In 1971, as already noted, the industry converted from exporting bananas by the bunch to exporting the fruit dehanded and boxed. Even when the boxing plants first opened, they were "relics of the past in the light of present state of boxing plant technology" (Prins, personal communication 1984), and they have not been altered since their inception. The plants created long delays for farmers and heavy pressure on selectors. As well, the poor facilities required more handling of the fruit, which increased the likelihood of damage, and often the lack of adequate water supply entailed inadequate chemical washing of the fruit and subsequent staining.

To solve some of the problems, the farmer was offered a higher price for field-packed fruit. With field-packing, there is less time wasted at the boxing plant and an apparent reduction in the rejection rate. However, this system is expensive in terms of equipment, adequate storage of boxes, transport costs, and labour; it has been estimated that the farmer must produce seventy boxes every time he harvests if he is to make any profit by this method. In 1983, there were only 212 growers who achieved this level of production, and they accounted for 31 per cent of the island's banana output. "In short, field pack [sic] transforms the banana growers enterprise from one essentially simple and risk free – generating a cash income with very little cash outlay – to a full commercial operation which, if it is to be profitably sustained, requires the exercise of more deft skills by the grower than hitherto needed" (Prins 1984, 15). While field-packing produces superior fruit, the programme has to be subsidized by the boxing-plant programme, and the entire extension service is taken up sustaining it. This has led to poor quality and insect control, with the result that insects were found on bananas when they were displayed on the British market. To rectify this, Geest began fumigating the bananas on their arrival in Britain, with the costs of this process being eventually borne by the Dominican peasants. The DBGA received the residual value of the banana (usually between 20 and 25 per cent of the UK retail price), after Geest deducted all costs and profits associated with shipping, ripening, and marketing, but these costs were increasing. Moreover, Geest boats were not carrying completely palletised cargo or maintaining precise temperature controls.

Nevertheless, many Dominicans remain heavily dependent on bananas, and the government has emphasized efficiency and quality in this sector of the economy by developing access to working agricultural lands and improving the road system. Although improving banana production has been part of the government's centring strategy since it attained independence from Britain, in 1978, it also has striven to diversify the economy and become more self-reliant. In 1987, Dominica's external trade was still characterized by imports (EC$ 179.2 million) exceeding exports (EC$ 129.6 million), and the major trading partners are the industrialized metropolitan centres. Imports (in EC$ millions) from the United States total 40.6; from Britain, 24.9; from Japan, 11.0; and from Canada, 7.1; exports (in EC$ millions) to Britain are 38.5.

POLITICS

The political changes in the 1980s, like the economic changes, reflected trends described earlier. Britain relinquished all political control of Dominica on 3 November 1978, 485 years after the island was first sighted by Columbus.[2] This time, however, the decision was made at the request of Dominica, and after considerable discussion and contumely in the country over the constitution and the size and type of parliament. Dominica was the only former British territory that moved directly to republican status, becoming the Commonwealth of Dominica.

These changes occurred in the midst of growing political trouble in the country. As early as 1973, a rift emerged between the administrative and legislative arms of government. In that year, just before the close of my fieldwork, the civil service went on strike over the transfer of a radio announcer, Daniel Caudeiron, to a desk job in the ministry. A state of emergency was declared. A year later, there was more unrest as the youth black-power movement became more aggressive. It was the time of the "Dreads" and the "Four Corner Boys," and of more radical activity from those who had aligned themselves with the Movement for a New Dominica. A white visitor, John Jirasek, was shot dead one evening in a park in Roseau during Mardi Gras. Violence also erupted in Grand Bay during Carnival festivities. Campbell (1985, 47) observes of this phenomenon, "Because the anti-capitalist stance of this force made itself felt in the community, the politicians in the Caribbean who were the transmission belt for Euro-American cultural values were horrified by the Dreads. They perceived Rasta and Dreads as repulsive and subversive, and responded by arresting the brethren and violently attempting to shave their locks." The deputy premier, Patrick John, gained popularity with his tough-sounding radio talks; in July, 1974, he replaced Edward Leblanc, who resigned as premier. But the "Dread issue" continued to escalate. Disaffected youths and intellectuals tried to force a confrontation with government, and the government countered with publication of the Prohibited and Unlawful Societies and Associations Act. In November 1974, a Canadian couple who had retired to Dominica were murdered in their home, and their house was set ablaze.

John won the election in March 1975 on the promise of controlling the Dreads. "Faced with the growing number of Dreads calling for an end of colonialism and neo-colonialism, the Dominican government of Patrick John passed a law giving every citizens the right to shoot, without fear of retribution, any individual suspected of being a Dread who entered the property of the said citizen" (Campbell 1987, 159). John increased the activities of the security forces in combing areas of the island that were suspected of harbouring such persons. The most violent group of Dreads was based in the interior, where maroons had once located themselves, and had similar success in forming an alternate society. In one attempt to flush them out, a member of the Defence Force was shot and killed. This led to the formation of the Dominica Defence Force (DDF), in November, 1975 (see Honychurch 1984, 186ff). Dread activity died down for a while, only to re-emerge with a vengeance at the end of the seventies. Two girls were kidnapped in Portsmouth and held captive for a while; a villager was killed on his way to his gardens in Giraudel, and another at La Plaine. A retired schoolmaster was murdered in Grand Bay.

While John, who had adopted the title of Colonel, was trying to contain these developments, he also proposed a "new socialism" after independence in 1978. To realize this, he promised whole tracts of land in Dominica to a couple of American investors and brought in large numbers of experts. In the view of one commentator, "After independence a new section of society developed, similar to the enclaves which dot the capitals of all Third World states: the Foreign Experts. Ironically the number of expatriates involved in the running of the country after independence rose out of all proportion to those few colonial officials who had served here before" (Honychurch 1984, 199).

John's own roots were in Newtown, a seaside suburb of Roseau, and he surrounded himself with town-based friends, increasingly alienating himself from the mass of supporters of the Dominica Labour Party. He hatched a plan with a Barbadian, Sydney Burnett-Alleyne, a self-declared international mercenary and gun-runner, to create a free port in Dominica. Although this never materialized, Burnett-Alleyne used Dominica as his base for various nefarious plans, including an invasion of Barbados to oust his arch-enemy, Tom Adams, who had become prime minister there. John's popularity declined ever further when it appeared that he and Leo Austin, the attorney general, had sold 45 square miles in the north of the island to a Texan business corporation for creation of a free-port zone. Public protest rose to such a pitch that John cancelled the deal before it took effect. He then faced a new threat from the Dominica Civil Service Association. The government tried to handle this with an amendment to the Industrial Relations Act limiting the right to strike. It also tried, in May of 1979, to amend the Libel and Slander Act to make mandatory disclosure of sources used in newspaper articles critical of individuals in their professional or official capacity.

The result of all this was what Dominicans refer to as "the little revolution." A crowd of some ten thousand demonstrators appeared around Government House protesting the proposed legislation. At first, it was a peaceful scene. But the DDF was called in and sprayed the crowd with tear-gas; when the protesters offered resistance, it opened fire with live ammunition, killing a youth, Phillip Timothy, and wounding some ten others. The government attempted to pass the legislation in the midst of this riot, but the opposition walked out and all trade unions and businesses went on strike until the government resigned. Ministers did resign, starting with Oliver Seraphin. The president, Fred Degazon, fled the country without informing anyone. A consensus emerged throughout the country opposing the continuing government-orchestrated police and military activity. The Committee for National Salvation was formed to press for John's resignation. This led to a multi-party coalition interim government under Seraphin as prime minister, and Jenner Armour as president. It had been operating for only two months when Hurricane David struck, in August 1979.

The Committee for National Survival died with the hurricane, as efforts to handle the devastation consumed everyone's energies. Seraphin tried to consolidate his own power within the interim government by delaying a general election as long as possible, but public feeling, the unions, and other interested parties pressured the government into calling a general election, as promised, and it was set for July 1980. The election was marked by a high degree of vituperation and name-calling, but, on 20 July the country elected the Dominica Freedom Party, led by Eugenia Charles, with 52.34 per cent of the vote, in seventeen of twenty-one electoral seats (Report of the House of Assembly General Elections, 1980).

John, his supporters, and elements of the DDF were outspoken in their opposition to the new government, and Charles's first year of office was dominated by fears for the island's security. She tried to curtail the power of the DDF, first by insisting on an arms inventory (some personnel had been suspected of trading arms for drugs, and some were seen in regular contact with a number of Dreads who operated behind Giraudel, an outlying community of Roseau), and then by disarming and disbanding it. Members of the DDF resisted and tried to make their way into government headquarters, supposedly in an attempt to reach Charles's office, but they were prevented from doing so.

The suspicious activities behind Giraudel increased. The Dreads met in a house that Eustace Francis, the speaker of the house in

Patrick John's government, had owned. The police became particularly suspicious after a co-operative shop was broken into and much of its stock stolen, along with some DDF uniforms. The president of the robbed co-operative was Ted Honychurch, a long-term white Dominican resident and town councillor. In February 1981, a special police squad moved in on the Gomier area and, in an armed clash, two Dread youths were killed. That afternoon, eight Dreads dressed in army fatigues surrounded Honychurch's house, seized him, his wife, his cook, and his gardener, and set the house on fire. They marched their captives into the valley at Beline, released all but Honychurch, and made demands for the release of prisoners. The government refused "to deal with terrorists" and the Dreads executed Honychurch, although this was not discovered until later.

Charles reported that a planned coup attempt by John and some senior DDF officers had been uncovered, and she put the individuals responsible, including John, under arrest. This led to the discovery of an extensive scheme involving mercenaries from the United States and Canada, DDF members, and a group of Dreads. The threat ended when the Ontario Provincial Police arrested two Canadians and US federal agents arrested eight Americans in New Orleans as they were preparing to embark on "Operation Red Dog," along with arms and ammunition, landing craft, and supplies. In October, the nine men involved in the plot in Dominica were bound over for trial in Roseau. In December, in an armed attempt to free John and co-defendants from prison, one policeman was killed and several others injured. A year later, a judge found no cause in the case of John and his co-defendants. The state won its appeal, and in 1983, six of the seven who were arrested in the failed attempt to release John were found guilty and sentenced to hang.

Charles was returned to power in July 1985, winning against a left-wing coalition of the Dominica Labour Party, the United Dominica Labour Party, and the Dominica Liberation Movement. She won fifteen of twenty-one electoral seats, and she won two more in by-elections in July, 1987. A fervent supporter of democracy, she entered the international arena when, in 1983, as chairperson of the Organization of East Caribbean States, she favoured United States intervention in Grenada, where Prime Minister Maurice Bishop, members of his cabinet, and some civilians had been murdered in a power struggle with the country's Revolutionary Government. Her conservative policies reflect a judicious mixture of external aid, self-reliance, and law and order.

In summary, Dominica has emerged, toward the close of this century, as a more complex but still very fragile and turbulent society. Despite the increased freedom to purchase that bananas brought, and the increased freedom to legislate and administer that political independence brought, the term "centring the periphery" still accurately portrays the Dominican experience. Recently, not only has Geest faced increasing financial problems, but the British government has said that it will withdraw protection of Windward Islands bananas on the British market. Furthermore, the demise of the Soviet bloc removes the strategic threat of communist incursions into the Caribbean. Thus, economic and political trends in the metropole make for a highly unpredictable future, as old relationships with a centre are severed in a society whose institutions were established to serve that centre.

DOMINICA, to use Cardoso's distinction (quoted in Hein and Stanzel 1979, 99–100) has moved from a situation of overt political dependence to one of "structural dependence where there is no direct determination of any policies by metropolitan states or companies, but nevertheless an indirect determination through a particular trade structure, through capital movements [and] communication flows." In the wake of waning metropolitan interest, the challenge for Dominica in the future is to create an order for itself in a historical context in which institutions have been generated from abroad.

APPENDIX

Some Additional Facts on Dominica

≈ 50% by 2000

In 1972, there were three "established" churches on the island: Catholic (comprising about 85 per cent of the population), Methodist (about 7 per cent) and Anglican (about 1.6 per cent). There were also eleven small, but growing, evangelical churches, including the Christian Union Mission, the Jehovah Witness, the Seventh Day Adventist, the Pentecostals, the Eli Brethren, and the Moravian Mission, which comprised about 6.4 per cent of the population in 1972 and have continued to attract converts since. In the 1981 census, Hindus (0.02 per cent) and Muslims (0.06 per cent) were counted for the time among Dominican believers.

Education is church-associated. Four of the nine secondary schools on the island are in Roseau, and three of them are church-operated. The Catholics run St Mary's Academy for Boys (fifty-two years old) and the Convent High School for Girls (one hundred and twenty-five years old), and the Methodists operate a girls' school. The remaining secondary schools are government-run; one of them, the Dominica Grammar School, has been in existence for one hundred years. High schools have been opened by the Dominica Government in Portsmouth, in the north, and Marigot, in the northeast. The government's education policy, however, has emphasized primary education. There are some sixty-six government primary schools and three Catholic primary schools. Most of the foreign aid allocated for education has gone to expanding this sector of education, which is offered at no charge. Dominicans place a high value upon education, for it has been a traditional path to upward social mobility. As a result, most of the schools are overcrowded, at both the primary and the secondary levels. There are also a sixth-form college, a teachers'-training college, a technical college, and an extension department of the University of the West Indies. A school of nursing and a school of pharmacy are attached to the Princess Margaret Hospital.

The Princess Margaret Hospital provides a number of medical services for the island; at the time of my fieldwork, all the medical specialists were Dominican. (For a fascinating history of health care on the island, see Clyde 1980.) For health-care purposes, the island is divided into four districts, each staffed by a medical officer. There are two small rural hospitals with varying facilities, but medical care in the rural areas is largely provided by public-health nurses and district midwives. A major change occurred in the late 1970s, when an offshore American medical school was created in Portsmouth, which also has a hospital with approximately fifty beds.

There has been a steady increase in Dominica's population, but it remains underpopulated compared to other Caribbean territories. Its population density was 194 per square mile in 1960 and 258 per square mile in 1970. (Table 20 compares population densities in the Caribbean in 1988.) Nevertheless, the population is expanding rapidly (0.57 per cent per annum), which is putting pressure on institutions such as education. Another characteristic feature of Dominica's population is its African or Euro-African composition. There are very few members of other ethnic groups on the island. In 1960, there were 251 whites, including aid personnel; in 1981, there were 341, most of whom were aid personnel. In 1970, there were 23 East Indians, 2 Portuguese, 68 Syrians, and 1,270 Amerindians; the ethnic composition had changed little by 1981, except for a decline in the number of Amerindians and the addition of four Chinese (*1980–1981 Population Census of the Commonwealth Caribbean*, 1: 104).

Industry is not well developed on the island. There is no forest industry, although "the forest resources of Dominica are incomparably the best among the Lesser Antilles" (Fentem 1960, 19). Dom-Can Timbers, a Canadian lumber company, was given cutting rights to the island's "total forest resources" for twenty-one years in 1967. It encountered serious shortfall problems in production because of difficulties with the terrain (Maximea 1972, 32) and in the process created serious soil-erosion problems (Weber 1973, 198). There has been some attempt to develop a local pumice industry and tourism, but neither have become large-scale employers. Most industry centres on processing agricultural products and is an offshoot of Dominica's reliance on its agricultural base. Agriculture is not

Table 20
Caribbean Islands: Area and Population Density, 1988

Territory	Area (Sq. Km.)	Density
Jamaica	10,991.0	214.5
Trinidad	5,128.0	240.9
Barbados	430.0	593.0
Grenada	344.5	273.2[a]
St Vincent	389.3	289.2[a]
St Lucia	616.3	231.0[a]
Dominica	749.8	108.3
Antigua	441.6	174.6[a]
St Kitts–Nevis	261.6	168.2[a]
Anguilla	96.0	70.8[b]
Monserrat	102.0	116.7[a]
Cayman Islands	259.0	96.1
Turks and Caicos	430.0	30.2

Source: Compiled from Europa World Yearbook 1990.
[a] 1967.
[b] 1966.

composed of large-scale, rationalized enterprises, but is peasant-based. The major crop is bananas, most of which are produced in small peasant gardens and exported to Britain. Citrus is produced on estates, but labour shortages and the sale of certain estates have reduced production and led to the underutilization of much of the small amount of agricultural land that exists on the island. Some of it has been used for housing development; for example, what was once the Bath lime estates on the western edge of Roseau, owned by the British firm Roses, is now a suburb.

Roseau is the capital town of the island, population 8,279 (*1980–1981 Population Census of the Commonwealth Caribbean*, 3:9). In the forties, it was "pretty, simple and innocent, and utterly different in feeling from the sultry, brooding, rather wicked atmosphere that hangs over Fort-de-France. The houses were built like chalets, and some had jutting, pillar-supported gables of trellis work, but most remarkable were the wooden houses built throughout of overlapping dark grey wooden shingles in the style of Bukovina. Little Union Jacks fluttered from carved roof-trees" (Fermor 1950, 99). And the town is still attractive. More recently, Cracknell (1973, 157) described it thus: "With its grey wooden shingled houses, its shuttered windows and wooden balconies, its streams [sic] running in channels down the streets as a necessary precaution to cope with the sudden torrential storms, the town of Roseau has retained much of its old-world charm."

Dominicans are independent and proud. Although they have been under British rule for most of their history, they are largely Catholic and speak a French patois. (There are two predominantly

English-speaking communities in the northeast of the island, Marigot and Wesley.) The women used to wear distinctive costumes and dance the Bellaire and the Quadrille, but these traditions have disappeared. Dominicans have important beliefs, including a belief in *obeah* and both sympathetic and contagious magic, and they use various potions to achieve specific goals and to make sense of their lives. They are also suspicious of others. There is a sobriety about the culture, which exhibits the dimension of peasant culture that Foster (1965) characterizes as the notion of "limited good." They are, however, above all a resourceful people.

Notes

PREFACE

1 As Sale (1990, 4) observes of Columbus's legacy, "It enabled humanity to achieve, and sanctify, the transformation of nature with unprecedented proficiency and thoroughness, to multiply, thrive, and dominate the earth as no single species ever has, altering the products and processes of the environment, modifying systems of soils and water and air, altering stable atmospheric and climatic balances, and now threatening, it is not too much to say, the existence of the earth as we know it and the greater proportion of its species, including the human."

2 Before 1961, the only air link to the outside was a twice-weekly Grumann amphibian aircraft service from the sheltered harbour at Portsmouth, and this was often cancelled because of the weather. A small, five-thousand-foot-runway airport was completed in 1961 at Melville Hall, but the mountainous nature of the island precluded the construction of a runway able to accommodate jets. More recently, the development of short-land-and-takeoff planes enabled a small airstrip to be constructed closer to the capital, and this has become the usual port of entry and exit for the island. A deepwater harbour has recently been completed at Woodbridge Bay, just north of Roseau. Previously, passengers and cargo were carried a half-mile from shore by boat.

3 Using the newer airstrip, planes now have to land parallel to the mountains and the sea, although the mountains are further inland and pose less of a threat.

4 "The mountains of this island are the highest in the whole range of the

Lesser Antilles, the highest peak of Morne Diablotin reaching the height of 5314 feet" (Imray 1848, 257). In fact, it is 4,750 feet (Cracknell 1973, 14).

5 The diablotin is the focus of much superstition and is feared for its eerie call and nocturnal habits. Remorselessly hunted by the French and Creole inhabitants as a delicacy, it was last seen in 1882 and thought to be extinct until a female was found alive but exhausted on a Roseau doorstep in the mid-1950s. It died and none have been sighted since, but they are believed to survive "in the heights."

6 Road-maintenance expenditures for the twenty-year period 1950–70 increased by 1,317 per cent (from $EC 65,425 in 1949 to $EC 927,206 in 1970) while the total mileage of road increased by only 119 per cent (from 203.8 miles, in 1949, to 447 miles, in 1970).

CHAPTER ONE

1 This perspective appears to have arisen independently of Marxian thought and converged with similar structuralist views that were being proposed at about the same time for Latin America by Raul Prebisch and others of the United Nations' Economic Commission for Latin America (ECLA) school. The perspective could easily be linked to Marxian views, despite the possibility that "Marxism in its deeper theoretical aspects is scarcely read, let alone understood, in these former colonies. It is an alien tradition" (Oxaal 1975, 47). Girvan (1973, 25–9), outlining the convergence of Latin American and Caribbean structuralist dependency thinking, hints at a collaboration with African and Asian scholars, specifically Amin and Rodney. However, while the New World Economists "tend to reject the conventional Marxist element ... they make free use of a class terminology adapted from Marx" (Cumper 1974, 469). Whatever the influence of Marx on these writings, it is wise to be aware that "one of the most striking features of many neo-Marxist writers ... is how little they quote from or otherwise attempt to articulate themselves to the classical canons of Marxism" (Foster-Carter 1974, 84).

2 The phenomenon of social differentiation based on colour in the Caribbean would be viewed, in this perspective, as a function of exploitative capitalism.

3 See, for example, Frank's (1967; 1972) discussion of capitalism and underdevelopment in Latin America.

4 Frank took the comments about the propertied class's inability to innovate and extended them to describe Latin American intellectuals. As a radical critic of ECLA, he was "led by the force of his own argument to adopt anticapitalist and ultimately Marxist positions." (Booth 1975, 64).

Amin (1976, 345) argued, similarly, for Africa, "Since the peripheral economy exists only as an appendage of the central economy, peripheral society is incomplete; what is missing from it is the metropolitan bourgeoisie, whose capital operates as the essential dominating force. Because of the weaker and unbalanced development of the local bourgeoisie, the bureaucracy appears to have much more weight."

5 Elsewhere, Wallerstein (1979, 276) says,

Capitalism, overall, has been the more exploitative (that is, extractive of surplus labor) and destructive of life and land, for the vast majority of persons located within the boundaries of the world-economy, than any previous mode of production in world history. (I know this will evoke howls of dismay among many as it seems to go against the grain of the "obvious" expansion of human well-being in the last two centuries. But this expansion of well-being has seemed to be obvious because it has been true of a highly visible minority, largely located in the core countries, and the perception of this rise in well-being has left out of account the populations that have been decimated and pauperized, largely in peripheral zones.)

6 Hopkins et al. (1982, 42) describe the world system in these terms:
The premise is that the arena within which social action takes place and social change occurs is not "society" in the abstract, but a definite "world," a spatio-temporal whole ... This "world-system" has since grown through cycles of expansion and contraction in its geographical scope (and now encompasses the globe), in its productive capacity (capital formation), in its integration as a whole (world-scale interdependence), and in its penetration and organization of social relations ("commodification" and class-formation) ... This arena of modern social action and modern social change has been and continues to be the modern world-system, which emerges in the sixteenth century as a European-centered world-economy.

7 Science, as a mode of thought, was used to dominate nature. Prigogine and Stengers (1984, 32), comment, "Any science that conceives of the world as being governed according to a universal theoretical plan that reduces its various riches to the drab applications of general laws thereby becomes an instrument of domination. And man, a stranger to the world, sets himself up as its master ... Martin Heidegger directs his criticism against the very core of the scientific endeavor, which he sees as fundamentally related to a permanent aim, the domination of nature."

8 The reason for this is that he derives his scheme partly through "a theoretical analysis of functional requirements of societies and partly through an examination of archaeological, anthropological, and historical evidence" (Parsons 1977, 11).

9 Besides the failure of functionalism to account for social change, there
were obvious difficulties in using a scientific approach to understand
social life. Unlike physical scientists, who could usually isolate the
things they wanted to study from their contexts and control them by
bringing them into the laboratory, sociologists could only study the
social world "as if" it were isolated. The period of dominance for
functional reasoning came to an end. Becker (1988, 265) sums it up
when he observes,

> Its most prominent representative, Parsonian sociology, came under
> attack in the sixties and early seventies and subsequently lost its
> overwhelming influence. A few years later the so-called "crisis of
> Marxism" eroded the Marxist functionalist approach, most notably
> expounded by the Althusserian school. In the sphere of methodol-
> ogy, Anthony Giddens observed in 1977 that with regard to function-
> alism "the battlefield is largely empty." Nowadays methodological
> individualism, game theory or as in Marxism, discourse theory seem
> to have filled the place once held by functionalist systems theory and
> "structuralist" Marxism. Even systems theorist Niklas Luhmann
> asserts in his recent work that functional explanation is nothing more
> than the "inquiry" into and "elimination" of functional equivalents.

10 Bloch (1983, 2) observes, "Marx attempted to rewrite the history of man-
kind for the use of the oppressed, so that they would be able to understand the nature of the oppression to which they were subjected, and
how it had come about. For Marx this historical word was also political, because he believed that understanding the workers' condition
through the study of history would enable them the better to fight it."

11 An example of this is the "butterfly effect" discovered by Lorenz
(1979), in which the turbulence produced by a butterfly's wings may be
translated into major weather effects hundreds of miles away.

12 An example of this sort of phenomenon is provided by Robert May's
study of the population biology of gypsy moths (May 1974, 1976; May
and Oster 1976). May was interested in what happened when a population's growth rate passed a critical point. He found that by trying
different values of his nonlinear parameter he could dramatically
change the system's character – not just the quantity of the outcome,
but also the quality. When the parameter was low, May's simple model
settled on a steady state. When the parameter was high, the steady
state would break apart, and the population would oscillate between
two alternating values. When the parameter was very high, the system
– *the very same system* – seemed to behave completely unp[redictably
(Gleick 1987, 70). In other words, in certain contexts, order (a patterned
activity) seemed to generate chaos.

Mitchell Feigenbaum, a scientist at Los Alamos, took May's equation and used the output or solution of one calculation as the input for the next. A predictable order was established that, like May's gypsy moths', bifurcated at apparently unpredictable points. The equation changed qualitatively, but Feigenbaum found that these splittings followed a pattern – numbers were converging geometrically. He discovered a cascade of period-doublings, the splitting of two-cycles into four-cycles, four-cycles into eight-cycles, and so on. As Gleick (1987, 172) observes, "Feigenbaum knew what he had, because geometric convergence meant that something in this equation was *scaling*, and he knew that scaling was important. All of renormalization theory depended on it. In an apparently unruly system, scaling meant that some quality was being preserved while everything else changed. Some regularity lay beneath the turbulent surface of the equation."

13 Mandelbrot was a research-staff member at IBM's Thomas J. Watson Research Center. He used "fractals" (a term he coined to describe irregular, but also fractional and fragmented, phenomena) to investigate the problem of noise in data transmission, and created a workable model out of a new geometry.

14 This perspective is an attempt to bridge the materialist–mentalist gulf that Wolf (1982, 148) argues besets the discussion of culture today:

> The days are over when American Anthropology was unified by a common concept of culture. Mentalists now battle the materialists for order of preference. The materialists cleave to the belief that human affairs are caused by the ways human beings cope with nature. In that struggle, the instrumental means for capturing energy from the universe appear primary, the proliferation of human consciousness as secondary. The mentalist, on the other hand, attract all those who believe in the primacy of Mind, who see humankind as spinning ever more complex webs of signification through autonomous process of the symbolic faculty.

15 Sahtouris (1989) notes that the logical opposite of the Greek term *chaos* is the Greek term *cosmos*. It may be useful to employ these terms, as distinct from order and disorder. Cosmos is a period when order prevails but gives way to chaos, while chaos is a period when disorder prevails but gives way to cosmos.

16 At another level, much human psychosocial development may be seen as centring activity in which an adequate centre (ego) is created and supported by an adequate peripheral social network. The "other" (periphery) is most important in the development of the "self" (centre) (see Mead 1962).

17 For a fuller theoretical discussion of this perspective, see Baker 1993a.

18 For a discussion of this approach, with particular reference to the notions of space and time, see Baker 1993b.

CHAPTER TWO

1 Taylor (1972, 5) observes, "No doubt even before the coming of white men a barter went on between the mainland and the islands. Crescent-shaped ornaments of a gold alloy called *carácuri*, green stone charms, and no doubt certain raw materials and products made of them must have been acquired from the mainland either by war or in exchange for something, perhaps canoes, that the islanders made with greater facility."

2 Taylor (1946, 212) observes, "Like other conquerors before and after them, the Island Carib seem to have begun by imposing a maximum of social change on their erstwhile Arawak wives; only to revert, albeit gradually, to a large part of the culture of the conquered (even in language: all recent Island Carib texts showing a large proportion of Arawak words and forms)."

3 Rouse (1964, 505) states, "Three dates, obtained by radio-carbon method, of about 15,000 to 13,000 years ago have been obtained, two from Muaco, on the coast near the mouth of the Rio Padernales (in Venezuela), and the third from Rancho Peludo, in the Maracaibo basin further west."

4 Some commentators have argued that Amerindians migrated from North America. Neveu-Lemaire (1921, 130), for example, writes, "Pour de Rochefort, le P. Labat et quelques autres, ils seraient venus du pays des Apalaches situé dans les terres avancées de la Floride, auraient gagné l'extrémité méridionale de cette presqu'île et traversé sur leur canots les bras de mer qui les séparait des îles Bahama, qu'ils auraient envahies ... en cheminant du nord au sud, dans toutes les petites îles de l'archipel antillais." [According to de Rochefort, Labat, and others, they would have come by canoe from the Appalachian region inland of Florida, reached the southerly tip of this promontory, and crossed the sea to the Bahamas, which they would have invaded ... They would have proceeded from the north to the south through all the little islands of the Antillean archipelago.] But, he goes on to note, "Le P. Dutertre et plusieurs autres historiens ont émis une opinion diamétralement opposée. Pour eux les Caraïbes des Antilles seraient au contraire venus des Guyanes, car ils ont toujours entendu dire à ces Indiens eux-mêmes qu'ils descendaient des *Galibis*, qui habitent encore aujourd'hui ces régions. Cela concorde avec l'hypothèse, généralement adoptée par les linguistes modernes." [Du Tertre and many other historians have a diametrically opposed opinion. For them, the Carib of the Antilles would have come from Guyana, because these Indians say that they are descended from the Galibi, who are still inhabiting these regions.

This is in agreement with the hypothesis that is generally adopted by modern linguists.] This is the argument presented by Taylor (1972, 3).

5 The remnants of pottery made by these peoples has often been used to document their progress through the Lesser Antilles. Kirby (1975, 19), for example, argues that the migrations took place in a series of waves expanding northward, until each series ran out of momentum, and posits that there were at least three or four series during Meso-Indian times.

6 For a discussion of the source of this term, see Taylor (1946, 180–1), who says that there were four names, with their variations, applied to the Carib: one by themselves, and the other three by their neighbours and enemies.

7 Kirby (1975, 19) argues that they were forced to bypass Trinidad because of its high density of Arawak.

8 This was one of the three main routes open to these early lithic peoples. Several writers have argued that pre-Columbian inhabitants of the Caribbean and northern South America were able sailors (Nicholson 1975, 102; see also McKusick 1960). For example, Nicholson (1975, 102) argues that the pre-Columbian seafarers "had knowledge and traditions built up through having lived on the water for a thousand years, since their start from near Saladero (a riverine context in north-eastern Venezuela). They were not at the mercy of the wind and currents to make chance inter-island passages and new discoveries, as is so often postulated by prehistorians." Thus, the first expansion in the Antilles was a systematic and deliberate one carried out by experienced sailors. As well, their seafaring occurred in the period of the last glaciation, when the sea level was about a hundred metres lower than it is today, and so there were many more islands and the distance between them would have been less. Travel up the Lesser Antilles would therefore have been easier, particularly as changes in winds and ocean currents accompanied the climatic changes and would have forced the stronger trade winds and ocean currents farther south. Haag (1967, 90) argues similarly against the drift hypothesis for the peopling of the Lesser Antilles, but posits that there was probably little difference between the ocean currents in those days and todays: "It is not conceivable that ocean currents now prevailing in the Caribbean and adjacent waters would have been appreciably different several thousand years ago."

9 For a fuller discussion of the creation of such stereotoypes, see Baker 1988.

10 Gullick (1985, 33) observes that the Carib claim that they departed from South America, "where they had been living with the Galibies, to fight the Arawaks who lived in the islands. They destroyed the males and

took the females as wives-cum-slaves. This, they said, explained the existence of male and female languages."

11 On the other hand, Boromé (1966, 32) suggests that when the troops went into the forest to carry off fruit, "the Indians promptly showered them with poisoned arrows."

12 While inspection of a map of Dominica reveals many bays that should be ideal for human occupation, field inspection of these places gives a different picture. "Some areas can be ruled out immediately as unsuitable for habitation sites. These include the entire north coast where high vertical cliffs, and the absence of sheltered bays or of a coastal shelf, made the region formidable and of no value to aboriginal man" (Evans 1968, 94). The two largest bays in the northwest are beautiful, with clear water and sandy bottoms, but they are almost devoid of resources to serve as a food supply. Nowhere are there mangrove swamps. The central part of Dominica contains high, rugged mountains with "superb flora for the botanist, but nothing of use to aboriginal man" (Evans 1968, 96). There remains the wind-swept, surf-pounded, eastern side, which upon first inspection would appear to be even more unsuitable for aboriginal habitation than the rest of the island. However, it is here that the few traces of Amerindian occupation of Dominica have been found. Evans (1968, 94) observes that "as soon as the unfavorable subsistence resources became evident, the Indians apparently moved on to the next island where prospects were better" and indicates that materials gathered from the twenty-four sites examined provide evidence of "three different phases ... spanning a time period from the time of Christ to European contact, sometimes with two different phases represented at the same site: 'Historical Carib,' 'Arawak' and 'Caribbean Saladoid-Barrancoid or Pre-Arawak' habitations."

13 Breton, incidentally, is the only author whose account of Island Carib culture in early colonial times is based on what amounted to extensive field experience, as well as knowledge of the language (see Taylor 1949, 344).

14 Gullick (1985, 71) comments, "The Carib relationship with the French involved almost as many wars as with the British. Despite this they got on much better together. This was in part due to the French readiness to unbend and mix with the Caribs, and provides a good example of courtesy paying off." Unbending and mixing is more likely, of course, if one has settled on their island than if one makes sporadic attempts to set up posts and evict other settlers, which was more the pattern of the British.

15 Elsewhere, Labat (1970, 102) notes, "I also know, and it is quite true, that when the English and French first settled in the islands, many men

of both nations were killed, *boucanned*, and eaten by the Caribs. But this was due to the inability of the Indians to take revenge on the Europeans for their injustices and cruelty, and it was impotent rage, and not custom, that urged them to commit this excess." What is interesting about this statement is the opening line. Usually, the context in which one feels a need to justify "truth" is when it is based upon hearsay – such as the information Labat gathered from the Frenchman he met when he first set foot on the island, who had "fled to Dominica and was living with the Caribs and knew their language and customs as intimately as a Carib would" (Labat 1970, 95).

The term *boucan* connotes a process for drying meat. It was learned from the Amerindians by the Frenchmen who survived in Hispaniola after the Spanish had left to seek riches on the South American mainland, who hunted the wild cattle. From them we get the words *bucanier*, in French and Buccaneer, in English (see Gosse 1931, ix).

16 Incidentally, Breton appears to provide the only first-hand evidence of Carib cannibalism: "At the beginning of my stay in Dominica, my host, Captain Baron, had killed and brought back an Arawak from South America. He had a great drinking party and invited anyone who wished to come. He gave each woman a part of the Arawak to cook in her own pot so that she should eat it with her husband and family who were in the assembly. This they did with great enjoyment during the day. After having drunk and been entertained in their harangues concerning their valor, as night fell they were reeling and their eyes rolled in their heads. They began to sing and dance and howled with such fury and hatred that I was completely terrified" (quoted in Myers 1984, 166–7). Myers (1984, 167) argues that nevertheless most of Breton's account remains hearsay and that there was "enough blurring between oral tradition and eyewitnessed events to make Breton's description less than totally convincing." The account suggests to me, however, that Breton witnessed at least the after-effects of an anthropophagous ritual.

17 Du Tertre accused de Rochefort of plagiarizing his work (even the errors had been copied) (Du Tertre 1667 1, *Preface*). Goveia (1956, 24) observes of de Rochefort, "Despite his protestations to the contrary, not all that he writes can be taken as authentic. His work lacks the fine balance and reliability which distinguishes the achievement of the Dominican [du Tertre]." Nevertheless, de Rochefort tried to ameliorate the image of the Carib in his description. His work was translated by John Davies into English, a year after a revised version appeared in Rotterdam. But, as Moore (1973, 119) observes, "Remarkably, this English edition bears two differing title pages – one beginning *The*

History of the Caribby-Islands ... and the other, *the History of Barbados* ... with the author's name omitted. This indicates responsibility." Whether de Rochefort made these observations is not at all discernible from Davies, who explicitly says that they eat only their archenemies, the *Arougues* (Arawaks): "They carried away men, women and children, whom they brought to Dominico [sic] and St. Vincents [sic]; but it was never heard that they did eat of them, it seems they reserve that cruelty for the *Arougues*" (Davies 1666, 2:323). The only context in which Davies indicates that the Carib make a distinction between Europeans is when he refers to the lack of comparative and superlative elements in their language: "Thus, when they would represent what they think of the *European* Nations which they are acquainted withal, they say of the *Spaniards* and the *English*, that they are not good at all; of the *Dutch*, that they have as much goodness as a man's hand, or as far as the elbow; and of the *French*, that they are as both the arms, which they stretch out to shew the greatness thereof" (Davies 1666, 2:265).

18 The Carib term *poito* was translated by Europeans as "slave," but probably meant "servant" or even just "helper," "assistant," or "follower." In Akawaio and some other Carib dialects on the South American mainland, "*poito-lu* can mean (1) nephew (sister's son); or (2) son-in-law; this is related to the former as in cross-cousin marriage a man's daughter marries her FZS [father's sister's son]. A son-in-law lived metrilocally with his WF [wife's father] and WM [wife's mother] who are also his FZ [father's sister] and MB [mother's brother], and worked in the family unit doing many tasks and thus they are assistants/servants/helpers/followers/sons-in-law/nephews" (Gullick 1978, 283).

19 "Du Tertre tells us that the Dominica Caribs had, by the middle of the seventeenth century, acquired a few Negro slaves, and it is probably with these that miscegenation started" (Taylor 1945, 507).

20 From a Eurocentric perspective, they were portrayed as a remnant Carib population, "buffeted between the British and French, each of whom obtained the aid of the savages in attacks on the other" (Rouse 1963b, 548).

21 "Overall, the disaster to Amerindian populations assumed a scale that is hard for us to imagine, living as we do in an age when epidemic disease hardly matters. Ratios of 20:1 or even 25:1 between pre-Columbian populations and the bottoming-out points in Amerindian population curves seem more or less correct, despite wide local variations. Behind such chill statistics lurks enormous and repeated human anguish, as whole societies fell apart, values crumbled, and old ways of life lost all shred of meaning" (McNeill 1976, 215).

CHAPTER THREE

1 There was still the traditional recognition of attaining political rights through conquest and occupation. In the conquest of Naples by Ferdinand II in 1503–04, the monarch simply took over the territory and completely ignored the Roman pontiff, who was feudally subject to the pope. But as far as new territories were concerned, the Pope had precisely divided North African conquests between Aragon and Castile in 1291 and the lands of the Atlantic between Castile and Portugal by the Treaty of Alvàçovas in 1479, the latter passing into the papal bull of Sixtus IV in 1481. Batlori (1976) argues that John II of Portugal and Ferdinand and Isabella of Spain could have settled the problems arising from Columbus's discoveries without an appeal to Rome. However, because the Spanish monarchs feared that John II might try to use the papal authority, they decided to pre-empt him and approached the pope themselves.

2 Besides bubonic and pulmonary plague (the latter new to Europe in the fourteenth century and particularly devastating) there were leprosy, ergotism, scurvy, chorea, smallpox, measles, diphtheria, typhus, tuberculosis, and influenza, every one of which was potentially deadly.

3 "Columbus did not take slaves with him to America, but he took the idea. He did more than that. As a good Catholic, he took with him the Catholic doctrines of his age, and among them a firm belief that heathen nations, because of their infidelity, had neither spiritual nor civil rights" (Sherrard 1959, 26).

4 Commenting on Columbus's first landing at Guadeloupe, Young (1906, 283) describes his thinking in these terms:

This was the first organized transaction of slavery on the part of Columbus, whose design was to send slaves regularly back to Spain in exchange for the cattle and supplies necessary for the colonies. There was not very much said now about religious conversion, but only about exchanging the natives for cattle. The fine point of Christopher's philosophy on this subject had been rubbed off; he had taken the first step a year ago on the beach of Guanahani, and after that the road opened out broad for him. Slaves for cattle, and cattle for the islands; and wealth from cattle and islands for Spain, and payment from Spain for Columbus, and money from Columbus for the redemption of the Holy Sepulchre – these were the links in the chain of hope that bound him to his pious idea.

5 Moore observes, "The 'discoverer' also declared that he heard some of the indigenous people using Carib and kindred names to indicate powerful enemies whom they feared. Under the influence of the mediaeval mythology and travel accounts he had read in *The Book of Marco*

Polo and Mandeville's *Travels*, Columbus confused such indigenous terms as *caritaba, cariba,* and *caribal* with *canima, caniba,* and *canibal.*" Moore also submits that "Columbus is quoted in his *Journal*: 'And so I repeat what I have said on other occasions, the Caniba are nothing else than the people of the Grand Khan, who must be very near here and possess ships, and they must come to take them captive, and as the prisoners do not return, they believe that they have been eaten.' Such a belief however was false" (Moore 1973, 120–1). (See also Weiner 1920–21, 1: 20 and 43; Winston 1896, 166.)

6 Taylor (1958, 157) argues, "If the hypothesis outlined above should be correct, our 'cannibal' and 'Carib' go back to Arawakan designations describing some tribe or clan as *manioc people.* Had the original name been pejorative, as those applied to foreigners often are, it would not have been widely adopted, as it has been, by the people so designated. And this in turn suggests that those arch-enemies of historical times, the Arawaks and the Caribs, were once close friends, as their traditions indeed relate." It is not even clear that the early Spanish were making "a clear ethnic distinction between the so-called *Caríbes* and other *Indios*" (Escardo 1978, 245). Escardo (1978, 248) argues that "the name *Caribe* was not used in any of the sources referred to with an ethnic connotation, but in a wider sense, meaning a 'daring and fierce people,' 'enemies of the Royal Crown and its subjects' and 'eaters of human flesh.' "

7 Wilson (1892, 270–1) has observed, "The story of cannibalism is a constant theme. To circulate such stories enhanced the wonder with which Europe was to be impressed. The cruelty of the custom was not altogether unwelcome to warrant a retaliatory mercilessness ... Fears and prejudices might do much to raise such a belief, or at least to magnify the habits. Irving remarks that the preservation of parts of the human body, among the natives of Española, was looked upon as a votive service to ancestors, and it may have needed only prejudice to convert such a custom into cannibalism when found with the Caribs."

8 Las Casas, the pope, and even the Spanish sovereign soon abolished slavery in the Greater Antilles and preached improving the Amerindians' condition. But, as Ober (1894, 29) cynically observes, "After the enslavement of the rapidly-decreasing natives of the larger islands was prohibited, it was not surprising to find how many 'cannibals' the Spanish discovered." To strike a compromise, in 1511 Las Casas accepted the argument that since "the labour of one Negro was more valuable than that of four Indians, every effort should be made to bring to Hispaniola many Negroes from Guinea" (Williams 1970, 37).

9 Dr Chanca, ship's physician on Columbus's second voyage, observed that even before the Spanish had met any of the Carib, they hated them

"on account of their cannibalism ... The customs of these Carib people are beastly ... As for the men, they are able to capture, they bring those who are alive home to be slaughtered and eat those who are dead on the spot. They say that human flesh is so good that there is nothing like it in the world; and this must be true, for the human bones found in their houses were so gnawed that no flesh was left on them except what was too tough to be eaten" (Cohen 1969, 135–6).

10 A measure of the lack of Spanish impact on the island may be gained from the fact that Dominica is the only Spanish name appearing on a 1776 map of the island, according to Wesche (1972, 86).

11 Sir Henry Colt, on his passage past Martinique, Dominica, and Guade-loupe in 1631, reported that *none* of the islands was yet occupied by Europeans (Dunn 1972, 7).

12 Some hundred years later, Labat (1970, 95) comments, "When we arrived in Dominica, we met a Frenchman who had committed a murder in Martinique and brought him with us as interpreter. This man had fled to Dominica and was living with the Caribs and knew their language and customs as intimately as a Carib would."

13 Colonel Phillip Warner "was charged with murdering his half-brother and sent home to England for trial, but was acquitted" (St Johnston 1932, 2).

14 In 1751, a prohibition was issued on all foreign trade in the neutral islands, but to little avail. The local residents continued to trade with vessels that had anchored "for refreshment" (Boromé 1967, 21).

15 Elizabeth (1972, 166) rightly observes, "Outwardly, the free coloured formed a racial group that some people have called the 'intermediate class.' The word class should not mislead us, however, for in this in-stance it encompasses various social levels or statuses. At the top were the people whose freedom had perhaps been recently secured but who, by education and way of life, were closely connected with the white aristocracy ... At the foot of the ladder were people whose status was much nearer that of the slaves; some of these had been born in Africa."

16 I have been unable to identify an equivalence for this measure. While *pieds* means feet, its use in the above context is strange, even if used to mean square feet. Boromé does not explain the measure, although he does comment on *fosse* in the same article. It has been suggested, in a personal communication, that it might have been a scribner's error for *pièces*, a measure defined in terms of whatever units the commodity is shipped in – sacks, boxes, casks, bunches, and so on.

17 The British, believing that possession was nine-tenths of the law, were particularly concerned at the evidence of a nascent French administra-tion on Dominica.

18 Many of the French from Martinique were free coloureds; all of the

French seemed an entrepreneurial lot. Indeed, the French administration in Martinique sometimes doubted their dependability in Dominica, and, when they surrendered to the British in 1673, branded them traitors and swore to banish them all to Louisiana once the island had been recaptured (see Boromé 1967, 36).

19 These, after the Amerindians, were the first Dominicans. It was their desire for separation from the French islands that prompted their migration to Dominica and accounted for a spirit of independence that caused the French administration some concern. They created a particular type of social structure based upon resident, small-scale, primary-resource economic activity and a racial mixture. The natural outcome of such a gene pool, given the cultural value of miscegenation of the earlier French Caribbean regimes, was, in time, to produce a largely coloured population. This predominance of French-speaking, Catholic, small-scale coloured entrepreneurs remains the hallmark of Dominica today.

20 One consequence of this was that the Carib retreated farther and farther from the Europeans. "From then [1748] on until the end of the century these two [European] pillars of civilization ousted one another from their respective nests as often as and whenever opportunity offered; and we can well imagine that between them 'the native Indian,' if not exterminated, was driven more and more into the fastnesses of forests and mountains" (Taylor 1938, 110).

CHAPTER FOUR

1 Colbert's l'exclusif with respect to the French territories was the apogee of this approach.

2 Williams (1970, 145–6) notes that between 1764 and 1771, 35,397 slaves were imported to Barbados and 31,897 died, accounting for a net population increase of only 3,500.

3 Klein provides a more complicated picture of the slave trade:
The example of Dominica, I would propose, strongly supports the idea of a mixed or intermediate trade, using either an island as an entrepot, or of vessels coming directly from Africa with one stop at Dominica before proceeding on to Havanna ... That some 16 per cent of the ships were bringing in between 100 and 199 slaves would seem to indicate that possibly a third variant route of the trade existed, that is, a type of mixed venture. Most likely these were ships that were arriving from Africa with the intention of supplying several island markets or were inter-island traders specializing in transporting large numbers of slaves. The fact that 65 per cent of the 293 middle range ships (carrying between 100 and 199 slaves) arrived before 1809, when the trade was still open with the British and

French islands, seems to support the thesis that these middle-rank ships were involved in some manner in supplying several islands. (Klein 1978, 217, 219)

4 Dunn (1972, 21) comments, "This static policy ... was not a sign of English apathy. Quite the contrary. It expressed the protectionist strength of the English sugar lobby."

5 Luke (1950, 127) is incorrect when he states, "The British Government, in order to encourage British settlers to the island, sold the French land in lots." Incidentally, the monies made from the sale of lands to Englishmen was not reinvested in the island, but used "to replenish an impoverished exchequer and was mostly ... to form a dowry for Queen Charlotte" (St Johnston 1921, 4).

6 For an indication of the variability in some of these figures see Boromé (1967, 38), who notes reports on the white population ranging between 600 and 2,020 and those on slaves of between 2,000 and 8,497!

7 Boromé (1967, 16) observes that there were some three hundred free Negroes in Dominica in 1763.

8 Boromé (1967, 38) discusses the varying population figures that scholars have given for this period.

9 Duchilleau, commandant in Martinique, had long seen the strategic value of Dominica for promoting communication between Martinique and Guadeloupe and preventing privateers from having a serviceable base (see Boromé 1969a, 36).

10 Rawley (1981, 120–1) observes, "The Free Port Act of 1766 legalized trade between Martinique and Guadeloupe and nearby Dominica. Almost immediately after acquisition, Dominica became a depot for British slaving in both French and Spanish islands. A contemporary note reads: 'The greater part of the Slaves sold at Dominica were purchased by the French and Spaniards, who paid for them in specie, Bills of Exchange, Cotton and Coffee.' Small French vessels came in great numbers to the two legal ports carrying away slaves left by English and New England slave traders ... Besides the legal trade, which operated under particularized regulations, a contraband traffic along the Dominica coast flourished."

11 Edwards (1819, 1: 434) commented on "the utter disregard which was manifested by the then administration towards the security of this and the other British islands in the West Indies ... It will scarcely be believed that the whole regular force allotted during the height of the war, for the protection of Dominica consisted of no more than six officers and 94 privates."

12 Boromé (1969a, 37) suggests that the haste was, rather, necessitated by the possibility of Admiral Samuel Barrington arriving with three ships of the line and twelve frigates from Barbados.

13 Cracknell (1973, 63) asserts that de Bouille attacked before he even knew of the outbreak of war between England and France. But Boromé indicates that the British were already alarmed at the presence of several foreign Frenchmen "all visiting the acquaintances in Dominica and that Lieutenant Governor Stuart had known of the French declaration of war and their intention to attack Dominica since the 20 August that year" (Boromé 1969a, 37).

14 In September, 1778, Duchilleau created a militia of French inhabitants that consisted mainly of "free Negroes" (Boromé 1969a, 42).

15 Captain John Ward, RN, was appointed governor of Dominica when he was thirty-three, but the English did not formally take possession of the island until 1784, "when the troops marched into Roseau amidst the greatest rejoicings" (St Johnston 1932, 6).

16 Hugues sent a detachment of about three hundred soldiers from Guadeloupe to join forces with the French inhabitants and the maroons and seize the island. They were defeated at Pagua Bay. Hugues then sent over another three hundred men, who were defeated at Colihaut (see Cracknell 1973, 65).

17 St Johnston observes, "The year 1805 was known among the inhabitants for many decades after as 'La Grange Year', and nurses would frighten their little charges with threats of La Grange" (St Johnston 1932, 13).

18 There was one other small incident, in 1806, in which a crew of a small sloop-of-war mutinied and fled to Guadeloupe, where the French general remanned it and sent it back with another vessel to try to cut out British merchant shipping. Both ships were captured by a British man-of-war that happened to be at Roseau (see St Johnston 1932, 13).

19 Marshall suggests that these runaways "founded" the Dominica maroons (Marshall 1982, 34), but Cracknell is probably right in stating that *marronage* "did not begin suddenly in 1763" (Cracknell 1973, 66). Indeed, a group of five hundred maroons were reported in Martinique as early as 1665 (Debien 1973, 108).

CHAPTER FIVE

1 Hatch (1973, 99) observes, "Kroeber speaks of value culture as 'embodying expression or sublimations of play impulses' ... he refers to 'a very strong latent impulse toward cultural play, innovation, and experiment, a true originality and inventiveness' in man" (Hatch 1973, 99).

2 Green (1976, 27) argues, "The whole edifice of British imperial power rested upon deeply held convictions of superiority – superior governing capabilities of the British, the superior culture of the metropolitan country. Britain's vaunted 'civilizing mission' was but one expression

of a profound and pervasive, though often subtle, sense of racial superiority."

3 Europeans did not simply rely on existing structures, however. The Portuguese, for example, actively undermined the structure of the Kongo in order to obtain slaves. They then used Kongo chiefs to extend their trade into the Mbudu Kingdom, south of the Dande River (see Wolf 1982a, 223).

4 Lady Nugent (1966) observed of Jamaica, "In this country it appears as if everything were bought and sold ... The Creole language is not confined to the negroes. Many of the ladies who have not been educated in England, speak a sort of broken English, with an indolent drawling out of their words, that is very tiresome if not disgusting." Edward Long (1754) notes, "Isolated from other whites, with daily contacts limited to slaves and free coloured servants, the Creole woman in particular took on folk speech, diet, and customs, 'gobbling pepperpot, seated on the floor, with her sable handmaids around her ... Her ideas were narrowed to ... the business of the plantation, the tittle-tattle of the parish, the tricks, superstitions, diversions, and profligate discourses of black servants' " (quoted in Lowenthal 1972, 38).

5 Bridenbaugh and Bridenbaugh (1972, 10) describe the early settlers in these terms: "Desire, verging on greed, for land, advancement, rank, and power, as well as desire to participate in the recently uncovered opportunities to exploit tropical soils for the production of exotic staple crops, animated the promoters of the first permanent English colonies begun at St. Christopher in 1624 and Barbados in 1627." Ragatz (1963, 3) further observes, "No considerable body of persons inspired by motives higher than the desire to extract the greatest possible amount of wealth from them in the shortest possible time reached the smiling shores of the Caribbean colonies ... Few landed to establish homes and to raise their station in a new world."

6 Edwards (1819) writes, "In countries where slavery is established, the leading principle on which the government is supported is fear: or a sense of the absolute coercive necessity which, leaving no choice of action, supersedes all questions of right. It is vain to deny that such actually is, and necessarily must be, the case in all countries where slavery is allowed" (quoted in Hart 1980, 89).

7 Mintz (1974b, 49) observes, "It is a commentary on slavery that Caribbean slave populations did not maintain themselves by reproduction. In the most lunatic periods of plantations expansion ... high mortality rates typified the plantation regimen, and the trade could barely keep pace with the proclaimed need for new slaves."

8 "Slave ratios were most meager and runaways most frequent on absentee owned estates" (Lowenthal 1972, 43).

9 Ragatz (1931, 17) wryly comments that government business could be

confounded by the private affairs of such individuals, "as when Mr. Isaacs, the receiver in Chancery, went before his mercantile partner, the master in Chancery, to effect an auditing of their accounts as merchants for wares supplied to estates in his charge and when Mr. Crabb, in his judicial capacity, decided on questions arising out of such a proceeding."

10 The French pattern of settlement also inhibited sugar production. Their "holdings were too small in many cases to make cane-growing a practical proposition" (Goodridge 1972, 154).

11 If we are to believe Goodridge's (1972, 153) figures, the population of Dominica increased significantly in the twenty years from 1730 to 1750, and many of those arriving were slaves. He suggests that, in 1753, Africans comprised some 3,528, or 75 per cent, of the settled population of 4,690. By the close of the Seven Years' War, "it was found that over 6,000 acres were under cultivation upon which were living close to 3,000 Frenchmen, who possessed nearly 6,000 slaves busily occupied in producing coffee, cacao and cotton" (Goodridge 1972, 154).

12 Certainly, the two major players in the abolitionist movement, Thomas Clarkson and William Wilberforce, were not motivated by economic considerations. Clarkson, the son of a clergyman in Cambridgeshire, received a direct revelation from God while riding from Hertfordshire to London. Wilberforce, the son of a rich merchant in Yorkshire who had tired of the fashionable life, converted to "muscular Christianity" and resolved to enter the missionary, but was persuaded by Pitt to stay on in Parliament and gladly agreed to become Clarkson's champion in Parliament for religious reasons (see Mannix 1981, 109–12).

13 In fact, Drescher suggests that the political activity of the free masses in the metropole, with the fifteen thousand abolition petitions to Parliament and the large numbers of signatories, was "a new variable in the history of slaves" (see Drescher 1987, 194, 207).

14 There had been a long-known tension, in Christian Europe, between "the Aristotelian dictum that from the hour of their birth 'some are marked out for subjection' and the awareness that slavery involved the treatment of one's own species as animals" (Anstey 1975, 93). This was thrown into sharp relief by the new values of the French Revolution – liberty, and equality – which argued for the mutability of the social order. Thus, "the more emphasis given to liberty and happiness, the more condemned and isolated did the slave system appear. The emphasis on benevolence and the invoking of the principles of nature and utility were the marks of a growing disposition to effect change in the area of natural, civil and political liberty, by legislative action" (Anstey 1975, 151). These seventeenth-century views were linked, late in the eighteenth century, by evangelical and Quaker thinkers to the concept

of Providence, which spurred them to lobby government to abolish slavery and the slave trade.

15 Williams probably underestimated the growth of the domestic market and overestimated the role that Africa and the Americas played in generating capital for English growth. The home market was important, and English exports to Europe exceeded in value those going to Africa and the Americas in the seventeenth and eighteenth centuries. Williams's thesis may thus be rephrased to suggest not that English industrial development was predicated mainly on the Atlantic trade, but that the Atlantic trade furnished English industrial development with a "principal dynamic element" (Wolf 1982a, 199–200).

16 In some cases, plantations were attacked after emancipation. Jean Rhys, whose grandfather, James Gibson Lockhart, arrived in Dominica from Scotland at the end of the eighteenth century, observes, "It was during my grandfather's life, sometime in the 1830s, that the first estate house was burnt down by the freed Negroes after the Emancipation Act was passed" (Rhys 1979, 25).

17 "Admitting that estates in general sustained damage proportionate to their size, which is a concession on my part, when it is considered that the buildings on larger properties are usually kept in much the best order and repair, and therefore, are the least likely to suffer injury, it is of import to observe that none but the chief could bear the expense of adequately supplying the wants of the Negroes and that, in proportion to the failure of doing so, have distress and misery accumulated" (Lovell 1818, 22).

18 As one commentator observes, "For at least a hundred years after the arrival of the English, the French planters remained numerically and economically superior" (Christie 1982, 42). Thus emancipation may have had a greater impact on the relative status of the French and their descendants.

19 It is difficult to reconcile these developments with Riviere's (1972, 15) assertion that "in Dominica the immense opportunities available for peasant farming allegedly went virtually untested, the majority of ex-slaves showing a remarkable preference for plantation labour."

20 In 1972, a senior civil servant remarked to me, "You know that Dominica is made up of four 'islands' – the north, the south, the east, and the west, and that people are different in each area!" Other Dominicans corroborated this, commenting on the characteristics of people from one area as opposed to another. The origins of this phenomenon lie both in the topography of the island, which for years hampered physical mobility, and in the settlement pattern that developed after emancipation.

CHAPTER SIX

1 As Besson and Momsen (1987, 5) observe, "Both family land and common land are forms of customary tenure in the anglophone Caribbean created in response to the constraints of agrarian relations and their legal codes. These have emerged at the margins of Caribbean plantation society as well as at its core."

2 Although Eguchi (1984, 45–6) states that "almost all peasants in Dominica originated directly from plantation slaves," his diagram on the formation of peasantry on the page following this statement clearly shows the influence of early squatter and yeoman "modes of production."

3 It should be noted, however, that these observations are based on anthropological works using data collected in the last few decades. Their relevance to the historical picture is assumed.

4 Eguchi (1984, 111) observes, "Family land works to secure blood-related relatives from desperate situations if it is necessary."

5 There was an indication from a survey of banana growers carried out by Cynthia Baker in 1971–72 (Baker 1973) that the practice of *coup de main* was being eroded, particularly in the more productive banana areas. It was noticeably more prevalent in the south than in the north, where the better banana lands are situated.

6 Spens states that the community she studied had a low incidence of consensual unions, but that it differed from other areas in Dominica. She also suggests that older women frequently married during their first pregnancies, while younger ones did not. Moreover, the latter appeared to start bearing children younger, but bore more illegitimate children. She is, however, somewhat skeptical of these data (see Spens 1969, 68, 190).

7 On the other hand, Eguchi (1984, 78) indicates that females formed only 28.9 per cent of household heads in Great Ridge.

8 Eguchi (1985, 320) observes that there has been increasing mobility between ranks and that occupation has become "especially critical in changing rank."

9 Eguchi (1984, 76) notes of Great Ridge, "Despite the clearly known history of the village, there is a legend among the villagers which claims that some of the first settlers were Maroons from Cross Plantation."

10 George Gilbert, a planter at Coulibri, reported that about four hundred rebels, armed with cutlasses, sticks, and other weapons, had surrounded his house, broken into it, and destroyed and plundered his property. Similarly, Henry Sorhaindo, another planter, reported that his house had been broken into and valuable articles had been stolen. In

some cases, buildings and crops were destroyed (see *Official Gazette, 1844*, Minutes of House of Assembly and Council, 28 August, 24 September, 15 October, 15 November, 19 November 1844; and Grell 1976, 145–6).

11 Honychurch (1984, 107) puts the date of the Batalie disturbances at 1856. However, he cites no references, whereas Grell (1976, 150) cites the *Dominica Colonist* for 28 January 1854. I would suggest that ownership was probably granted in 1853, for it would have taken some weeks for the information to be relayed to the administrators in Dominica and for them to draw up eviction procedures.

12 There are several discrepancies between the accounts of Grell (1976, 147–52) and Honychurch (1984, 106–7) concerning "The Black Revolt at Batalie" (Grell 1976, 147). Among them, Grell argues that Blackhall attempted to address the people *after* the policemen had failed to evict the villagers. There is also some disagreement over which regiment was involved.

13 Why this was so is not clear. Honychurch (1984, 107) states, "This delayed the Marshal for many days, and when he did eventually reach Batalie he was only successful in arresting three women." Grell (1976, 151) argues that "black resistance made it impossible for the marshal to arrest any of the stipulated Dominicans. Probably out of frustration, the marshal and his agents arrested three black women, for whom no arrest warrants were issued, and carried them back to Roseau."

14 In the process, according to Grell (1976, 152), "homes belonging to the people were destroyed." On the other hand, according to Honychurch (1984, 107), "the police broke one hut and formal possession was taken of the other buildings in order to get the squatters to agree to the conditions of rental and ownership."

15 One suspects that sometimes their readiness to assert themselves in defence of their rights was used by interested parties in Roseau to further their own causes. There were, for instance, the "Religious Riots" (Honychurch 1984, 105) of 1847. The basis for these disturbances lay in the religious structure of the island: the vast majority of the population were Catholic, but a majority of the whites and some of the mulatto élite were Protestant. The Protestant church received an annual dowry from public funds in the island, but the Catholic church did not. The secretary of the Catholics and a member of the House of Assembly, T.R. Lockhart, tried to have this matter redressed in the House. He was vociferously opposed by Falconer, a staunch Methodist, who argued that no church should get monies from the public purse. Lockhart warned that "the Catholic majority would not submit meekly" (Grell 1976, 156). In October, some Catholics who were working on an extension to the cathedral, which is situated next to the Methodist church,

disrupted a Methodist meeting, and the fracas quickly turned into a riot involving some three thousand individuals over several days. The *Dominican* proclaimed that "the island is on the brink of revolution" (*Dominican*, October 27, 1847). Martial law was proclaimed and troops were held in readiness, but the promise to redress the dowry issue seemed to defuse the matter. Nevertheless, the legislature saw fit, the following year, to pass laws specifying sanctions against rioters who tampered with religious property and "molested persons descending from the steps of the United Church of England and Ireland" (Grell 1976, 157).

16 A house and land tax existed only in Roseau, outlying villages, and on the Queen's Chains. Many large landowners lived outside the tax areas. Moreover, merchants, many of whom were relatively prosperous, could avoid taxes by taking out trade licenses (see Honychurch 1984, 108).

17 Income tax was set at 2 per cent on incomes of £50–£100 and 3 per cent on incomes over £100 (see Boromé 1969b, 60).

18 A few weeks before, when the police had tried to stop carnival masquerading, which had exceeded the three-day limit, they had been beaten up and driven back into Fort Young, the police station (Boromé 1969b, 40). In response to this, Haynes-Smith confidentially recommended to the Secretary for the Colonies that Dominica become a Crown colony. In response, a commission of inquiry headed by Sir Robert Hamilton visited the island in November 1893 and recommended some sweeping changes that were not well received in London.

CHAPTER SEVEN

1 According to the figures given by Martin (1844, 284) the white population of Dominica comprised 4.1 per cent of the total population in 1832.

2 There had been squabbles between the Executive Council and the Assembly ever since Britain was ceded the island in 1763. The entire Assembly had refused to bid farewell to the first governor, William Young, at his departure in 1773. Governor John Orde exclaimed, in 1775, "Never certainly were such a set of men got together" (Orde to King, 16 March 1796, CO 71/28). In 1814, Governor Ainslie was appalled at the furious dissensions in the House, and in 1823, the Earl of Huntingdon asked for an immediate transfer "anywhere in the world" (see Boromé 1969b, 26).

3 The first "coloured" Dominican paper started and failed in 1837. No copy is extant of this paper, which was entitled either the *Dominican Standard* or the *Dominican Observer* (see Boromé 1960, 17, n1).

4 Falconer's supporters in the Assembly included "his brother-in-law,

three uncles, a half-brother, and a nephew, who was also the assistant editor of the *Dominican*," together with "two men amenable to Falconer's desires" (Boromé 1969b, 27). Thus, they were known as "the Family Party." Falconer was a staunch Methodist, as were his relatives, so they were also known as "the Methodist Clique" (see Boromé 1960, 13).

5 Much of the acrimonious debate in the House (which became something of a tradition in Dominica) in the previous decade had concerned the qualifications of those admitted to sit in the House. It had passed a bill in 1850 to widen the franchise and increase the numbers of voters and candidates for office by reducing qualifications. At this time, 80 per cent of the population of twenty-five thousand were illiterate. Whitehall withheld assent of this bill until a registry of voters had been compiled that would determine the eligibility of individuals to vote and hold office. Many members of the Assembly opposed this demand, as it was known that some of them had produced fictitious conveyances, temporarily transferred property ownerships to themselves, and held land they had never seen or occupied. This matter was still an issue when Price arrived.

6 This was in spite of a setback in January, 1863. He was forced to dissolve the House on a technicality and contend with a re-elected Falconer, who thundered, "My mission is to crush this House, and it shall be crushed" (Boromé 1969b, 28).

7 Hamilton held seven hearings in Roseau and another seven around the island. He heard from seven elected representatives, six merchants, twelve proprietors or managers of large estates, seven government officials, one magistrate, four schoolteachers, three priests, and thirty-nine peasant proprietors, small shopkeepers, estate tenants, and labourers (Hamilton 1894).

CHAPTER EIGHT

1 Knight (1978, 143) comments that "the Caribbean was not discriminating in its search for laborers, buying them from Ireland, Germany, Portugal, Spain, the Madeiras, West Africa and Japan, as well as India and China."

2 Also in 1930, the United States, "to protect its growing citrus industry, placed a tariff against lime juice imports" (Maguire 1981, 199).

3 For a fuller discussion of this change in attitude by British officials toward the West Indian peasantry, see Lobdell (1988). He argues that there are at least three explanations, including the economic crisis of the West Indies after 1880, the role of the "Colonial Office Mind" in altering attitudes toward the peasantry, and the role played by specific

individuals, particularly Sir Henry Norman and Sydney Olivier (Lobdell 1988, 202–3).

4 A measure of the firm's success is noted by Trouillot (1988, 174, 182) who observes, "Geest Industries made a profit of £3.18 million in 1980 alone ... [and its] payroll of nineteen million pounds sterling was, in 1979, six times more than the total revenues of the Government of Dominica."

5 O'Loughlin (1968, 39) observes, "Before 1950 banana production for export was negligible; in 1955 exports were valued at EC $500,000 and numbered 1.4 million stems. By 1963 they were valued at EC $3,700,000 and numbered 2.5 million stems. This represents a considerable increase in the acreage under this crop; it is estimated to have more than trebled in the past fifteen years. Much of this came from new lands cleared, but probably nearly half was idle land belonging to both peasants and estates which at one time was cultivated but had been allowed to revert to bush."

6 Watty (1974, 54) says that foreigners held 6,630 acres in 1970, of which 5,802 were in thirteen holdings of 50 acres or more. Watson (1974, 54) gives figures of 8,800 acres held under aliens' licenses.

7 Welch (1968, 229) observes, "Dominica has extensive land holdings belonging to entire families or groups of families equal or varying in proportions – a most unsatisfactory form of land tenure."

8 While Dominica yet again became a largely monocrop producer, bananas were significantly different from previous crops with respect to who produced them, a point at least obscured in Riviere's remark, "Production in Dominica, then, is centered around the monocrop culture of bananas *in the same way* that coffee dominated the economy in the late eighteenth and first half of the nineteenth century, sugar the second half, vanillas the first quarters of the twentieth and limes the second quarter" (Riviere 1981, 266–7, my italics).

9 This phenomenon is reminiscent of Weber's description of the agricultural problems east of the Elbe, where workers were motivated to leave their "secure" serfdom for an insecure "free" labour market, motivated by ideals of liberty and self-determination (see Bendix 1962, 22).

10 A parallel concern was expressed by many peasants, who indicated that there was less and less *coup de main* and that people wanted money for their services instead.

CHAPTER NINE

1 Riviere (1982, 369) argues that Nicholls single-handedly brought unionism to Dominica: "In fact, unionism came to Dominica in the nineteen forties through the single-handed efforts of Nichols [sic], an employer,

who is said to have earned the disgust of his class allies for his radicalism and benevolence towards workers." Unfortunately, there is no supporting evidence for this assertion.

2 For a comprehensive study of Dominican migration, see Myers 1976.

3 For a discussion of these developments, see Baker 1978 and Draper 1982.

CHAPTER TEN

1 This substantiates Christie's (1982, 47) comment, "English is spreading to domains formerly considered the prerogative of the Creole; for example, it is being more widely used than formerly in the home and in popular songs composed locally. The Creole, too, has extended its functions in recent years and has come to be used in some radio broadcasting, for example."

2 However, British government aid was part of the independence arrangement agreed upon with Dominica. It is necessary because, first, Geest, as a privately owned company, is the major beneficiary, which inhibits other aid doners from investing in the industry, and, second, "the residual value left to the islands for their bananas by Geests is insufficient to finance the investment needed to modernize the industry as well as meet recurrent costs" (Prins 1984, xlv).

Bibliography

PRIMARY SOURCES

THE BRITISH LIBRARY

The Censuses of Dominica, 1849–1921.

DOMINICA ARCHIVES

Byers' Survey of Dominica, 1835.
Dominica. H.A.A. Nicholls, n.d.
Dominica Almanac 1861, The. London: W.D. Thomson (For C.A. Filan, clerk of Assembly).
Dominica Almanac and Register, The. 1821. W.F. Stewart.
Dominica Blue Books, 1838–40, 1843, 1845, 1847–60.
Dominican, The, 1847.
Dominica Pocket Alamack, The. 1844. George Falconer.
Leeward Islands Almanack, in which is incorporated the Dominica Almanack, The. 1879. Alex R. Lockhart, comp.
Manumission registers, 1783.
Register of Births, Marriages and Deaths.
Register of Land Sales 1756–73.

THE FOREIGN AND COMMONWEALTH OFFICE

2365   Bell, Sir H.H.J. *Notes on Dominica 1903.*

– *Notes on Dominica and hints to settlers*, 1909, 1919.
Cullen, Pearson. *Notes on Dominica*, 1891.
Eliot, E.C. *Broken Atoms*. n.d.
Grieve, S. *Notes on Dominica*, 1906.
Lovell, L. *Present State of Dominica*, 1818.
Nicholls, H.A.A. *Natural Resources of the Layou Flats*, 1883.
Sterns-Fadelle. *Dominica: a Fertile Island*, 1902.
Watts, Sir F. *Soils of Dominica*, 1903.
– *The Boiling Lake*, 1904.
– *Agricultural Conditions of Dominica*, 1925.

OVERSEAS DEVELOPMENT AGENCY

A2228	*Tourist Trade*. 1971.
A2444	Shankland, Cox. *Economic Policy*. 1972.
A2524	Lang, D.M. *Land*. 1970.
A3928	*Water Power Electricity*, 2 vols. 1965.
A4662	Prosser, A. *Social Development*. 1976.
A5224	Thornton, J. *Education*. 1977.
A5979	*Resource Management on Agricultural Marketing*. 1975.
A6499	Paddon, A. *Charcoal*. 1979.
A6871	– *Charcoal*. 1980.
A8000	Lewis, R. *Fruit*. 1975.
	– *Vegetables*. 1975.
A8398	Cronshaw, D. *Bananas: Diseases and Pests*. 1979.
A8671	– *Sigatoka*. n.d.
A8759	Lewis, R. *Land Resources*. 1975.
A8844	Stoneham, J. *Fisheries*. 1975
A9231	Coopers and Lybrand. *Industrialization*.
HC157.D3	*Economic Policy – Development Programme*. 1959–64.
HC157.D3	Campbell, L. *Economic Conditoins*. 1965.
HC160.D3	*Dominica: Economic Conditions*. 1967.
HC157.D5	*Dominica: Economic Conditions*. 1971.

THE PUBLIC RECORDS OFFICE (KEW GARDENS, LONDON)

CO71/	Original Correspondence.
CO72/	Entry Books.
CO73/	Dominica Acts, 1830–1889.
CO74/33	Dominica Minutes of the Legislative Assembly, January 1860–January 1880.
CO75/1	Dominica Official Gazette.

co76   Miscellanea.
co152/   Leeward Islands. Correspondence, Secretary of State, Administrator of Dominica, Despatches, 1903–1934.
co700/1–15   Maps 1765–1907.
co884/6   Land settlement and road construction in St Vincent and Dominica.
co950/490   Pidduck, H.B., 1938. Memorandum on Agricultural Problems, Dominica, for the Royal Commission.
co884/7   Hesketh Bell, Report on Caribs.
co1031/141   Windward – monthly political reports.
co1745–1766/590 Acts of the Privy Council.
                   Minutes of the Privy Council 1844.

THE DOMINICA GOVERNMENT

Annual Overseas Trade Report, 1969.
Annual Overseas Trade Report, 1980.
Annual Report of the Chief Medical Officer, 1983.
Annual Statistical Digest No. 4, 1970–1972, Dominica.
Aspects of Health Care in Dominica, 1984.
Commonwealth of Dominica Natoinal Health Plan, 1982–1987.
Dominica Banana Growers Association Annual Report 1967.
Dominica Banana Growers Association Annual Report 1968.
Dominica Banana Growers Association Annual Report 1971.
Dominica Banana Growers Association Annual Report 1972.
Dominica Development Plan, 1971–1975.
Minutes of the House of Assembly 1823. 1844.
Net Domestic Income, Dominica. 1972.
Official Gazette. 1844.
Report of Committee of Inquiry into Disturbances at the St Mary's Academy.
Report on the House of Assembly General Elections, 1975.
Report on the House of Assembly General Elections, 1980.
1950 Estimates of Dominica.
1970 Estimates of Dominica.
1972 Estimates of Dominica.

CENSUSES

West Indies Census of Agriculture 1946. Barbados: Government Printery, 1948.
West Indies Census of Agriculture, 1961: The Eastern Caribbean Territories. Barbados: The British Development Division in the Caribbean 1967.

1946 West Indies Census, Windward Islands.

1960 Eastern Caribbean Population Census: Windward Island, Dominica. 2 vols. Trinidad and Tobago: Central Statistical Office.

1967 Dominica: Report for the Years 1963, 1964 and 1965. London: Her Majesty's Stationery Office.

1970 Population Census of the Commonwealth Caribbean, vols 4–10. University of West Indies.

1970 Population Census Preliminary Report.

1980–1981 Population Census of the Commonwealth Caribbean, Dominica. 3 vols. Port of Spain, 1985.

SECONDARY SOURCES

Adams, R.N. *Energy and Structure: A Theory of Social Power.* Austin: University of Texas Press 1975.

– *The Eighth Day: Social Evolution as the Self-Organization of Energy.* Austin: University of Texas Press 1988.

Allaire, Louis. "On the Historicity of Carib Migrations in the Lesser Antilles." *American Antiquity* 45 (1980): 238–45.

Allfrey, Phyllis Shand. *Palm and Oak II.* Roseau: Star Printery n.d.

Allfrey, Robert E. "The Story of Indian Warner." *Dies Dominica*, 24–5. Roseau: Government Headquarters, Publication Division 1972.

Amin, Samir. *Unequal Development: An Essay on the Social Formation of Periphery Capitalism.* Translated by Brian Pearce. Hassocks: Harvester 1976.

Andrews, Kenneth R., ed. *English Privateering Voyages to the 'West Indies 1588–1595.* The Hakluyt Society, Series 2, no. 111. Cambridge: Cambridge University Press 1959.

Anonymous (A Resident). *Sketches and Recollections of the West Indies.* London: Smith, Elder & Co. 1828.

Anstey, Roger. *The Atlantic Slave Trade and British Abolition, 1760–1810.* London: Macmillan 1975.

– "Slavery and the Protestant Ethic." In Michael Craton, ed., *Roots and Branches: Current Directions in Slave Studies. Historical Reflexions* 6, no. 1 (1979): 157–72.

Armytage, Francis. *The Freeport System of the British West Indies: A Study in Commercial Policy, 1766–1822.* London: Longman, Green and Co. 1953.

Aspinall, Algernon. *The Handbook of the British West Indies, 1926–1927.* London: The West India Committee n.d.

Atwood, Thomas. *The History of the Island of Dominica.* London: J. Johnson 1791.

Bailey, Kenneth D. "Equilibrium, Entropy and Homeostasis: A Multidisciplinary Legacy." *Systems Research* 1, no. 1 (1984): 25–43.

Baker, Cynthia J. *Some Problems of the Banana Industry of Dominica. An Interim Report.* Swansea: FCO, Overseas Development Administration, and University of Wales 1973.

– *Economic and Social Aspects of Banana Production in Dominica.* Great Britain: Overseas Development Administration 1975.

Baker, E.C. *A Guide to Records in the Windward Islands.* Oxford: Basil Blackwell for University of the West Indies 1968.

Baker, Patrick L. "Ideology and Agrarian Reform: Élite Reactions to Social Change on a Dominican Estate." Paper presented at the Canadian Ethnology Society Conference 1978.

– "Social Differentiation in Roseau: Political-Economic Change and the Realignment of Class, Status Group and Party among Élites in a Caribbean Capital." Ph.D. diss., University of Wales, University College 1982. *—9 years after field work!*

– "Ethnogenesis: The Case of the Dominica Caribs." *América Indígena* 48, no. 2 (1988): 377–401.

– "Chaos, Order and Sociological Theory." *Sociological Inquiry* 63, no. 2 (1993a): 123–49.

– "Spacetime and Society." *Sociological Inquiry* 63, no. 4 (1993b). Forthcoming.

Barbour, Philip L., ed. *The Jamestown Voyages Under the First Charter 1606–1609.* 2 vols. The Hakluyt Society, Series 2, nos 136–137. Cambridge: Cambridge University Press 1969.

Barbour, T. *Third List of Antillean Reptiles and Amphibians.* Bulletin of the Museum of Comparative Zoology, no. 82 (1937).

Batllori, Miguel. "The Papal Division of the World and Its Consequences." In Fredi Chiappelli, ed., *First Images of America: The Impact of the New World on the Old,* 1: 211–20. Berkeley: University of California Press 1976.

Bayley, F.W.N. *Four Years Residence in the West Indies, during the Years 1826–1829.* London: William Kidd 1832.

Beck, Horace. "The Bubble Trade." *Natural History* 85, no. 10 (1976): 38–47.

Becker, Uwe. "From Social Scientific Functionalism to Open Functional Logic." *Theory and Society* 17 (1988): 865–83.

Bell, Herbert, et al. *Guide to the British West Indian Archive Materials, in London and in the Islands, for the History of the United States.* Washington, DC: Carnegie Institution of Washington 1926.

Bell, Sir Henry Hesketh. "The Caribs of Dominica." *Journal of the Barbados Museum and Historical Society* 1 (1937): 18–31.

– *Glimpses of a Governor's Life from Diaries, Letters, and Memoranda.* London: Sampson, Low and Marston 1946.

Bendix, Reinhard. *Max Weber: An Intellectual Portrait.* Garden City: Anchor 1962.

Berger, Peter L., and Thomas Luckman. *The Social Construction of Reality: A Treatise in the Sociology of Knowledge.* New York: Doubleday/Anchor 1967.

Besson, Jean. "A Paradox in Caribbean Attitudes to Land." In Jean Besson and Janet Momsen, eds., *Land and Development in the Caribbean*, 13–45. Warwick University Caribbean Studies. London: MacMillan Caribbean 1987.

Besson, Jean, and Janet Momsen. "Introduction." In Jean Besson and Janet Momsen, eds., *Land and Development in the Caribbean*, 1–9. Warwick University Caribbean Studies. London: MacMillan Caribbean 1987.

Bloch, Maurice. *Marxism and Anthropology*. Oxford: Clarendon 1983.

Bodley, John H. *Victims of Progress*. Menlo Park: Cummings 1975.

Bogat, Raphael. "Dominique terre de refuge." *Société d'Histoire de la Guadeloupe Bulletin* 8 (1967): 79–94.

– "Dominique terre de refuge." *Société d'Histoire de la Guadeloupe Bulletin* 10 (1969): 149–54.

Booth, David. "Andre Gunder Frank: An Introduction and Appreciation." In Ivar Oxaal and David Booth, eds., *Beyond the Sociology of Development: Economy and Society in Latin America and Africa*, 50–85. London: Routledge and Kegan Paul 1975.

Boromé, Joseph. "Charles Gordon Falconer." *Caribbean Quarterly* 6, no. 1 (1960): 11–17.

– "Spain and Dominica, 1493–1647." *Caribbean Quarterly* 12, no. 4 (1966): 30–46.

– "The French and Dominica, 1699–1763." *Jamaican Historical Review* 7 (1967): 9–39.

– "Dominica during French Occupation." *English Historical Review* 84, no. 330 (1969a): 36–58.

– "How Crown Colony Government Came to Dominica by 1898." *Caribbean Studies* 9, no. 3 (1969b): 26–67.

– "Origin and Growth of the Public Libraries of Dominica." *Journal of Library History* 5, no. 3 (1972): 200–36.

Bradford, Ernle. *Christopher Columbus*. New York: Viking 1973.

Braithwaite, L. "Social Stratification in Trinidad: A Preliminary Analysis." *Social and Economic Studies* 2, no 2 & 3 (1953): 5–175.

– "The Problem of Cultural Integration in Trinidad." *Social and Economic Studies* 3, no. 1 (1954): 82–96.

Breton, Raymond. "Dictionnaire Caraïbe–Français, mêlé de quantité de remarques historiques pour l'éclaircissement de la langue; Catéchisme en langue Caraïbe; Dictionnaire Français–Caraïbe." In Abbé Renard, *Les Caraïbes de la Guadeloupe, 1635–1656*. Paris: Librairie G. Flicker 1929.

Brewster, Havelock, and Clive Thomas. *The Dynamic of West Indian Economic Integration*. Mona, Jamaica: Institute of Social and Economic Research, University of the West Indies 1967.

Bridenbaugh, Carl, and Roberta Bridenbaugh. *No Peace Beyond the Line: The English in the Caribbean, 1624–1690*. New York: Oxford University Press 1972.

Bridge, William S. *Roseau: Reminiscences of Life as I Found It in the Island of Dominica, and among the Carib Indians.* New York: Isaac H. Blanchard 1900.

Briggs, John, and David F. Peat. *Turbulent Mirror: An Illustrated Guide to Chaos Theory and the Science of Wholeness.* New York: Harper and Row 1989.

Broom, Leonard. "The Social Differentiation of Jamaica." *American Sociological Review* 19 (1954): 115–25.

Buisseret, David. "The Elusive Deodand: A Study of the Fortified Refuges of the Lesser Antilles." *Journal of Caribbean History* 6 (1973): 43–80.

Bullen, Ripley, and Adelaide K. Bullen. *Archaeological Investigations of St Vincent and the Grenadines, West Indies.* Wm. L. Bryant Foundation, American Studies, Study no. 8, 1972.

– "Culture Areas and Climaxes in Antillean Prehistory." In Ripley P. Bullen, ed., *Proceedings of the 6th International Congress for the Study of Pre-Colombian Cultures of the Lesser Antilles,* 1–10. Guadeloupe 1975.

Bunge, William. "The Cave of Coulibistrie." *Political Geography Quarterly* 2, no. 1 (1983): 57–70.

Burns, Sir Alan. *History of the British West Indies.* London: George Allen and Unwin 1954.

Burns, W.L. *Emancipation and Apprenticeship in the British West Indies.* London: Jonathan Cape 1937.

Burrage, Henry S., ed. *Early English and French Voyages Chiefly from Hakluyt 1534–1608.* New York: Barnes and Noble 1906.

Byers, J. *Plan of the Island of Dominica Laid Down by Actual Survey under the Direction of the Honorable Commissioners for the Sale of Lands in the Ceded Islands.* London: S. Hooper 1776.

Campbell, Horace. "The Rastafarians in the Eastern Caribbean." *Rastafari,* Caribbean Quarterly monograph series. Kingston: University of the West Indies 1985.

– *Rasta and Resistance: from Marcus Garvey to Walter Rodney.* Trenton, NJ: Africa World Press 1987.

Campbell, John. *Candid and Impartial Considerations on the Nature of the Sugar Trade.* London: R. Baldwin 1763.

Campbell, L.C. *The Development of Natural Resources in Dominica.* Institute of Social and Economic Research, series 3. Trinidad: University of the West Indies 1965.

Canon, Jo Ann. "Mating Patterns as Environmental Adaptations in Dominica, British West Indies." Ph.D. diss., University of California 1970.

Carew, Jan. "Columbus and the Origins of Racism in the Americas: Part Two." *Race and Class* 30, no. 1 (1988): 31–57.

Carneiro, Robert L. "The Evolution of Complexity in Human Societies and Its Mathematical Expression." *International Journal of Comparative Sociology* 28, nos 3 & 4 (1987): 111–27.

Carrington, Selwyn H.H. "The American Revolution and the British West Indies' Economy." In Barbara L. Solow and Stanley L. Engerman, eds., *British Capitalism and Caribbean Slavery: The Legacy of Eric Williams*, 135–62. Cambridge: Cambridge University Press 1987.

Carrison, Daniel J. *Christopher Columbus: Navigator to the New World*. New York: Franklin Watts 1967.

Chardon, J.P. *La population d'une petite antille: la Dominique*. Étude et documents no. 11. Pointe à Pitre: Groupe Universitaire de recherches inter-Caraïbes, Centre d'Enseignement Supérieur Littéraire 1971.

Christie, Pauline. "Language Maintenance and Language Shift in Dominica." *Caribbean Quarterly* 28, no. 4 (1982): 41–51.

Clarke, William C. *Notes on the Geography and History of Dominica*. Berkeley: University of California, Department of Geography 1962.

Clyde, David F. *Two Centuries of Health Care in Dominica*. New Delhi: Mrs Sushima Gopal 1980.

Cohen, J.M., ed. and trans. "The Letter Written by Dr Chanca to the City of Seville." In *The Four Voyages of Christopher Columbus*, 129–52. Hammondsworth: Penguin 1969.

Coke, Thomas. *A History of the West Indies, Containing the Natural, Civil, and Ecclesiastical History of Each Island: With an Account of the Missions Instituted in Those Islands, from the Commencement of Their Civilizations; but More Especially of the Missions which Have Been Established in that Archipelago by the Society Late in Connexion with the Rev. John Wesley*. 3 vols. London: A. Paris 1810. Reprint. Cass Library of West Indian Studies, no. 21. London: Frank Cass 1971.

Coleridge, Henry Nelson. *Six Months in the West Indies in 1825*. London: J. Murray 1826.

Columbus, Christopher. *The Journal of Christopher Columbus*. Translated by Cecil Jane. New York: Clarkson N. Potter 1960.

Comitas, Lambrose. *Caribbeana 1900–1965*. Seattle: University of Washington Press 1968.

– *A Complete Caribbeana 1900–1975: A Bibliographic Guide to the Scholarly Literature*. 4 vols. New York: KTO 1977.

Cottrell, Fred. *Energy and Society*. New York: McGraw-Hill 1955.

Cracknell, Basil. *Dominica*. Newton Abbot: David and Charles 1973.

Craton, Michael. *Sinews of Empire: A Short History of British Slavery*. New York: Anchor 1974.

– *Testing the Chains: Resistance to Slavery in the British West Indies*. Ithaca: Cornell University Press 1982.

Craton, Michael, James Walvin, and David Wright. *Slavery, Abolition and Emancipation: Black Slaves and the British Empire*. London: Longman 1976.

Cross, Malcolm, and Gad Heuman, eds. "Introduction." In *Labour in the Caribbean: from Emancipation to Independence*, 1–11. London: MacMillan Caribbean 1988.

Cumper, George E. "Dependence, Development, and the Sociology of Economic Thought." *Social and Economic Studies* 23, no. 3 (1974): 465–82.

Curtin, Philip D. *The Atlantic Slave Trade*. Wisconsin: University of Wisconsin Press 1969.

Davey, John. *The West Indies before and since Emancipation*. London: W. & F.A. Cash 1854.

Davies, John, trans. *The History of the Caribby–Islands, viz Barbados, St Christophers, St Vincents, Martinico, Barbanthos, Monserrat, Mevis, Autego etc. in all XXVIII*. London: Printer by J.M. for Thomas Dring and John Starbey 1666.

Dawe, Alan. "The Two Sociologies." *The British Journal of Sociology* 21 (1970): 207–18.

Debien, Gabriel. "Marronage in the French Caribbean." In Richard Price, ed., *Maroon Societies: Rebel Slave Communities in the Americas*, 107–34. Garden City, NY: Anchor Books 1973.

De Las Casas, Bartolomé. "Spanish Treatment of the Indians." In Roberta Marx Delson, ed., *Readings in Caribbean History and Economics: an Introduction to the Region*. New York: Gordon and Breach Science Publishers 1981.

De Rochefort, Charles. *Histoire naturelle et morale des isles Antilles de l'Amérique*. Vol 4. Rotterdam: A. Leers 1658.

Dookhan, Isaac. *A Post-Emancipation History of the West Indies*. London: Collins 1975.

Douglas, Rosie. *Chains or Change: Focus on Dominica*. Toronto: Committee in Defence of Black Prisoners 1974.

Draper, Gordon M. "The Castle Bruce Farmers Co-operative: Dominica." In Susan Craig, ed., *Contemporary Caribbean: a Sociological Reader* vol. 2, 97–110. Maracas, Trinidad: Susan Craig 1982.

Drescher, Seymour. *Econocide: British Slavery in the Era of Abolition*. Pittsburgh: University of Pittsburgh Press 1977a.

– "Capitalism and Decline of Slavery: The British Case in Comparative Perspective." *Annals of the New York Academy of Sciences* 292 (1977b): 132–42.

– "Paradigms Tossed: Capitalism and the Political Sources of Abolition." In Barbara L. Solow and Stanley L. Engerman, eds., *British Capitalism and Caribbean Slavery: The Legacy of Eric Williams*, 191–208. Cambridge: Cambridge University Press 1987.

Dunn, Richard S. *Sugar and Slaves: The Rise of the Planter Class in the English West Indies, 1624–1713*. New York: W.W. Norton 1972.

– "Dreadful Idlers' in the Cane Fields: The Slave Labor Pattern on a Jamaican Sugar Estate, 1762–1831." In Barbara L. Solow and Stanley L. Engerman, eds., *British Capitalism and Caribbean Slavery: The Legacy of Eric Williams*, 163–190. Cambridge: Cambridge University Press 1987.

Du Tertre, Jean-Baptiste. *Histoire Générale des Antilles Habitées parles François*.

Divisée en deus Tomes. Et Enrichie de Cartes et de Figures Par le R.P. du Tertre de l'Ordre des F.F. Prescheurs de la Congregation de S. Louis Missionnaires Apostoloques dans les Antilles. 2 vols. Paris, 1667.

– "Concerning the Natives of the Antilles." 1667. In Marshall McKusick and Pierre Verin, trans. *Histoire générale des isles de S. Christophe, de la Guadeloupe, de la Martinique et autre dan [sic] l'Amérique,* vol. 4, 1–42. Human Relations Area Files, ST 13, Callinago, 1958.

Early, Eleanor. *Ports of the Sun.* Boston: Houghton Mifflin 1937.

Edwards, Bryan. *The History, Civil and Commercial, of the British West Indies.* 5th ed. 5 vols. London: Miller 1819.

Eguchi, Nobukiyo. "Relative Wealth and Adaptive Strategy among Peasants in a Small Village Community of Dominica, West Indies." Ph.D. diss., University of North Carolina 1984.

– "Inequality and Ranking among Peasants: A Case Study of the Dominican Peasants." *Japanese Journal of Ethnology* 49, no. 4 (1985): 320–42.

Elizabeth, Leo. "The French Antilles." In David W. Cohen and Jack P. Greene, eds., *Neither Slave Nor Free: The Freedman of African Descent in the Slave Societies of the New World,* 134–71. Baltimore: John Hopkins University Press 1972.

Escardo, Mauricio E. "Who Were the Inhabitants of the Virgin Islands at the Time of Columbus' Arrival?" In Jean Benoist and Francine-M. Mayer, eds., *Proceedings of the 7th International Congress for the Study of Pre-Colombian Cultures of the Lesser Antilles, Caracas, Venezuela,* 245–57. Montreal: Centre de Recherches Caraïbes, Université de Montréal 1978.

Europa World Year Book 1990. 2 vols. London: Europa Publications 1990.

Evans, Clifford. "The Lack of Archeology on Dominica." In Ripley B. Bullen, ed., *Proceedings of the 2nd International Congress for the Study of Pre-Colombian Cultures of the Lesser Antilles,* 93–102. Barbados: Barbados Museum and Historical Society 1967.

Feigenbaum, Mitchell. "Quantitative Universality for a Class of Nonlinear Transformations." *Journal of Statistical Physics* 19 (1978): 25–52.

– "The Universal Metric Properties of Nonlinear Transformations." *Journal of Statistical Physics* 21 (1979): 669–706.

Fentem, Arlin D. *Commercial Geography of Dominica.* Indiana: Indiana University, Department of Geography 1960.

Fermor, Patrick. *The Traveller's Tree: A Journey through the Caribbean Islands.* London: John Murray 1960.

Figueredo, Alfredo E. "The Virgin Islands as an Historical Frontier Between the Tainos and the Caribs." *Revista/Review Interamericana* 8, no. 3 (1979): 393–9.

Forsythe, Dennis. "West Indian Culture Through the Prism of Rastafarianism." *Rastafari,* Caribbean Quarterly monograph, 62–81. Kingston: University of West Indies 1985.

Foster, George. "Peasant Society and the Image of Limited Good." *American Anthropologist* 67 (1965): 293–315.

Foster-Carter, Aiden. "Neo-Marxist Approaches to Development and Underdevelopment." In Emanuel de Kadt and Gavin Williams, eds., *sociology and Development*, 67–105. London: Tavistock 1974.

Franck, Harry A. *Roaming through the West Indies*. New York: Century 1920.

Frank, Andre Gunder. *Capitalism and Underdevelopment in Latin America: Historical Studies of Chile and Brazil*. New York: Monthly Review Press 1967.

– *Lumpen Bourgeoisie: Lumpen Development – Dependence, Class and Politics in Latin America*. New York: Monthly Review Press 1972.

Gardiner, Richard Eugene. "The Allocation of Scarce Goods and Values: A Comparative Analysis of Mating Patterns in Dominica, West Indies." Ph.D. diss., University of California 1974.

Garrison, Fielding H. *An Introduction to the History of Medicine*. Philadelphia: W.B. Saunders 1929.

Gaspar, David Barry. *Bondmen and Rebels: A Study of Master-Slave Relations in Antigua with Implications for Colonial British America*. Baltimore: Johns Hopkins University Press 1985.

Giddens, Anthony. *Studies in Social and Political Theory*. London: MacMillan 1977.

Girvan, Norman. "The Development of Dependency Economics in the Caribbean and Latin America: Review and Comparison." *Social and Economic Studies* 22, no. 1 (1973): 1–33.

Gleick, James. *Chaos: Making a New Science*. New York: Viking Penguin 1987.

Goodridge, Cecil A. "Dominica: The French Connection." In Dominica Government, *Aspects of Dominican History*, 151–62. Roseau: Government Printery 1972.

Gorenstein, Shirley. "The Indigenous Caribbean." In Roberta Marx Delson, ed., *Readings in Caribbean History and Economics: An Introduction to the Region*, 101–3. New York: Gordon and Breach Science Publishers 1981.

Gosse, Philip. "Introduction." In Jean Baptiste Labat, *The Memoirs of Père Labat*, translated and abridged by J. Eaden, vii–xv. London: Constable 1931.

Goulbourne, Harry. *Politics and State in the Third World*. London: MacMillan 1979.

Gouldner, Alvin W. *The Coming Crisis of Western Sociology*. New York: Avon 1970.

Goveia, Elsa V. *A Study of the Historiography of the British West Indies to the End of the Nineteenth Century*. Instituto Panamericano de Geografia e Historia, no. 186. Mexico: 1956.

– *Slave Society in the British Leeward Islands at the End of the Eighteenth Century*. New Haven: Yale University Press 1965.

Green, William A. *British Slave Emancipation: The Sugar Colonies and the Great Experiment, 1830–1865.* Oxford: Clarendon 1976.

Greenfield, Sidney M. "Socio-Economic Factors and Family Form: A Barbadian Case Study." *Social and Economic Studies* 10, no. 1 (1961): 72–85.

– *English Rustics in Black Skins: A Study of Modern Family Forms in a Preindustrial Society.* New Haven: College and University Publishers 1966.

– "Plantations: Sugar Cane and Slavery." In Michael Craton, ed., *Roots and Branches: Current Directions in Slave Studies*, 85–119. *Historical Reflexions* 6, no. 1 (1979).

Grell, Francis. "Politics of Survival and Change in Dominica, 1763–1973: An Interpretation of the Political Life Experience of Dominicans in the Colonial and Post-Colonial Situation." Ph.D. diss., Carleton University 1976.

Grieve, Symington. *Notes upon the Island of Dominica.* London: Adam and Charles 1906.

Gullick, C.J.M.R. "Black Carib Origins and Early Society." In Jean Benoist and Francine-M. Mayer, eds., *Proceedings of the 7th International Congress for the Study of Pre-Colombian Cultures of the Lesser Antilles, Caras, Venezuela*, 283–90. Montreal: Université de Montréal 1978.

– *Myths of a Minority: The Changing Traditions of the Vincentian Caribs.* Assen: Van Gorcum 1985.

Haag, William G. "A Comparison of Arawak Sites in the Lesser Antilles." In *Proceedings of the First International Convention for the Study of Pre-Colombian Culture in the Lesser Antilles*, 9–16. Fort-de-France: Société d'histoire de la Martinique 1961.

– "The Lesser Antilles: Their Ecological Setting and Function as a Diffusion Route." In *Proceedings of the 2nd International Congress for the Study of Pre-Colombian Cultures in the Lesser Antilles*, 87–92. Barbados: Barbados Museum and Historical Society 1967.

Halcrow, Elizabeth M. *Canes and Chains: A Study of Sugar and Slavery.* London: Heinemann 1982.

Hall, Douglas. "Slaves and Slavery." *Social and Economic Studies* 11 (1962): 305–18.

Hall, Gwendolyn Midlo. "Saint Dominigue." In David W. Cohen and Jack P. Greene, eds., *Neither Slave Nor Free: The Freedman of African Descent in the Slave Societies of the New World*, 172–92. Baltimore: John Hopkins University 1972.

Hamilton, Robert. *Report of the Royal Commission to Inquire into the Conditions and Affairs of the Island of Dominica and Correspondence Relating Thereto.* London: H.M. Stationery Office (House of Commons Sessional Papers, Cd. 7477) 1894.

Hamshere, Cyril. *The British in the Caribbean: A Social History of the British Overseas.* London: Weidenfeld and Nicolson 1972.

Harrison, Lucia Carolyn. "Dominica: A Wet Tropical Human Habitat." *Economic Geography* 5, no. 1 (1935): 62–76.

Hart, Richard. *Black Jamaicans' Struggle against Slavery*. Kingston: Institute of Jamaica for the African-Caribbean Institute 1977.

– *Slaves who Abolished Slavery: Blacks in Bondage*. Vol 1. Kingston: Institute of Social and Economic Research, University of the West Indies 1980.

Harvey, E.E. "Economic Conditions – Taxation, Unemployment, Population, Agriculture and Indebtedness." Memorandum prepared by the Treasurer for presentation to the Royal Commission. CO 950/489, 1938.

Hatch, Elvin. *Theories of Man and Culture*. New York: Columbia University Press 1973.

Hawys, Stephen. *Mount Joy*. London: Gerald Duckworth & Co. 1968.

Hein, Wolfgang, and Konrad Stenzel. "The Capitalist State and Underdevelopment in Latin America: The Case of Venezuela." In Harry Goulbourne, ed., *Politics and State in the Third world*, 92–116. London: Macmillan 1979.

Henriques, Fernando. *Family and Colour in Jamaica*. 2d ed. London: MacGibbon and Kee 1968.

Higman, B.W. *Slave Populations of the British Caribbean, 1807–1834*. Baltimore: John Hopkins University Press 1984.

Hodge, W.H. "The Vegetation of Dominica." *The Geographical Review* 33, no. 3 (1943): 349–75.

– "The Flora of Dominica, British West Indies. Part 1." *Lloydia* 17, nos 1, 2, 3 (1954): 1–238.

Hodge, W.H., and Douglas Taylor. "The Ethnobotany of the Island Caribs of Dominica." *Webbia* 12, no. 2 (1957): 513–627.

Homiak, John, and Phillip Decker. "The Hucksters of Dominica." *Grassroots Development* 10, no. 1 (1986): 30–7.

Honychurch, Lennox. *Our Island Culture*. Roseau: Dominica Cultural Council 1982.

– *The Cabrits and Prince Rupert's Bay: History and Nature Notes*. Roseau: The Dominica Institute 1983.

– *The Dominica Story: A History of the Island*. Roseau: The Dominica Institute 1984.

Hopkins, Terrence K. "The Study of the Capitalist World-Economy: Some Introductory Considerations." In Terrence K. Hopkins et al., eds., *World-Systems Analysis: Theory and Methodology*, 9–38. Beverley Hills: Sage 1982.

Hopkins, Terrence K., et al. "Patterns of Development of the Modern World-System." In Terrence K. Hopkins et al., eds., *World-Systems Analysis: Theory and Methodology*, 41–82. Beverley Hills: Sage 1982.

Hughes, Robert. *The Fatal Shore: The Epic of Australia's Founding*. New York: Alfred A. Knopf 1987.

Imray, J. "Observations on the Characters of Endemic Fever in the Island of

Dominica." *The Edinburgh Medical and Surgical Journal* 70, no. 177 (1848): 253–87.

– "Memoir on Yaws in Dominica." In G. Milroy, ed., *Report on Leprosy and Yaws in the West Indies*, 72–83. London: H.M. Stationery Office 1873.

Irving, Washington. *The Life and Voyages of Christopher Columbus: To Which Are Added Those of His Companions*. 1889. Rev. ed. vol. 1. New York: AMS 1973.

Jackson, J. "Social Organization in St Vincent." B. Litt. thesis, Oxford University 1972.

James, C.L.R. *The Black Jacobins: Toussaint L'Ouverture and the San Domingo Revolution*. 1938. London: Allison & Busby 1980.

– "The Slaves." *Caribbean Quarterly* 35, no. 4 (1989): 1–10.

Jesse, Rev. C. "The Spanish Cedula of December 23, 1511, on the Subject of the Caribs." *Caribbean Quarterly* 9, no. 3 (1963): 22–32.

Jordan, Winthrop D. "American Chiaroscuro: The Status and Definition of Mulattoes in the British Colonies." *William and Mary Quarterly* 9 (1962): 183–200.

Kirby, Earle. "The Pre-Hispanic Peopling of the Antilles." In Ripley P. Bullen, ed., *Proceedings of the 6th International Congress for the Study of Pre-Colombian Cultures of the Lesser Antilles*, 14–20. Guadeloupe 1975.

Klein, Herbert S. *The Middle Passage: Comparative Studies of the Atlantic Slave Trade*. Princeton: Princeton University Press 1978.

Knight, Derrick. *Gentlemen of Fortune: The Men who Made their Fortunes in Britain Slave Colonies*. London: Frederick Muller 1978.

Knight, Franklin W. *The Caribbean: The Genesis of a Fragmented Nationalism*. New York: Oxford University Press 1978.

Kroeber, Alfred L. *The Nature of Culture*. Chicago: University of Chicago Press 1952.

– *An Anthropologist Looks at History*. Edited by Theodora Kroeber. Berkeley: University of California Press 1963.

Kuusi, Pekka. *This World of Man*. Toronto: Pergamon Press 1985.

Labat, Jean Baptiste. *Voyage du Père Labat aux isles de l'Amérique*. 6 vols. The Hague: P. Husson 1724.

– *The Memoirs of Père Labat, 1693–1705*. Translated by John Eaden. London: Constable and Co. 1931.

Laszlo, Ervin. "Cybernetics in an Evolving Social System." *Kybernetics* 13 (1984): 141–5.

Layng, Anthony. "Dominica, an Island in Need of an Historian." *Caribbean Quarterly* 19, no. 4 (1973): 36–41.

– *The Carib Reserve: Identity and Security in the West Indies*. Lanham: University Press of America 1983.

Lévi-Strauss, Claude. *Triste Tropiques*. Translated by John Weightman and Doreen Weightman. New York: Atheneum 1974.

Levitt, Kari, and Lloyd Best. "Character of Caribbean Economy." In George L. Beckford, ed., *Caribbean Economy: Dependency and Backwardness*. Mona, Jamaica: Institute of Social and Economic Research, University of the West Indies 1975.

Lobdell, Richard A. "British Officials and the West Indian Peasantry, 1842–1938." In Malcolm Cross and Gad Heuman, eds., *Labour in the Caribbean: From Emancipation to Independence*. London: MacMillan Caribbean 1988.

Lockhart, R., ed. *Fillan's Almanac and Dominica Yearbook*. Roseau: Official Gazette Office 1876.

Long, Edward. *The History of Jamaica, or General Survey of the Ancient and Modern State of That Island*. 3 vols. London: T. Lowndes 1754.

Lorenz, Edward. "Predictability: Does the Flap of a Butterfly's Wings in Brazil Set Off a Tornado in Texas?" Address to the Annual Meeting of American Association for the Advancement of Science, Washington, 29 December 1979.

Lovell, Langford. *A Letter to a Friend to the Present State of the Island of Dominica*. Winchester: James Robins 1818.

Lowenthal, David. *West Indian Societies*. London: Oxford University Press 1972.

Luhmann, Niklas. *Soziale Systeme: Grundriß einer allgemeinen Theorie*. Frankfurt: Suhrkamp 1984.

Luke, Sir Harry. *Caribbean Circuit*. London: Nicholson and Watson 1950.

MacMillan, Allister, ed. *The West Indies (Illustrated Including the Isthmus of Panama and Bermuda)*. London: G.L. Colingridge 1912.

Maguire, Robert E. "Dominica's Ill-fated Lime Industry." In Roberta Marx Delson, ed., *Readings in Caribbean History and Economics: An Introduction to the Region*, 197–200. New York: Gordon and Breach Science Publishers 1981.

Major, R.R., trans. & ed. *Selected Letters of Christopher Columbus with Other Original Documents Relating to His Four Voyages to the New World*. 2d ed. London: Hakluyt Society 1870.

Mandelbrot, Benoit. *The Fractal Geometry of Nature*. New York: Freeman 1977.

Mannix, Daniel P. "The Humanitarian Influence in Abolition." In Roberta Marx Delson, ed., *Readings in Caribbean History and Economics: An Introduction to the Region*, 108–17. New York: Gordon and Breach Science Publishers 1981.

Marshall, Bernard A. "Maronage in Slave Plantation Societies: A Case Study of Dominica, 1785–1865." *Caribbean Quarterly* 22 (1976): 26–32.

– "Slave Resistance and White Reaction in the British Windward Islands." *Caribbean Quarterly* 28, no. 3 (1982): 33–46.

Marshall, Woodville. "Notes on Peasant Development in the West Indies since 1838." *Social and Economic Studies* 17, no. 3 (1968): 252–63.

– "Peasant Movements and Agrarian Problems in the West Indies. Part 1, Development of the Peasantry." *Caribbean Quarterly* 18, no. 1 (1972): 31–8.

Martin, R. Montgomery. *The British Colonial Library: Comprising a Popular and Authentic Description of all the Colonies of the British Empire.* 10 vols. London: Henry G. Bohn 1844. Reprint of vol. 2 as *History of the West Indies.* London: Whittaker & Co. 1937.

Maximea, Christopher. "The Development of Forestry in Dominica." *Dies Dominica*, 30–3. Roseau: Government Headquarters, Public Relations Division 1972.

May, Robert. "Biological Populations with Nonverlapping Generations, Stable Points, Stable Cycles, and Chaos." *Science* 186 (1974): 645–7.

– "Single Mathematical Models with Very Complicated Dynamics." *Nature* 261 (1976): 459–567.

May, Robert, and George F. Oster. "Bifurcations and Dynamic Complexity in Simple Ecological Models." *The American Naturalist* 110 (1976): 573–99.

McKusick, Marshall. "The Distribution of Ceramic Styles in the Lesser Antilles." Ph.D. diss., Yale University 1959.

– *The Aboriginal Canoes of the West Indies.* Yale University Publications in Anthropology, no. 63. New Haven 1960.

McNeill, William H. *Plagues and Peoples.* New York: Anchor/Doubleday 1976.

Mead, George Herbert. *Mind, Self, and Society from the Standpoint of a Social Behaviorist.* Edited by Charles W. Morris. Chicago: University of Chicago Press 1962.

Menzies, Ken. *Talcott Parsons and the Social Image of Man.* London: Routledge and Kegan Paul 1977.

Mintz, Sidney. "The Origins of Reconstituted Peasantries." In Sidney W. Mintz, ed., *Caribbean Transformations*, 146–56. Chicago: Aldine 1974a.

– "The Caribbean Region." *Daedalus* 103, no. 2 (1974b): 45–71.

Momsen, Janet. "The Geography of Land and Population in the Caribbean (with Special Reference to Barbados and the Windward Islands)." Ph.D. diss., University of London 1970.

– "Land Settlement as an Imposed Solution." In Jean Besson and Janet Momsen, eds., *Land and Development in the Caribbean.* Warwick University Caribbean Studies. London: MacMillan Caribbean 1987.

Moore, Richard B. "Carib 'Cannibalism': A Study in Anthropological Stereotyping." *Caribbean Studies* 13, no. 3 (1973): 117–35.

Moyne Commission. *West India Royal Commission Report.* Cmd 6607. 1945.

Mullin, Michael. "Slave Obeahmen and Slaveowning Patriarches in an Era of War and Revolution (1776–1807)." In Vera Rubin and Arthur Tuden, eds., *Comparative Perspectives on Slavery in New World Plantation Societies*, 481–90. Annals of New York Academy of Sciences, vol. 292. New York 1977.

Murch, Arvin. *Black Frenchmen: The Political Integration of the French Antilles.* Boston: Schenkman 1971.

Myers, Robert A. " 'I Love My Home Bad, But ...': The Historical and Contemporary Contexts of Migration on Dominica, West Indies." Ph.D. diss., University of North Carolina 1976.

– "Ethnohistorical vs. Ecological Considerations: The Case of Dominica's Amerindians." In Jean Benoist and Francine-M. Mayer, eds., *Proceedings of 7th International congress for the Study of Pre-Colombian Cultures of the Lesser Antilles, Caracas, Venezuela,* 325–41. Montreal: Centre de Recherches Caraïbes, Université de Montréal 1978.

– *Amerindians of the Lesser Antilles: A Bibliography.* HRFlex Books ST1-001 Bibliography Series. New Haven: Human Relations Area Files 1981.

– "Island Carib Cannibalism." *New West Indian Guide* 58, no. 3/4 (1984): 147–84.

– *A Resource Guide to dominica, 1493–1986.* New Haven: Human Relations Area Files 1987a.

– *Dominica.* World Bibliographical Series vol. 82, Santa Barbara: Clio Press 1987b.

Naftel, C.O. *Report on the Forest Lands and Estates of Dominica, and on the Agricultural Capabilities of the Island.* Roseau: Guardian Office 1897. Colonial Reports, Misc. no. 9, C.8801. London: HM Stationery Office: Darling & Sons, 1898.

Neveu-Lemaire, M. "Les Caraïbes des Antilles: Leurs representants actuels dans l'île de la Dominique." *La Géographie* 35, no. 2 (1921): 127–46.

Nicholson, Desmond. "Pre-Colombian Seafaring Capabilities in the Lesser Antilles." In Ripley P. Bullen, ed., *Proceedings of the 6th International Congress for the Study of Pre-Colombian Cultures of the Lesser Antilles,* 98–105. Guadeloupe 1975.

Nicole, Christopher. *The West Indies: Their People and History.* London: Hutchinson 1965.

Niddrie, D.L. "Eighteenth-Century Settlement in the British Caribbean." *Institute of British Geographers Transactions* 40 (1966): 67–80.

Norris, Oliver. "Situations et perspectives de la démographie dominicaine." *Cahiers du Centre d'études régionales antilles Guyane* 2 (1964): 1–71.

Nugent, Maria. *Lady Nugent's Journal.* Edited by Philip Wright. Kingston: Institute of Jamaica 1966.

Ober, Frederick Albion. "Aborigines of the West Indies." *Proceedings of the American Antiquarian Society* 9 (1894): 270–313.

O'Loughlin, Carleen. *A Survey of Economic Potential and Capital Needs of the Leeward Islands, Windward Islands and Barbados.* London: HMSO 1963.

– *Economic and Political Change in the Leeward and Windward Islands.* New Haven: Yale University Press 1968.

Olsen, Fred. "Did the Ciboney Precede the Arawaks of Antigua?" In *Proceedings of the 4th International Congress for the Study of Pre-Colombian*

Cultures of the Lesser Antilles, St Lucia, 94–102. Montreal: Centre de Recherches Caraïbes, Université de Montréal 1971.

Owen, Nancy Hammack. "Land and Politics in a Carib Indian Community: A Study of Ethnicity." Ph.D. diss., University of Massachusetts 1974.

Oxaal, Ivar. "The Dependency Economist as Grassroots Politician in the Caribbean." In Ivar Oxaal, Tony Barnett, and David Booth, eds., *Beyond the Sociology of Development: Economy and Society in Latin America and Africa*, 28–49. London: Routledge and Kegan Paul 1975.

Palgrave, William gifford. *Ulysses: Or Scenes and Studies in Many Lands*. London: MacMillan 1887.

Parry, J.H., and Phillip Sherlock. *A Short History of the West Indies*. 3d ed. London and Basingstoke: Macmillan 1971.

Parsons, Talcott. *The Social System*. New York: Free Press 1964.

– *The Evolution of Societies*. Edited by Jackson Toby. Englewood Cliffs: Prentice-Hall 1977.

Patterson, H. Orlando. *The Sociology of Slavery*. London: MacGibbon and Kee 1967.

Peters, Rev. C. *Two Sermons Preached at Dominica on the 11th and 13th April, 1800*. London: John Hatchard n.d.

Petitjean-Roget, Jacques. "The Caribs as Seen through the Dictionary of Reverent Father Breton." In *Proceedings of the First International convention for the Study of Pre-Colombian Cultures in the Lesser Antilles*, Part I, 43–68. Fort-de-France: Société d'Histoire de la Martinique 1961.

Pope-Hennessy, James. *The Baths of Absalom*. London: Allan Wingate 1954.

Prebisch, Raul. *The Economic Development of Latin America and its Principal Problems*. New York: United Nations Department of Economic Affairs 1950.

Prestoe, Henry. *Report on Coffee Cultivation in Dominica*. CO 74/33, 1875.

Price, Richard. "Introduction." In Richard Price, ed., *Maroon Societies: Rebel Communities in the Americas*, 1–30. Garden City: Anchor 1974.

Prigogine, Ilya, and Grégoire Nicolis. *Exploring Complexity: An Introduction*. New York: W.H. Freeman 1989.

Prigogine, Ilya, and Isabelle Stenger. *Order out of Chaos, Man's New Dialogue with Nature*. New York: Bantam 1984.

Prins, Nicholas. *Notes on the Dominica Banana Industry*. 1984. Mimeo.

Proesmans, Raymond Rev. *The History of Dominica*. Unpublished manuscript n.d.

– "Notes on the Slaves of the French." In Government of Dominica, *Aspects of Dominican History*, 163–72. Roseau: Government Printing Division 1972.

Pusinelli, P.N.F. *Report on the Review of the Structure, Salaries, and Conditions of Service of the Dominica Public Service*. 1970.

Ragatz, Lowell Joseph. "Absentee Landlordism in the British Caribbean, 1750–1833." *Agricultural History* 5 (1931): 7–24.

- *The Fall of the Planter Class in the British Caribbean, 1763–1833*. New York: Octagon 1963.
- *A Guide for the Study of British Caribbean History, 1763–1834, Including the Abolition and Emancipation Movements*. Washington, DC: Government Printing Office, 1932. Reprint. New York: Da Capo 1970.

Ransford, Oliver. *The Slave Trade: The Story of Transatlantic Slavery*. London: John Murray 1971.

Rawley, James A. *The Transatlantic Slave Trade: A History*. New York: W.W. Norton 1981.

Rhys, Jean. *Wide Sargasso Sea*. London: Andre Deutsch 1966.
- *Smile Please: An Unfinished Autobiography*. New York: Harper and Row 1979.

Richardson, David. "The Slave Trade, Sugar, and British Economic Growth, 1748–1776." In Barbara L. Solow and Stanley L. engerman, eds., *British Capitalism and Caribbean Slavery: The Legacy of Eric Williams*, 103–33. Cambridge: Cambridge University Press 1987.

Rifkin, Jeremy. *Entropy: A New World View*. New York: Bantam Books 1980.

Riviere, Bill "Para." "Contemporary Class Structure in Dominica." In Susan Craig, ed., *Contemporary Caribbean: A Sociological Reader*, vol. 1, 265–82. Maracas, Trinidad: Susan Craig 1981.
- "Contemporary Class Struggles and the Revolutionary Potential of Social Classes in Dominica." In Susan Craig, ed., *Contemporary Caribbean: A Sociological Reader*, vol. 2, 365–83. Maracas, Trinidad: Susan Craig 1982.

Riviere, W. Emanuel. "Labour Shortage in the British West Indies after Emancipation." *Journal of Caribbean History* 4 (1972): 1–30.

Rocher, Guy. *Talcott Parsons and American Sociology*. Don Mills: Thomas Nelson & Sons (Canada) 1974.

Rodgers, William B., and Miriam Morris. "Environmental Modification and System Response: Development Change in Dominica, West Indies." *Human Organization* 30, no. 1 (1971): 165–72.

Rodney, Walter. *Groundings with My Brothers*. London: Bogle-L'Ouverture 1969.

Rosa, Eugene A., Gary E. Machlis, and Kenneth M. Keating. "Energy and Society." *Annual Review of Sociology* 14 (1988): 149–72.

Ross, Charlesworth. "Caribs and Arawaks." *Caribbean Quarterly* 16 (1970): 52–9.

Rouse, Irving. "The Development of Pre-Colombian Art in the West Indies." In *Proceedings of the First International Convention for the Study of Pre-Colombian Culture in the Lesser Antilles*, 39–48. Fort-de-France: Société d'histoire de la Martinique 1961.
- "The Arawaks." In Julian Steward, ed., *Handbook of South American Indians* vol. 4, 507–46. New York: Cooper Square 1963a.
- "The Carib." In Julian Steward, ed., *Handbook of South American Indians* vol. 4, 547–65. New York: Cooper Square 1963b.

– "Prehistory of the West Indies." *Science* 144 (1964): 499–513.

Rouse, Irving, and Jose M. Cruxent. "Early Man in the West Indies." *Scientific American* 221, no. 5, (1969): 42–52.

Sahtouris, Elizabet. *Gaia: The Human Journey from Chaos to Cosmos.* New York: Pocket Books 1989.

Sale, Kirkpatrick. *The Conquest of Paradise: Christopher Columbus and the Columbian Legacy.* New York: Alfred A. Knopf 1990.

Schrödinger, Erwin. *What is Life & Mind and Matter.* Cambridge: Cambridge University Press 1944.

Sciulli, David, and Dean Gerstein. "Social Theory and Talcott Parsons in the 1980s." *Annual Review of Sociology* 11 (1985): 369–87.

Sewell, William Grant. *The Ordeal of Free Labour in the West Indies.* 1861. London: Frank Cass 1968.

Sheridan, Richard B. "The Plantation Revolution and the Industrial Revolution 1625–1775." *Caribbean Studies* 9, no. 3 (1969): 5–25.

– *Doctors and Slaves: A Medical and Demographic History of Slavery in the British West Indies, 1680–1834.* London: Cambridge University Press 1985.

Sherlock, Philip Manderson. "The Development of the Middle Class in the Caribbean." In *Middle Classes in Tropical and Sub-Tropical Countries,* 324–30. Brussels: INCIDI 1955.

– *West Indian Nations: A New History.* New York: St Martin's Press 1973.

Sherrard, O.A. *Freedom from Fear: The Slave and His Emancipation.* London: The Bodely Head 1959.

Shillingford, John D. *A Survey of the Institutions Serving Agriculture on the Island of Dominica, WI.* Cornell International Agricultural Mimeograph 35. Ithaca, NY: Department of Agricultural Economics, Cornell University 1972.

Silverman, Sydel. "The Peasant Concept in Anthropology." *Journal of Peasant Studies* 7, no. 1 (1979): 49–69.

Simpson, George E. "Haiti's Social Structure." *American Sociological Review* 6 (1941): 640–9.

Singham, A.W. "Legislative: Executive Relations in Smaller Territories." In Burton Benedict, ed., *Problems of Smaller Territories,* 134–48. London: Athlone Press 1967.

– *The Hero and the Crowd in a Colonial Polity.* New Haven: Yale University Press 1968.

Skinner, Elliott P. "Group Dynamics and Social Stratification in British Guiana." In Vera Rubin, ed., *Social and Cultural Pluralism,* 904–12. Annals of the New York Academy of Sciences vol. 18, article 5. New York: New York Academy of Sciences 1960.

Smith, Karl. "The Need for a Family Planning Programme in Dominica, West Indies." *West Indies Medical Journal* 21 (1972): 125–34.

Smith, Michael G. "Some Aspects of Social Structure in the British Caribbean about 1820." *Social and Economic Studies* 1, no. 4 (1953): 55–79.
- "Community Organization in Plural Jamaica." *Social and Economic Studies* 5, no. 3 (1956): 295–312.
- "Social and Cultural Pluralism." In Vera Rubin, ed., *Social and Cultural Pluralism*. Annals of the New York Academy of Sciences, vol. 83, article 5. New York: New York Academy of Sciences 1960.
- *The Plural Society in the British West Indies*. Berkeley: University of California Press 1965.
- *Corporations and Society: The Social Anthropology of Collective Action*. Chicago: Aldine 1975.
Smith, Raymond T. *The Negro Family in British Guiana*. London: Routledge and Kegan Paul 1956.
- *British Guiana*. London: Oxford University Press for the Royal Institute of International Affairs 1962.
Smith, Tony. "A Comparative Study of French and British Decolonization." *Comparative Studies in Society and History* 20 (1978): 70–102.
Soddy, F. *Matter and Energy*. London: Oxford University Press 1912.
- *Cartesian Economics: The Bearing of Physical Science Upon State Stewardship*. London: Hendersons 1922.
- *Wealth, Virtual Wealth and Debt: The Solution of Economic Paradox*. New York: Allen and Unwin 1926.
Solow, Barbara L. "Capitalism and Slavery in the Exceedingly Long Run." In Barbara L. Solow and Stanley L. Engerman, eds., *British Capitalism and Caribbean Slavery: The Legacy of Eric Williams*, 51–77. Cambridge: Cambridge University Press 1987.
Southey, Thomas. *Chronological History of the West Indies*. 3 vols. London: Longman, Rees, Orme, Brown and Green 1827.
Spencer, Herbert. *First Principles*. 1862. New York: A.L. Burt 1880.
Spens, Terry. "Family Structure in a Dominican Village." Ph.D. diss., Cambridge University 1969.
St Johnston, Sir Reginald. *The French Invasions of Dominica*. Antigua: Leeward Island Government Printery Office 1932.
- *From a Colonial Governor's Notebook*. London: Hutchinson & Co. 1936.
Sturge, Joseph, and Thomas Harvey. *The West Indies in 1837*. London: Hutchinson & Co. 1838.
Sunkel, Oswaldo. "National Development Policy and External Dependence in Latin America." *Journal of Development Studies* 6, no. 1 (1969): 23–48.
Taylor, Douglas. "The Island Caribs of Dominica, BWI." *American Anthropologist* 37, no. 2 (1935): 265–72.
- "The Caribs of Dominica." *Bureau of American Ethnology Bulletin* 119, Anthropological Papers no. 3 (1938): 103–59.

- "Columbus Saw Them First." *Natural History* 48, no. 1 (1941): 40–9.
- "Carib Folk-Beliefs and Customs from Dominica, B.W.I." *Southwestern Journal of Anthropology* 1 (1945): 507–30.
- "Kinship and Social Structure of the Island Carib." *Southwestern Journal of Anthropology* 2, no. 2 (1946): 180–212.
- "The Interpretation of Some Documentary Evidence on Carib Culture." *Southwestern Journal of Anthropology* 5, no. 4 (1949): 379–92.
- "Tales and Legend of the Dominica Caribs." *Journal of American Folklore* 65, no. 257 (1952): 267–79.
- "Carib, Caliban, Cannibal." *International Journal of American Linguistics* 24, no. 2 (1958): 156–7.
Temperley, Howard. "Eric Williams and Abolition: the Birth of a New Orthodoxy." In Barbara L. Solow and Stanley L. Engerman, eds., *British Capitalism and Caribbean Slavery: The Legacy of Eric Williams*, 229–57. Cambridge: Cambridge University Press 1987.
Thomas, Cuthbert. "From Crown Colony to Associate Statehood: Political Change in Dominica, the Commonwealth West Indies." Ph.D. diss., University of Massachusetts 1973.
Tribus, Myron, and Edward C. McIrvine. "Energy and Information." *Scientific American* 3 (1971): 179–88.
Trollope, Anthony. *The West Indies and the Spanish Main.* 2d ed. London: Thomson 1860.
Trouillot, Michel-Rolph. "Caribbean Peasantries and World Capitalism: An Approach to Micro-Level Studies." *Nieuwe West-Indische Gids/New West Indian Guide* 58, nos. 1 & 2 (1984a): 37–59.
- "The Economic Integration of a Caribbean Peasantry: The Case of Dominica." Ph.D. diss., Johns Hopkins University 1984b.
- "Labour and Emancipation in Dominica: Contribution to a Debate." *Caribbean Quarterly* 30, no. 3 & 4 (1984c): 73–84.
- *Peasants and Capital: Dominica in the World Economy.* Baltimore: Johns Hopkins University Press 1988.
UNESCO. *The Commonwealth of Dominica: Education Sector Survey.* Paris: UNESCO 1982.
United Nations. *Demographic Yearbook: Historical Supplement 1948–1978.* New York 1979.
- *Yearbook of National Accounts Statistics,* vol. 1, 1979. New York 1980.
Wallerstein, Immanuel. *The Modern World-System: Capitalist Agriculture and the Origins of the European World-Economy in the Sixteenth Century.* New York: Academic Press 1974.
- "World Networks and the Politics of the World-Economy." In Amos H. Hawley, ed., *Societal Growth: Process and Implications,* 269–78. New York: Free Press 1979.
Watson, Beverley. *Supplementary Notes on Foreign Investment in the Common-*

wealth Caribbean. Working Paper no. 1, Institute of Social and Economic Research, University of the West Indies 1974.

Watts, Francis. *Report on the Agricultural Conditions of Dominica with Recommendations for their Amelioration.* Antigua: Government Printing Office, CO 152/398, 1902.

- "The Development of Dominica." *West Indian Bulletin* 6 (1906): 204–8.
- "The Development of Dominica." *West Indian Bulletin* 15 (1916): 198–207.

Watty, Frank. "Aliens Land Ownership and Agricultural Development Issues, Problems, and Policy Framework." *Proceedings of the Fifth West Indian Agricultural Economic Conference*, 41–6. Trinidad: Department of Agricultural Economics and Farm Management, University of the West Indies 1970.

Waugh, Alec. *The Sugar Islands: A Caribbean Travelogue.* New York: Farrar, Straus 1949.

Weber, Bruce. "National Park Creation in a Developing Nation: A Case Study of Dominica, West Indies." Ph.D. diss., Colorado State University 1973.

Weber, Max. *Economy and Society.* 2 vols. Berkeley: University of California Press 1978.

Weiner, Leo. *Africa and the Discover of America.* 3 vols. Philadelphia: Innes and Sons 1920–22.

Welch, Barbara. "Population Density and Emigration in Dominica." *Geographical Journal* 134 (1968): 226–35.

Wesche, Marjorie Bingham. "Place Names as a Reflection of Cultural Change: An Example from the Lesser Antilles." *Caribbean Studies* 12, no. 2 (1972): 74–98.

White, Leslie. *The Science of Culture.* New York: Farrar, Straus 1949.

- *The Evolution of Culture.* New York: McGraw-Hill 1959.

White, Michael. "The Dominican Banana Industry – An Economic Hazard." *Proceedings of the Second West Indian Agricultural Economics Conference*, 56–70. Trinidad: University of the West Indies 1967.

Williams, Eric. *The Negro in the Caribbean.* Manchester: Panaj Service 1942.

- *Documents of West Indian History, 1492–1655.* Trinidad: PNM 1963.
- *Capitalism and Slavery.* New York: Russell and Russell 1964.
- *From Columbus to Castro: The History of the Caribbean, 1492–1969.* London: Andre Deutsch 1970.

Williams, R.L. *Industrial Development of Dominica.* Jamaica: Institute of Social and Economic Research 1971.

Wilson, Justin. *Christopher Columbus.* Boston: Houghton Mifflin and Co. 1892.

Wolf, Eric. *Europe and the People without History.* Berkeley: University of California Press 1982a.

- "Materialists vs. Mentalists: A Review Article." *Comparative Studies of Society and History* 24 (1982b): 148–52.
Woolley, S.F. "The Personnel of the Parliament of 1833." *English Historical Review* 53 (1938): 240–62.
World Bank. *Dominica: Economic Memorandum*. Report No. 4740–DOM. [New York: World Bank 1983.]
Yankey, Joseph Barnard. "A Study of the Situation in Agriculture and the Problems of Small Scale Farming in Dominica, West Indies." Ph.D. diss., University of Wisconsin 1969.
Young, Filson. *Christopher Columbus and the New World of His Discovery*. Vol. 1. London: E. Grant Richards 1906.

Index